BLACK DRAMA

An Anthology

BLACK DRAMA

An Anthology

Edited by
WILLIAM BRASMER
Denison University

DOMINICK CONSOLO
Denison University

With an Introduction by
DARWIN T. TURNER
*North Carolina Agricultural and
Technical State University*

Charles E. Merrill Publishing Company
A Bell & Howell Company
Columbus, Ohio

Standard Book Number: 675-09380-5 (paperback edition)
675-09347-3 (hardbound edition)

Library of Congress Catalog Number: 74-103048

1 2 3 4 5 6 7 8 9 10 — 77 76 75 74 73 72 71 70

Printed in the United States of America

Contents

The Black Playwright in the Professional Theatre of the United States of America, 1858-1959

Although professional theatre in the United States of America is more than two hundred years old, professional playwrights of African ancestry are relatively unknown because opportunities for black writers have been restricted far more severely in drama than in other literary fields. An African slave, Phillis Wheatley, published a collection of poems as early as 1773.[1] A fugitive slave, William Wells Brown, published an autobiography in 1847, a book of travels in 1852, and a novel in 1853.[2] But the first play by a black American was not written until 1858.[3] No Afro-American had a full-length serious drama produced in a Broadway theatre in New York City until 1925,[4] and only ten additional plays written totally or partly by Afro-Americans were produced on Broadway from 1926 until 1959, when Lorraine Hansberry's *A Raisin in the Sun* began the longest run on Broadway ever experienced by a play of Afro-American authorship.

---

[1] Phillis Wheatley, kidnapped from Senegal and taken to the United States at the age of seven, published *Poems* in London.

[2] Born a slave in Lexington, Kentucky, Brown escaped in 1835. He published *The Narrative of William Wells Brown* (1847), *My Three Years in Europe* (1852), and *Clotel, or the President's Daughter* (1853).

[3] *The Escape, or a Leap for Freedom* by William Wells Brown. Even though Brown gave public readings from this drama, there is no evidence that it was ever staged.

[4] Garland Anderson's *Appearances*, 1925.

1

The dearth of black playwrights cannot be attributed to a lack of literary talent among Afro-Americans. Phillis Wheatley, Frederick Douglass, William Wells Brown, W. E. B. DuBois, and Paul Laurence Dunbar earned international fame in other fields of letters before 1920. Langston Hughes, Gwendolyn Brooks, Richard Wright, Chester Himes, James Baldwin, and Ralph Ellison are only a few of the Afro-American writers who have earned international acclaim since 1920.

Instead, the shortage must be blamed on a lack of opportunity for recognition. A combination of economic, cultural, and social circumstances has restricted the black playwright.

In the United States, a reputation in drama is more expensive than in any other literary field. A poet may publish in magazines or on mimeographed sheets. He can read his work in lecture halls or on street corners. If he is heard or read by influential people, his work may be collected and published in book form at a reasonable cost. A fiction writer may publish in small literary magazines. His first novel may appear as a limited printing which does not represent a major financial gamble by a publishing house.

But a dramatist needs a cast of people and an auditorium with stage, lights, scenery, and seats. Even then, he is rarely recognized in the United States until his drama appears in one of the large theatres near Broadway in New York City, the theatrical capital of the United States. A Broadway production, needless to say, is a costly experiment which producers approach cautiously. Unwilling to lose money, they rarely gamble on new materials; instead, they revive and reshape the traditional in an effort to pander to the tastes which they presume to be characteristic of their potential audience of middle-class and upper-class white Americans.

Even daring directors and producers recognize this fact. Joseph Papp, a rejected director, has earned a reputation for presenting Shakespearean plays without charging admission and for staging artistic works by little-known dramatists. Yet he has written,

With few exceptions the large theatres in New York attract
theatregoers who both have money and are settled in their attitudes. These people . . . have no desire to spend money to hear
their ideals assaulted. They cannot tolerate doubts, and if they
have any they certainly do not want them exposed. . . . It is perfectly human to cultivate, and cater to, the status quo. It is certainly more reasonable to mount a production for an audience
that already exists than to do shows that must find their audience
(or, indeed, create it.) [5]

This combination of economic and cultural circumstances is
intensified by a social fact. Since Afro-Americans represent a
minority of the entire population and an even less significant
percentage of the Broadway audience, Negro life is regarded
as an exotic subject for the American theatre. Therefore, only
a limited number of plays on Negro themes are approved.
Furthermore, to please his predominantly white audience, the
cautious producer wishes to have these themes developed in
accordance with his customers' expectations. Too frequently,
therefore, he wants the stereotypes of Negro life and character
which white playwrights popularized and which many black
playwrights refuse to perpetuate. For example, in the years
between 1769, when the first black character appeared in a
play in America, and 1923, when the first black playwright had
a one-act play produced on Broadway, white playwrights es-
tablished five major stereotypes: the Buffoon, a comically ignorant type; the Tragic Mulatto, the product of miscegenation
who is destined to tragic exclusion from white society, which
will not accept her, and black society, which she will not accept;
the Christian Slave, a docile individual who worships both his
mortal white master and his immortal master; the Carefree
Primitive, an exotic, amoral savage; and the Black Beast, a
villain who seeks equality with white people. And when white
playwrights wrote of Negro life, they most frequently wrote
folk comedy. By repetition, white playwrights had given reality

---

5 *New York*, II (April 21, 1969) , p. 55.

to these stereotypes of Afro-American character and life for numerous white Americans who rarely experienced intimate personal relationships with black Americans. Therefore, producers did not seek plays written about the actual characters and lives of Afro-Americans; from black and white playwrights, they wanted dramas which would repeat the familiar.

Finally, playwrights, more than other writers, depend upon acquaintance with people who have money. Poets and novelists may submit manuscripts to publishing firms; a dramatist needs to know someone who knows a producer. In the segregated society of the United States, personal contact between black artists and wealthy producers has been very limited.

For all of these reasons, black American playwrights developed very slowly in the years between Brown in 1858 and Hansberry in 1959. The first significant efforts in dramatic writing, in fact, were not serious dramas but "coon" shows, musical variety shows. Very popular in the years between 1895 and 1905, these attracted and utilized the talents of such black writers as Paul Laurence Dunbar, one of America's most popular poets at the beginning of the twentieth century, and James Weldon Johnson, a poet and novelist who later earned a reputation as an American consul and as secretary of the National Association for the Advancement of Colored People. In these shows, which emphasized comedy, singing, and dancing rather than a story line, black poets and actors shamelessly pandered to the expectations of their white audiences. They wrote of Buffoons and Carefree Primitives. Afro-American performers put cork-black on their faces and painted red make-up around their lips to transform themselves into the grinning gargoyles popularized in the black-face minstrel shows which employed white actors. James Weldon Johnson later described the manner in which black song writers even avoided love duets for their heroes and heroines because American audiences, presuming sexual amorality to be characteristic of Negro life, refused to believe that romance could be a serious topic for Afro-Americans.

Although these all-black musical shows disappeared from Broadway for more than a decade while black writers and performers were refused opportunity, musical comedy about black people has remained popular in the American theatre. *Shuffle Along* (1921), an all-black musical, written and directed by blacks, is frequently praised as one of the works which revived American interest not only in black talent but also black culture during the 1920's. It was the first of many such musicals produced during that decade. *Porgy and Bess* (1935), a folk opera by George Gershwin based on a play by Dubose Heyward (both white), is so highly esteemed by white Americans that, during the 1950's, the United States government selected it to be presented in Europe as the theatrical work best exemplifying American art and culture. In each decade, musical comedies about black people have extraordinary success in the theatre. The continuation of the pattern is evidenced in the present by *Golden Boy* and *Hello, Dolly!* both written originally for white performers but adopted into musicals for blacks. The perennial popularity of such shows evidences both the talent of black performers and the persistence of white Americans' predilection for viewing black Americans primarily as gay, or occasionally pathetic, people continually expressing their emotions in song and dance.

In contrast to the success of musical shows is the relative failure of serious professional drama by black American playwrights, the focus of this essay.

The first to be produced on Broadway was *The Chip Woman's Fortune* (1923), a one-act play by Willis Richardson. Because of debts, Silas Green, a porter in a store, is about to lose his job and the record player he has purchased on credit. He turns for assistance to Aunt Nancy, a chip woman, who has helped him previously. But Aunt Nancy plans to give her savings to her son Jim, just released from prison after serving a term for assaulting his unfaithful sweetheart and her lover. When Jim arrives, he agrees to give Silas enough money to pay the debts. As the opener on a program which included a revival of Oscar Wilde's *Salome, The Chip Woman's Fortune,* presented by the Ethiopian Art Players of Chicago, lasted only two weeks on Broadway.

The first full-length play, Garland Anderson's *Appearances,* first produced on October 13, 1925, treated a more serious subject—a Negro bell-hop's successful defense of himself from a false charge of rape.

Three years later, Frank Wilson, an actor, created an unusual protagonist in *Meek Mose,* which opened February 6, 1928. Most black playwrights have refused to write about docile blacks or have portrayed them as villains who must either be converted to self-respect or destroyed before the final curtain. Frank Wilson, however, not only made such a character a protagonist but even rewarded him. When white community leaders propose to move the blacks to a different section of town, peace-loving Mose, a leader of the black community, advises the blacks to agree. The blacks turn on him when disease and death result from the new living conditions, but he is rewarded for his faith when oil is discovered on the new property. Historically, of course, *Meek Mose* retells the success of some American Indians who, driven from their fertile farmland in the East, were forced to relocate in Oklahoma, where oil was later discovered. Nevertheless, it is an unusual theme for a black playwright. The play lasted only twenty-four performances.

Harlem, the final play to appear on Broadway during the 1920's, was a collaboration between Wallace Thurman, a talented, satirical black novelist, and a white playwright, William Jordan Rapp. Thurman, who had written two novels about Harlem, blended melodrama and the exoticism of Harlem into a play which continued for ninety-three performances. The plot of *Harlem* retraces themes familiar to individuals who have read widely in literature by blacks. After migrating from South Carolina to Harlem, the Williamses find unhappiness instead of the anticipated opportunity. Impoverished, they are forced to give parties to which they charge admission so that they can pay the rent. The daughter Cordelia becomes intoxicated by the wild life of the city. After rejecting a West Indian suitor, Cordelia becomes the mistress of a Harlem gambler. When he is killed, the West Indian is suspected but acquitted. Cordelia and her family continue to search for happiness in the cold city.

Paul Laurence Dunbar had told a comparable story in *The Sport of the Gods* (1901) when he novelized the misfortunes of Southern blacks who corrupt their souls in Harlem. In the 1920's, novelist Rudolph Fisher repeated the theme in fiction, and in the following decade Randolph Edmonds developed it in drama. Sometimes white American critics have misinterpreted this theme as evidence of the black author's willingness to perpetuate the myth that life is better for black people in the South than it is in the North. To the contrary, the black writer was often more concerned with dispelling the myth that white Americans created about Harlem—that it was a world where black people enjoyed a gay, carefree existence.

In these four Broadway productions, black playwrights worked within the framework set by white playwrights. *The Chip Woman's Fortune* tells of black peasants. *Meek Mose* presents docile blacks. While *Harlem* suggests actuality, it nevertheless perfumes the stage with exoticism and amorality, and it capitalizes upon the national popularity which Harlem enjoyed during the 1920's.

In 1929, a severe economic depression hit America, and in 1930 Marc Connelly adapted Roark Bradford's *Ol' Man Adam and His Children* into *Green Pastures*, a comic fantasy about religion as practised by blacks. These two events motivated four dramas by black playwrights on Broadway and two in the more experimental, less costly theatres off Broadway.

Marc Connelly's play is a white man's fantasy about black people's conceptions of Biblical stories. The central character is De Lawd, a magnificent, white-haired, cigar-smoking black man—excellently acted by Richard B. Harrison, a college teacher of speech who, according to Langston Hughes, re-

quired the services of a white actor to train him to speak the
"Negro" dialect which Marc Connelly had written. The heavenly fish fries and carryings-on amused white audiences but
both irritated and intrigued black playwrights, who capitalized
upon the interest in Negroes' religion as background for their
works.

Staged by the Negro Theatre Guild, Augustus Smith's
Louisiana (1933), melodramatically, but much more realistically than *Green Pastures*, depicted religious forces in a black
community in Louisiana. The two most powerful community
leaders are Amos Berry, minister of a Baptist church, and
Aunt Hagar, who practices voodoo. When a disreputable tavern
keeper attempts to force his attentions on the minister's niece,
Berry and Aunt Hagar combine the powers of Christianity and
voodoo to crush him.

This was not the first American drama to portray voodoo
prominently. In 1922, Mary Wiborg, a white playwright, had
presented *Taboo*, and within the same decade Em Jo Basshe
had written *Earth*. Despite its exoticism, however, voodoo has
not excited American audiences. *Taboo* barely lasted through
three performances; Smith's *Louisiana* lasted only eight.

Two days after *Louisiana* opened, Hall Johnson's *Run, Little
Chillun* began a more successful run of 126 performances. It too
told a story of different religious forces. This time, however,
there is conflict between the pagan New Day Pilgrims and the
Hope Baptists. Sulamai, a New Day Pilgrim, entices married
Jim Jones, who is the son of the minister of the Baptist church.
Finally, Christianity triumphs when Jim returns to his faith
and Sulamai is stricken during a revival meeting.

Five years later, George Norford, in a theatre off Broadway,
dramatized a different religious element in black life when he
wrote about Father Divine, a black, self-proclaimed re-incar-
nation of God, who attracted a large following during the
Depression.

The economic depression influenced black playwrights less
directly than had *Green Pastures*. The severity of life during

the 1930's prompted writers to question all aspects of life in the United States and to protest against conditions which mitigated against poor people. This concern spread even to the Broadway stages. Here again, however, black dramatists seem to have been granted opportunity to tell their stories only after paths had been prepared by white playwrights.

In 1932, white James Miller wrote *Never No More*, a protest against lynching. In 1934, white John Wexley presented *They Shall Not Die*, based on an actual incident in which nine Negro youths from Scottsboro, Alabama, were convicted of alleged rape of two white prostitutes; and in *Stevedore*, in the same year, George Sklar and Paul Peters, white playwrights, described the manner in which a militant black youth was made to seem responsible for a crime which he did not commit.

In 1934 also, Dennis Donoghue, a black playwright with a non-black name, wrote *Legal Murder*, another version of the case of the Scottsboro boys. In Donoghue's play, the nine youths have hopped aboard a freight train to ride to Chicago to seek work as singers. Their car is invaded by two white men and two women. One white man, who is armed, orders the youths to jump from the moving train, but the youths seize the gun. At the next stop, they are arrested and falsely accused of rape. In court, they and their Jewish lawyer are ridiculed, and they are convicted.

Legal Murder lasted only seven days, but in 1935, Langston Hughes' *Mulatto* began the longest Broadway run of any play by a black dramatist before Lorraine Hansberry. Produced in 1935, but written in 1930, *Mulatto* is an emotionally engaging drama, marred by melodrama, propaganda, and crudities common to inexperienced playwrights. Developed from a short story, "Father and Son," *Mulatto* dramatizes the conflict between Colonel Norwood, a wealthy white man, and Robert, his yard child. Since the age of seven, Robert has hated his father for refusing to recognize their relationship, of which he himself had been proud. During his summer's vacation from college, Robert has strained tension to a breaking point by defying the mores of his father and of the Georgia town in which they live. Finally, on the day of Bert's scheduled return to college, the tension snaps. Incensed to learn that Bert has defied a white woman, has driven faster than a white man, and has entered the front door of the house regularly, Norwood threatens to kill Bert. Bert kills his father and flees; but, chased by a posse, he returns to the house, where he kills himself.

Much of the power of the play derives from the subject itself. A traditional subject in drama, father-son conflict inevitably generates excitement and frequently produces memorable characters and confrontations: Laius and Oedipus, Claudius and Hamlet, Theseus and Hippolytus are only a few. In this instance, the excitement was intensified for American audiences by the first professional dramatization of a conflict between a mulatto and his father.

The play gains strength also from Hughes' characterizations of Bert and his mother Cora. Although he is obviously modeled on the proud and noble slaves of Negro literary tradition, Bert is an interesting character. His contempt for other Negroes, his stubborn insistence that he be recognized as a man, and his arrogant defiance of custom symptomize a fatal *hubris*. In his deliberate provocation of trouble, a manifestation of what seems almost a suicidal complex, he anticipates James Baldwin's protagonist in *Blues for Mr. Charlie*, written a generation later (1964).

The theme of protest was continued off Broadway in Langston Hughes' *Don't You Want To Be Free?* (1937), a musical history of blacks in America, and in Theodore Ward's *Big White Fog* (1940). Although it lasted only sixty-four performances, *Big White Fog* dramatized a black man's frustrated and tragic existence more bitterly than any play previously presented professionally in the United States.

Set in Chicago and covering a period from 1922 to 1931, the play recounts the misadventures of Victor Mason and his family. Convinced that black people cannot live profitably in the United States, Victor Mason buys stock in the Black Star liner on which Marcus Garvey, a West Indian, plans to help black people return to Africa, where they will re-establish themselves in a new community. Events intensify Mason's conviction that he must leave: His son Lester is denied a scholarship because of his race; his daughter Wanda abandons her education in hopes of earning money to purchase some of the luxuries she desires. But, despite the opposition of his wife, Mason idealistically clings to the hope that Garvey's plan will succeed. The hope collapses when Garvey is arrested and convicted of fraud.

Nine years later, the Masons have hit bottom. Wanda has become a prostitute. Les has become a Communist. Mason's wife, Ella, pawns their few valuables in order to feed the family. When bailiffs come to evict the family for failure to pay rent, Victor Mason is killed attempting to stop them. The play ends with the glimmering hope that union of blacks and whites may improve conditions in America, but one remembers more vividly Les's despairing cry: "Seems like the world ain't nothing but a big white fog, and we can't see no light no where."

Typically, in contrast to the short life of *Big White Fog* off Broadway, *Cabin in the Sky* in the same year titillated Broadway audiences for 156 performances. A comic fantasy written by whites, it repeated the familiar Negro stereotypes in a story heavily laden with primitive religious faith, comedy, and song.

The decade of protest reached its climax in Richard Wright's *Native Son* (1941), adapted for the stage by Paul Green, a white regional dramatist who had written more plays about Negroes than any other American dramatist. Written originally as a novel, *Native Son* tells the story of Bigger Thomas, a twenty-year-old black youth from Mississippi, who lives with his mother and his younger sister and brother in a rat-infested room in the slums of Chicago's black ghetto. A monster created by America's economic and social system, Bigger is characterized by envy, fear, and hatred. He envies, fears, and hates white people who control the society, own the houses and the stores in the slums, acquire education and jobs, and deny opportunity and free movement to black people. Bigger, however, also hates

Negroes because they occupy inferior positions in America. To stave off awareness of his impotence to assist his family, he even erects a wall of hate between himself and them. But, because he cannot completely conceal his impotence from himself, he also hates himself.

Hired as a chauffeur by the Daltons, white "liberals" who derive part of their fortune from slum houses such as Bigger's, Bigger is ordered to drive the Daltons' daughter, Mary, to her evening classes at the University of Chicago. Mary, however, insists that Bigger take her to an assignation with her Communist sweetheart, Jan, who attempts to enlist Bigger in the Party. At the end of the evening, Bigger assists the drunken girl to her room, where he is surprised by her blind mother. Fearing that he will be discovered and accused of rape, Bigger accidentally smothers the girl while trying to prevent her from responding to her mother's questions. After a melodramatic chase during which he rapes and kills his Negro sweetheart, Bigger is caught, tried, and executed.

As a novel, *Native Son* was a powerful and shocking indictment of America. Much of the emotional impact resulted from the subjective presentation of Bigger; readers saw the United States through his eyes, and for them also it became a world of white horror. The adaptation of the work into a drama transformed the character and the theme. Bigger was humanized and made less fearful, less brutal. In the novel, Bigger fights his black associates to prevent himself from realizing that he is too cowardly to rob a white man; in the play, his temper is the only reason for his fight. In the novel, he brutally assaults his sweetheart to prevent her betraying him to the police; in the play, she is killed by policemen. Although these character changes made Bigger a more sympathetic individual for a theater audience, they erased Wright's major thesis: that American society has shaped this Bigger and other Biggers into monsters who are brutal because they are fearful. Furthermore, in the play, a white reporter, suspecting Bigger, skillfully proves

Bigger's guilt. In contrast, emphasis in the novel is placed upon the fact that, as a result of his accidental murder, Bigger, for the first time, realizes that he can outwit white people. In the novel, his guilt is discovered accidentally by reporters who suspect him no more than Captain Delano suspected the innocent-looking black mutineers in Melville's "Benito Cereno." Finally, without the introspective examination of Bigger, *Native Son* is more a cops-and-robbers melodrama than a thesis play. Nevertheless, it ran for ninety-four performances and was even nominated for a Drama Critics Circle award for the year. This anthology presents an updated, revised version by Paul Green.

Protest did not disappear from the theater during the 1940s, but the end of World War II and the apparent triumph of democracy revived idealistic hopes for brotherhood and understanding. While white dramatists wrote pleas for integration of Negroes into the opportunities, black dramatists sought to educate white audiences by writing more realistically about problems of the past and the present.

In *Our Lan'* (1947), Theodore Ward described the efforts of black freedmen after the Civil War. Although the play focuses on the United States' betrayal of freed slaves, who were promised land, then forced to sign away their rights, and finally driven off by Union troops, considerable attention is given to the character of the slaves themselves and to their problems not related to land.

In 1954, in a theatre off Broadway, William Branch presented *In Splendid Error*, the story of an important episode in the life of Frederick Douglass, who, after escaping from slavery, dedicated himself to abolishing that evil from the United States. For a period of time, Douglass supported John Brown's efforts to help slaves liberate themselves by flight and by guerilla attacks upon Southern planters. When Brown, however, decided to attack federal property at Harper's Ferry, Douglass was forced to choose between unpleasant alternatives: if he accompanied Brown, he would sacrifice his life in a mission which he considered suicidal; if he refused, some would suspect him of cowardly betrayal of the cause. The play is the story of Douglass's effort to make a choice.

In 1956, off Broadway, Loften Mitchell's *A Land Beyond the River* dramatized a more recent incident in the history of black Americans. It recounted the valiant efforts of Mr. Dulane, a minister in South Carolina, to help Negro children enroll in schools reserved for white children, where facilities, supplies, and equipment promised a higher quality of education than was possible in the antiquated structures assigned to black children. Historically, Mr. Dulane succeeded; his case was one of those which persuaded the Supreme Court to rule in 1954 that all publicly supported schools must admit students without restriction based on race or religion. Nonetheless, historically, as in the play, Mr. Dulane was forced to save his life by fleeing at night from embittered white neighbors resentful of the changing conditions.

Professional drama by Afro-Americans came of age on Broadway during the 1950's. In 1953, Louis Peterson told the story, in *Take a Giant Step*, of educated northern Negroes, who are neither primitive nor pathetic but who have problems. Spencer Scott, the protagonist, is a member of the only Negro family in a neighborhood in Philadelphia, Pennsylvania. When he reaches the age of sexual maturity, he becomes isolated from his former white friends, who no longer invite him to their homes or visit him. He attempts to discover companionship among members of his race, but he cannot adjust to the Negroes whom he sees in taverns. Isolated by race and by social position, he is alone except for a grandmother who loves him but cannot provide the companionship required by a teen-aged youth. Peterson did not pretend to have a solution. At the end of the play, Scott remains isolated.

Take a Giant Step continued for seventy-six performances and was followed in the next year by *Mrs. Patterson*, a happier tale of the daydreams of a Negro girl, co-authored by Charles Sebree, black, and Greer Johnson, white. Teddy Hicks wants to be a wealthy white woman, like Mrs. Patterson, her mother's employer; but she also dreams of an exciting life with "Mr. D." from Hell. Eventually, the dreams are crushed, and Teddy faces reality. This play lasted for 101 performances, undoubtedly benefitting from the casting of popular Eartha Kitt as Teddy.

The trend towards verisimilitude, however, was interrupted by Langston Hughes's *Simply Heavenly* (1957), which, designed for the commercial theater, reached Broadway in a state weaker than Hughes's *Simple Takes a Wife*, the book upon which the play was based. The major sufferer in the adaptation is Jesse B. Simple himself. In the tales and dialogues of the Simple books, Jesse assumes the dimensions of a folk hero. Even though he drinks, cavorts with women, has difficulty paying rent, talks ungrammatically and excessively, his foibles never detract from his dignity, for, like the Greek gods and the heroes of various mythologies, he is larger than life. It may be appropriate even to say that he, like Joseph Conrad's Kurtz, is remembered primarily as a voice, in this instance a voice which utters common sense even when the speaker seems emotional and illogical. Reduced to actable dimensions, however, Simple loses his grandeur. In the play, he peeks beneath his legs to watch Joyce, his fiancée, change clothes; he turns somersaults; he is thrown from a car to land on his "sit-downer"; he is propped comically in a hospital bed with his legs in traction; sentimentally and pathetically, he tries to reform and to win Joyce. In short, Simple's reality as the embodied spirit of the Negro working class is reduced to the Harlem barfly; the Chaplinesque Comic Hero shrinks to a farcical fall guy of the model made familiar earlier by Stan Laurel and Lou Costello.

The second major injury resulting in the adaptation is suffered by the material itself. Even though incidents occur in the book, they generally serve merely as acceptable devices to generate Simple's philosophizing. Consequently, what is important is not the event itself but the reaction which it stimulates from Simple. For a Broadway show, however, Hughes needed to emphasize action and to minimize Simple's reflections. As a result, undue attention is given to Simple's unsuccessful efforts to seduce Joyce, to the Watermelon Man's pursuit of Mamie, and to the domestic difficulties of Bodidilly and Arcie. The effort to please Broadway failed; the show closed after sixty-two performances.

Two years later Lorraine Hansberry achieved the kind of success which earlier black American playwrights had dreamed of. Her drama, *A Raisin in the Sun*, won the Drama Critics Circle Award as the best play of 1958-59. It continued for 530 performances in its initial run.

Appropriately, *A Raisin in the Sun* is a play about the dreams of ghetto dwellers. Descended from five generations of slaves and sharecroppers, the Youngers have moved north in the hope of realizing their dreams. In Chicago, however, their dreams are dying. Thirty-five-year-old Walter Lee Younger is merely a chauffeur who cannot support his family adequately, cannot even provide a bedroom for his young son, who sleeps on a couch in the living room. Beneatha, Walter Lee's sister, wants to be a doctor even though she realizes the financial strain that her education places upon the children. Walter Lee's wife, who is pregnant, suffers with the realization that the family cannot afford another child. Walter Lee's mother wants happiness for her children and a garden for herself; but she sees weariness and sorrow in her children, and in the concrete wasteland of Chicago's ghetto she can find space enough only for a window box plant for herself.

In order to earn money to support his family, Walter Lee wants to purchase a share of a liquor store with the money his mother has received from the insurance of his father, who died from overwork. His mother refuses because she believes liquor stores are immoral and because she wants to use the money to purchase a home for the family. Walter Lee steals part of the money but loses it in a swindle. The mother makes a down payment on a home, but it is in a neighborhood where black people have never lived: exorbitant costs have prevented her buying a home in Negro neighborhoods. Despite warnings of opposition by their new neighbors, the Youngers decide to move, hoping at last to realize one dream.

Lorraine Hansberry did not idealize the Younger family. Walter Lee Younger experiences bitter frustration because no one else in his family agrees to his scheme to invest his mother's insurance money in a liquor store. Far from epitomizing nobility, he searches for pride and for maturity. As he says, "I'm thirty-five years old; I been married eleven years and I got a boy who sleeps in the living room—and all I got to give him is stories about how rich white people live." He believes that the Negro who wishes to succeed must imitate white people.

In contrast, his sister, Beneatha (Bennie), inspired partly by racial pride and partly by the lectures of her African suitor, argues against the assimilation of the Negro race into the American culture. Whereas Walter materialistically concentrates upon acquiring money, Bennie wants to become a doctor because her desire since childhood has been to help other people.

Concerned neither with money nor with crusades, their mother desires merely to provide cleanliness and decency for her family. When she receives the insurance money left by her husband, she restrains herself from donating the ten thousand dollars to the church only because she wishes to help her children realize their dreams. She wants her children to respect themselves and to respect others.

The Youngers disagree even in their attitudes toward their race. Although Walter blames the backwardness of the race for the inferior economic status of the Negro, he responds to the rhythms of recordings of African music. Bennie recognizes the barrier which separates her from the snobbish Negroes who possess wealth; yet she considers herself a crusader for and a defender of her race. Individual in their characters and their attitudes towards life, the Youngers find unity only in their common belief in the importance of self-respect, a philosophy not unique to the Negro race.

The play also includes a wealthier Negro—well-dressed, well-educated, condescending toward lower-class blacks and ridiculed in turn by people of that lower economic class. Contrasted with him is an African, who is proud of his nationality and contemptuous of the assimilationist behavior of American blacks.

The play has been judged a comedy because it is amusing, but it remains the most perceptive presentation of Negroes in the history of American theater.

It is encouraging to observe that Afro-American dramatists since the 1950's have had the freedom to people their plays with individualized blacks rather than stereotypes. Clearly, this indicates that the popular images are changing. Nevertheless, the Afro-American remains an exotic subject for American professional theatre. As long as this condition continues, the major opportunities for Afro-American dramatists will lie in the amateur theatrical of the colleges and in the semi-professional performances of black community groups. Despite recent awards, the black dramatist is not yet a significant force in American professional theatre.

Darwin T. Turner

MULATTO

A Tragedy of the Deep South

Langston Hughes

LANGSTON HUGHES was the most prolific Black writer in America. At his death he had written some forty volumes of poetry, short stories, plays, and anthologies. Hughes was part of the Harlem Renaissance movement in the 1920's and as such was one of the driving forces in bringing recognition to the Black Culture of Harlem at that period.

Mulatto was first produced at the Vanderbilt Theatre on October 24, 1935, and played 373 consecutive performances— a phenomenal number for a play by a Black author and especially during the depression years, a time when the Establishment concerned itself with problems of a different order.

In 1950 Langston Hughes adapted *Mulatto* into an opera with music by Jan Meyerowitz. Starring Lawrence Tibbett and Muriel Rahn this work lasted but four performances on Broadway. Later, Hughes was to achieve success with the dramatization of his remarkable "Simple" short stories in the musical comedy work, *Simply Heavenly*.

Mulatto remains a classic of its time, a period piece if you will, with its theme of miscegenation, responsibility, and ambiguous "Uncle Tomism." Yet in its powerful dramatic recreation of the tragic confrontation between White father and Black son, it also symbolically portrays the necessity to repudiate "tradition" at whatever cost to affirm the unnegotiable basis of one's humanity. To the extent that the Colonel relies on tradition to support his own "outraged" benevolence and ignores the necessity of affirmation thereby denying *both* the son and the human, the tragedy is of that time but of this place.

MULATTO

Characters

COLONEL THOMAS NORWOOD   *Plantation owner, a still vigorous man of about sixty, nervous, refined, quick-tempered, and commanding; a widower who is the father of four living mulatto children by his Negro housekeeper*

CORA LEWIS   *A brown woman in her forties who has kept the house and been the mistress of Colonel Norwood for some thirty years*

WILLIAM LEWIS   *The oldest son of Cora Lewis and the Colonel; a fat, easy-going, soft-looking mulatto of twenty-eight; married*

SALLIE LEWIS   *The seventeen-year-old daughter, very light with sandy hair and freckles, who could pass for white*

ROBERT LEWIS   *Eighteen, the youngest boy; strong and well-built; a light mulatto with ivory-yellow skin and proud thin features like his father's; as tall as the Colonel, with the same gray-blue eyes, but with curly black hair instead of brown; of a fiery, impetuous temper—immature and willful—resenting his blood and the circumstances of his birth*

FRED HIGGINS   *A close friend of Colonel Norwood; a county politician; fat and elderly, conventionally Southern*

SAM   *An old Negro retainer, a personal servant of the Colonel*

BILLY   *The small son of William Lewis; a chubby brown kid about five*

TALBOT   *The overseer*

MOSE   *An elderly Negro, chauffeur for Mr. Higgins*

A STOREKEEPER

AN UNDERTAKER

UNDERTAKER'S HELPER   *Voice off-stage only*

THE MOB

24

Act I

TIME   *An afternoon in early fall.*

THE SETTING   *The living room of the Big House on a plan-*
tation in Georgia. Rear center of the room, a vestibule with
double doors leading to the porch; at each side of the doors,
a large window with lace curtains and green shades; at left
a broad flight of stairs leading to the second floor; near the
stairs, downstage, a doorway leading to the dining room and
kitchen; opposite, at right of stage, a door to the library.
The room is furnished in the long out-dated horsehair and
walnut style of the nineties; a crystal chandelier, a large old-
fashioned rug, a marble-topped table, upholstered chairs. At
the right there is a small cabinet. It is a very clean, but
somewhat shabby and rather depressing room, dominated
by a large oil painting of NORWOOD'S *wife of his youth on the*
center wall. The windows are raised. The afternoon sun-
light streams in.

ACTION   *As the curtain rises, the stage is empty. The door*
at the right opens and COLONEL NORWOOD *enters, crossing*
the stage toward the stairs, his watch in his hand. Looking
up, he shouts:

NORWOOD   Cora! Oh, Cora!

CORA   (*Heard above*)   Yes, sir, Colonel Tom.

NORWOOD   I want to know if that child of yours means to
leave here this afternoon?

CORA   (*At head of steps now*)   Yes, sir, she's goin' directly.
I's gettin' her ready now, packin' up an' all. 'Course, she
wants to tell you goodbye 'fore she leaves.

NORWOOD   Well, send her down here. Who's going to drive
her to the railroad? The train leaves at three—and it's
after two now. You ought to know you can't drive ten
miles in no time.

The text printed here is from *Five Plays* by Langston Hughes (Bloomington:
Indiana University Press, Midland Book Edition, 1968).

25

CORA   (*Above*)   Her brother's gonna drive her. Bert. He
ought to be back here most any time now with the Ford.

NORWOOD   (*Stopping on his way back to the library*)
Ought to be *back* here? Where's he gone?

CORA   (*Coming downstairs nervously*)   Why, he driv in
town 'fore noon, Colonel Tom. Said he were lookin' for
some tubes or somethin' 'nother by de mornin' mail for de
radio he's been riggin' up out in de shed.

NORWOOD   Who gave him permission to be driving off in
the middle of the morning? I bought that Ford to be used
when I gave orders for it to be used, not . . .

CORA   Yes, sir, Colonel Tom, but . . .

NORWOOD   But what? (*Pausing. Then deliberately*)   Cora,
if you want that hardheaded yellow son of yours to get
along around here, he'd better listen to me. He's no more
than any other black buck on this plantation—due to work
like the rest of 'em. I don't take such a performance from
nobody under me—driving off in the middle of the day to
town, after I've told him to bend his back in that cotton.
How's Talbot going to keep the rest of those darkies working right if that boy's allowed to set that kind of an example? Just because Bert's your son, and I've been damn fool
enough to send him off to school for five or six years, he
thinks he has a right to privileges, acting as if he owned this
place since he's been back here this summer.

CORA   But, Colonel Tom. . .

NORWOOD   Yes, I know what you're going to say. I don't
give a damn about him! There's no nigger-child of mine,
yours, ours—no darkie—going to disobey me. I put him
in that field to work, and he'll stay on this plantation till
I get ready to let him go. I'll tell Talbot to use the whip on
him, too, if he needs it. If it hadn't been that he's yours,
he'd-a had a taste of it the other day. Talbot's a damn good
overseer, and no saucy, lazy Nigras stay on this plantation

and get away with it. (*To* CORA) Go on back upstairs and see about getting Sallie out of here. Another word from you and I won't send your (*Sarcastically*) pretty little half-white daughter anywhere, either. Schools for darkies! Huh! If you take that boy of yours for an example, they do 'em more harm than good. He's learned nothing in college but impudence, and he'll stay here on this place and work for me awhile before he gets back to any more schools. (*He starts across the room.*)

CORA   Yes, sir, Colonel Tom. (*Hesitating*) But he's just young, sir. And he was mighty broke up when you said last week he couldn't go back to de campus. (COLONEL NORWOOD *turns and looks at* CORA *commandingly. Understanding, she murmurs*) Yes, sir. (*She starts upstairs, but turns back.*) Can't I run and fix you a cool drink, Colonel Tom?

NORWOOD   No, damn you! Sam'll do it.

CORA   (*Sweetly*) Go set down in de cool, then, Colonel. 'Taint good for you to be going' on this way in de heat. I'll talk to Robert maself soon's he comes in. He don't mean nothing—just smart and young and kinder careless, Colonel Tom, like ma mother said you used to be when you was eighteen.

NORWOOD   Get on upstairs, Cora. Do I have to speak again? Get on! (*He pulls the cord of the servants' bell.*)

CORA   (*On the steps*) Does you still be in the mind to tell Sallie good-bye?

NORWOOD   Send her down here as I told you. (*Impatiently*) Where's Sam? Send him here first. (*Fuming*) Looks like he takes his time to answer that bell. You colored folks are running the house to suit yourself nowadays.

CORA   (*Coming downstairs again and going toward door under the steps*) I'll get Sam for you.

(CORA *exits left.* NORWOOD *paces nervously across the floor. Goes to the window and looks out down the road. Takes a cigar from his pocket, sits in a chair with it unlighted, scowling. Rises, goes toward servants' bell and rings it again violently as* SAM *enters, out of breath.*)

NORWOOD   What the hell kind of a tortoise race is this? I suppose you were out in the sun somewhere sleeping?

SAM   No, sah, Colonel Norwood. Just tryin' to get Miss Sallie's valises down to de yard so's we can put 'em in de Ford, sah.

NORWOOD   (*Out of patience*) Huh! Darkies waiting on darkies! I can't get service in my own house. Very well. (*Loudly*) Bring me some whiskey and soda, and ice in a glass. Is that damn Frigidaire working right? Or is Livonia still too thickheaded to know how to run it? Any ice cubes in the thing?

SAM   Yes, sah, Colonel, yes, sah. (*Backing toward door left*) 'Scuse me, please sah, but (*as* NORWOOD *turns toward library*) Cora say for me to ask you is it all right to bring that big old trunk what you give Sallie down by de front steps. We ain't been able to tote it down them narrer little back steps, sah. Cora, say, can we bring it down de front way through here?

NORWOOD   No other way? (*Sam shakes his head*) Then pack it on through the back, quick. Don't let me catch you carrying any of Sallie's baggage out of that front door here. You-all'll be wanting to go in and out the front way next. (*Turning away, complaining to himself*) Darkies have been getting mighty fresh in this part of the country since the war. The damn Germans should've . . . (*To* SAM) Don't take that trunk out that front door.

SAM   (*Evilly, in a cunning voice*) I's seen Robert usin' de front door—when you ain't here, and he comes up from de cabin to see his mammy.

(SALLIE, *the daughter, appears at the top of the stairs, but hesitates about coming down.*)

NORWOOD   Oh, you have, have you? Let me catch him and I'll break his young neck for him. (*Yelling at* SAM) Didn't I tell you some whiskey and soda an hour ago?
    (SAM *exits left.* SALLIE *comes shyly down the stairs and approaches her father. She is dressed in a little country-style coat-suit ready for traveling. Her features are Negroid, although her skin is very fair.* COLONEL NORWOOD *gazes down at her without saying a word as she comes meekly toward him, half-frightened.*)

SALLIE   I just wanted to tell you goodbye, Colonel Norwood, and thank you for letting me go back to school another year, and for letting me work here in the house all summer where mama is. (NORWOOD *says nothing. The girl continues in a strained voice as if making a speech*) You mighty nice to us colored folks certainly, and mama says you the best white man in Georgia. (*Still* NORWOOD *says nothing. The girl continues.*) You been mighty nice to your—I mean to us colored children, letting my sister and me go off to school. The principal says I'm doing pretty well and next year I can go to Normal and learn to be a teacher. (*Raising her eyes*) You reckon I can, Colonel Tom?

NORWOOD   Stand up straight and let me see how you look. (*Backing away*) Hum-m-m! Getting kinder grown, ain't you? Do they teach you in that school to have good manners, and not be afraid of work, *and to respect white folks?*

SALLIE   Yes, sir, I been taking up cooking and sewing, too.

NORWOOD   Well, that's good. As I recall it, that school turned your sister out a right smart cook. Cora tells me she's got a good job in some big hotel in Chicago. I'm thinking about you going on up North there with her in a

year or two. You're getting too old to be around here, and
too womanish. (*He puts his hands on her arms as if feeling her flesh*)

SALLIE   (*Drawing back slightly*)   But I want to live down
here with mama. I want to teach school in that there
empty school house by the Cross Roads what hasn't had
a teacher for five years.

(SAM *has been standing with the door cracked, over-
hearing the conversation. He enters with the drink
and places it on the table, right.* NORWOOD *sits down,
leaving the girl standing, as* SAM *pours out a drink.*)

NORWOOD   Don't get that into your head, now. There's been
no teacher there for years—and there won't be any teacher
there, either. Cotton teaches these pickaninnies enough
around here. Some of 'em's too smart as it is. The only
reason I did have a teacher there once was to get you
young ones o' Cora's educated. I gave you all a chance
and I hope you appreciate it. (*He takes a long drink.*)
Don't know why I did it. No other white man in these
parts ever did it, as I know of. (*To* SAM)   Get out of
here! (SAM *exits left*)   Guess I couldn't stand to see
Cora's kids working around here dumb as the rest of these
no good darkies—need a dozen of 'em to chop one row of
cotton, or to keep a house clean. Or maybe I didn't want
Talbot eyeing you gals. (*Taking another drink*)   Anyhow, I'm glad you and Bertha turned out right well. Yes,
hum-m-m! (*Straightening up*)   You know I tried to do
something for those brothers of yours, too, but William's
stupid as an ox—good for work, though—and that Robert's just an impudent, hardheaded, yellow young fool.
I'm gonna break his damn neck for him if he don't watch
out. Or else put Talbot on him.

SALLIE   (*Suddenly frightened*)   Please, sir, don't put the
overseer on Bert, Colonel Tom. He was the smartest boy
at school, Bert was. On the football team, too. Please, sir,

Colonel Tom. Let brother work here in the house, or somewhere else where Talbot can't mistreat him. He ain't used . . .

NORWOOD   (*Rising*) Telling me what to do, heh? (*Staring at her sternly*) I'll use the back of my hand across your face if you don't hush. (*He takes another drink. The noise of a Ford is heard outside.*) That's Bert now, I reckon. He's to take you to the railroad line, and while you're riding with him, you better put some sense into his head. And tell him I want to see him as soon as he gets back here. (CORA *enters left with a bundle and an umbrella.* SAM *and* WILLIAM *come downstairs with a big square trunk, and exit hurriedly, left.*)

SALLIE   Yes, sir, I'll tell him.

CORA   Colonel Tom, Sallie ain't got much time now. (*To the girl*) Come on, chile. Bert's here. Yo' big brother and Sam and Livonia and everybody's all waiting at de back door to say goodbye. And your baggage is being packed in. (*Noise of another car is heard outside.*) Who else is that there coming up de drive? (CORA *looks out the window.*) Mr. Higgins' car, Colonel Tom. Reckon he's coming to see you . . . Hurry up out o' this front room, Sallie. Here, take these things of your'n (*Hands her the bundle and parasol*) while I opens de door for Mr. Higgins. (*In a whisper*) Hurry up, chile! Get out! (NORWOOD *turns toward the front door as* CORA *goes to open it*)

SALLIE   (*Shyly to her father*) Goodbye, Colonel Tom.

NORWOOD   (*His eyes on the front door, scarcely noticing the departing* SALLIE, *he motions.*) Yes, yes goodbye! Get on now! (CORA *opens the front door as her daughter exits left.*) Well, well! Howdy do, Fred. Come in, come in! (CORA *holds the outer door of the vestibule wide as* FRED HIGGINS *enters with rheumatic dignity, supported on the arm of his chauffeur,* MOSE, *a very black Negro in a slouchy uniform.* CORA *closes the door and exits left hurriedly, following* SALLIE.)

NORWOOD   (*Smiling*) How's the rheumatiz today? Women or licker or heat must've made it worse—from the looks of your speed!

HIGGINS   (*Testily, sitting down puffing and blowing in a big chair*) I'm in no mood for fooling, Tom, not now. (*To* MOSE) All right. (*The* CHAUFFEUR *exits front.* HIGGINS *continues angrily.*) Norwood, that damned yellow nigger buck of yours that drives that new Ford tried his best just now to push my car off the road, then got in front of me and blew dust in my face for the last mile coming down to your gate, trying to beat me in here—which he did. Such a deliberate piece of impudence I don't know if I've ever seen out of a nigger before in all the sixty years I've lived in this country. (*The noise of the Ford is heard going out the drive, and the cries of the* NEGROES *shouting farewells to* SALLIE. HIGGINS *listens indignantly.*) What kind of crazy coons have you got on your place, anyhow? Sounds like a black Baptist picnic to me. (*Pointing to the window with his cane*) Tom, listen to that.

NORWOOD   (*Flushing*) I apologize to you, Fred, for each and every one of my darkies. (SAM *enters with more ice and another glass.*) Permit me to offer you a drink. I realize I've got to tighten down here.

HIGGINS   Mose tells me that was Cora's boy in that Ford—and that young black fool is what I was coming here to talk to you about today. That boy! He's not gonna be around here long—not the way he's acting. The white folks in town'll see to that. Knowing he's one of your yard niggers, Norwood, I thought I ought to come and tell you. The white folks at the Junction aren't intending to put up with him much longer. And I don't know what good the jail would do him once he got in there.

NORWOOD   (*Tensely*) What do you mean, Fred—jail? Don't I always take care of the folks on my plantation without any help from the Junction's police force? Talbot can do more with an unruly black buck than your marshal.

HIGGINS   Warn't lookin' at it that way, Tom. I was thinking how weak the doors to that jail is. They've broke 'em down and lynched four niggers to my memory since it's been built. After what happened this morning, you better keep that yellow young fool out o' town from now on. It might not be safe for him around there—today, nor no other time.

NORWOOD   What the hell? (*Perturbed*) He went in just now to take his sister to the depot. Damn it, I hope no ruffians'll break up my new Ford. What was it, Fred, about this morning?

HIGGINS   You haven't heard? Why, it's all over town already. He sassed out Miss Gray in the post office over a box of radio tubes that come by mail.

NORWOOD   He did, heh?

HIGGINS   Seems like the stuff was sent C.O.D. and got here all smashed up, so he wouldn't take it. Paid his money first before he saw the box was broke. Then wanted the money order back. Seems like the post office can't give money orders back—rule against it. Your nigger started to argue, and the girl at the window—Miss Gray—got scared and yelled for some of the mail clerks. They threw Bert out of the office, that's all. But that's enough. Lucky nothing more didn't happen. (*Indignantly*) That Bert needs a damn good beating—talking back to a white woman—and I'd like to give it to him myself, the way he kicked the dust up in my eyes all the way down the road coming out here. He was mad, I reckon. That's one yellow buck don't know his place, Tom, and it's your fault he don't—sending 'em off to be educated.

NORWOOD   Well, by God, I'll show him. I wish I'd have known it before he left here just now.

HIGGINS   Well, he's sure got mighty aggravating ways for a buck his color to have. Drives down the main street and don't stop for nobody, white or black. Comes in my store and if he ain't waited on as quick as the white folks are, he walks out and tells the clerk his money's as good as a white man's any day. Said last week standing out on my store front that he wasn't *all* nigger no how; said his name was Norwood—not Lewis, like the rest of his family—and part of your plantation here would be his when you passed out—and all that kind of stuff, boasting to the walleyed coons listening to him.

NORWOOD   (*Astounded*) Well, I'll be damned!

HIGGINS   Now, Tom, you know that don't go 'round these parts 'o Georgia, nor nowhere else in the South. A darkie's got to keep in his place down here. Ruinous to other niggers hearing that talk, too. All this postwar propaganda on the radio about freedom and democracy—why the niggers think it's meant for them! And that Eleanor Roosevelt, she ought to been muzzled. She's driving our niggers crazy—your boy included! Crazy! Talking about civil rights. Ain't been no race trouble in our country for three years—since the Deekin's lynching—but I'm telling you, Norwood, you better see that that buck of yours goes away from here. I'm speaking on the quiet, but I can see ahead. And what happened this morning about them radio tubes wasn't none too good.

NORWOOD   (*Beside himself with rage*) A black ape! I——I . . .

HIGGINS   You been too decent to your darkies, Norwood. That's what's the matter with you. And then the whole country suffers from a lot of impudent bucks who take lessons from your crowd. Folks been kicking about that, too. Guess you know it. Maybe that's the reason you didn't get that nomination for committeeman a few years back.

NORWOOD   Maybe 'tis, Higgins. (*Rising and pacing the room*)   God damn niggers! (*Furiously*)   Everything turns on niggers, niggers, niggers! No wonder Yankees call this the Black Belt! (*He pours a large drink of whiskey.*)

HIGGINS   (*Soothingly*)   Well, let's change the subject. Hand me my glass, there, too.

NORWOOD   Pardon me, Fred. (*He puts ice in his friend's glass and passes him the bottle.*)

HIGGINS   Tom, you get excited too easy for warm weather … Don't ever show black folks they got you going, though. I think sometimes that's where you make your mistake. Keep calm, keep calm—and then you command. Best plantation manager I ever had never raised his voice to a nigger—and they were scared to death of him.

NORWOOD   Have a smoke. (*Pushes cigars toward* HIGGINS)

HIGGINS   You ought've married again, Tom—brought a white woman out here on this damn place o' yours. A woman could help you run things. Women have soft ways, but they can keep things humming. Nothing but blacks in the house—a man gets soft like niggers are inside. (*Puffing at cigar*)   And living with a colored woman! Of course, I know we all have 'em—I didn't know you could make use of a white girl till I was past twenty. Thought too much o' white women for that—but I've given many a yellow gal a baby in my time. (*Long puff at cigar*)   But for a man's own house you need a wife, not a black woman.

NORWOOD   Reckon you're right, Fred, but it's too late to marry again now. (*Shrugging his shoulders*)   Let's get off of darkies and women for awhile. How's crops? (*Sitting down*)   How's politics going?

HIGGINS   Well, I guess you know the Republicans is trying
     to stir up trouble for us in Washington. I wish the South
     had more men like Bilbo and Rankin there. But, say, by
     the way, Lawyer Hotchkiss wants to see us both about that
     budget money next week. He's got some real Canadian
     stuff at his office, in his filing case, too—brought back from
     his vacation last summer. Taste better'n this old mountain
     juice we get around here. Not meaning to insult your
     drinks, Tom, but just remarking. I serve the same as you
     myself, label and all.

NORWOOD   (*Laughing*) I'll have you know, sir, that this is
     prewar licker, sir!

HIGGINS   Hum-m-m! Well, it's got me feelin' better'n I did
     when I come in here—whatever it is. (*Puffs at his cigar*)
     Say, how's your cotton this year?

NORWOOD   Doin' right well, specially down in the south
     field. Why not drive out that road when you leave and
     take a look at it? I'll ride down with you. I want to see
     Talbot, anyhow.

HIGGINS   Well, let's be starting. I got to be back at the Junc-
     tion by four o'clock. Promised to let that boy of mine have
     the car to drive over to Thomasville for a dance tonight.

NORWOOD   One more shot before we go. (*He pours out
     drinks.*) The young ones must have their fling, I reckon.
     When you and I grew up down here it used to be a car-
     riage and the best pair of black horses when you took the
     ladies out—now it's an automobile. That's a good lookin'
     new car of yours, too.

HIGGINS   Right nice.

NORWOOD   Been thinking about getting a new one myself,
     but money's been kinder tight this year, and conditions are
     none too good yet, either. Reckon that's why everybody's
     so restless. (*He walks toward stairs calling.*) Cora! Oh,
     Cora! . . . If I didn't have a few thousand put away, I'd

feel the pinch myself. (*As* CORA *appears on the stairs.*) Bring me my glasses up there by the side of my bed . . . Better whistle for Mose, hadn't I, Higgins? He's probably 'round back with some of his women. (*Winking*) You know I got some nice black women in this yard.

HIGGINS   Oh, no, not Mose. I got my servants trained to stay in their places—right where I want 'em—while they're working for me. Just open the door and tell him to come in here and help me out. (NORWOOD *goes to the door and calls the* CHAUFFEUR. MOSE *enters and assists his master out to the car.* CORA *appears with the glasses, goes to the vestibule and gets the* COLONEL'S *hat and cane which she hands him.*)

NORWOOD   (*To* CORA) I want to see that boy o' yours soon as I get back. That won't be long, either. And tell him to put up that Ford of mine and don't touch it again.

CORA   Yes, sir, I'll have him waiting here. (*In a whisper*) It's hot weather, Colonel Tom. Too much of this licker makes your heart upset. It ain't good for you, you know. (NORWOOD *pays her no attention as he exits toward the car. The noise of the departing motor is heard.* CORA *begins to tidy up the room. She takes a glass from a side table. She picks up a doily that was beneath the glass and looks at it long and lovingly. Suddenly she goes to the door left and calls toward the kitchen.*) William, you William! Com'ere, I want to show you something. Make haste, son. (*As* CORA *goes back toward the table, her eldest son,* WILLIAM *enters carrying a five-year-old boy.*) Look here at this purty doily yo' sister made this summer while she been here. She done learned all about sewing and making purty things at school. Ain't it nice, son?

WILLIAM   Sho' is. Sallie takes after you, I reckon. She's a smart little crittur, ma. (*Sighs*) De Lawd knows, I was dumb at school. (*To his child*) Get down, Billy, you's too heavy. (*He puts the boy on the floor*) This here sewin's really fine.

BILLY   (*Running toward the big upholstered chair and jumping up and down on the spring seat*) Gityap! I's a mule driver. Haw! Gee!

CORA   You Billy, get out of that chair 'fore I skins you alive. Get on into de kitchen, sah.

BILLY   I'm playin' horsie, grandma. (*Jumps up in the chair*) Horsie! Horsie!

CORA   Get! That's de Colonel's favorite chair. If he knows any little darkie's been jumpin' on it, he raise sand. Get on, now.

BILLY   Ole Colonel's ma grandpa, ain't he? Ain' he ma white grandpa?

WILLIAM   (*Snatching the child out of the chair*) Boy, I'm gonna fan your hide if you don't hush!

CORA   Shs-ss-s! You Billy, hush yo' mouth! Chile, where you hear that? (*To her son*) Some o' you all been talking too much in front o' this chile. (*To the boy*) Honey, go on in de kitchen till yo' daddy come. Get a cookie from 'Vonia and set down on de back porch. (*Little* BILLY *exists left*)

WILLIAM   Ma, you know it 'twarn't me told him. Bert's the one been goin' all over de plantation since he come back from Atlanta remindin' folks right out we's Colonel Norwood's chilluns.

CORA   (*Catching her breath*) Huh!

WILLIAM   He comes down to my shack tellin' Billy and Marybell they got a white man for grandpa. He's gonna get my chilluns in trouble sho'—like he got himself in trouble when Colonel Tom whipped him.

CORA   Ten or 'leven years ago, warn't it?

WILLIAM   And Bert's *sho'* in trouble now. Can't go back to that college like he could-a if he'd-a had any sense. You can't fool with white folks—an de Colonel ain't never really liked Bert since that there first time he beat him, either.

CORA   No, he ain't. Leastwise, he ain't understood him. (*Musing sadly in a low voice*) Time Bert was 'bout seven, warn't it? Just a little bigger'n yo' Billy.

WILLIAM   Yes.

CORA   Went runnin' up to Colonel Tom out in de horse stables when de Colonel was showin' off his horses—I 'members so well—to fine white company from town. Lawd, that boy's always been foolish! He went runnin' up and grabbed a-holt de Colonel and yelled right in front o' de white folks' faces, "O, papa, Cora say de dinner's ready, papa!" Ain't never called him papa before, and I don't know where he got it from. And Colonel Tom knocked him right backwards under de horse's feet.

WILLIAM   And when de company were gone, he beat that boy unmerciful.

CORA   I thought sho' he were gonna kill ma chile that day. And he were mad at me, too, for months. Said I was teaching you chilluns who they pappy were. Up till then Bert had been his favorite little colored child round here.

WILLIAM   Sho' had.

CORA   But he never like him no more. That's why he sent him off to school so soon to stay, winter and summer, all these years. I had to beg and plead to have him home this summer—but I's sorry now I ever got that boy back here again.

WILLIAM   He's sho' growed more like de Colonel all de time, ain't he? Bert thinks he's a real white man hisself now. Look at de first thing he did when he come home, he ain't seen de Colonel in six years—and Bert sticks out his hand fo' to shake hands with him!

CORA   Lawd! That chile!

WILLIAM   Just like white folks! And de Colonel turns his back and walks off. Can't blame him. He ain't used to such doings from colored folks. God knows what's got into Bert since he come back. He's acting like a fool—just like he was a boss man round here. Won't even say "Yes, sir" and "No, sir" no more to de white folks. Talbot asked him warn't he gonna work in de field this mornin'. Bert say "No!" and turn and walk away. White man so mad, I could see him nearly foam at de mouth. If he warn't yo' chile, ma, he'd been knocked in de head fo' now.

CORA   You's right.

WILLIAM   And you can't talk to him. I tried to tell him something the other day, but he just laughed at me, and said we's all just scared niggers on this plantation. Says he ain't no nigger, no how. He's a Norwood. He's half-white, and he's gonna act like it. (*In amazement at his brother's daring*) And this is Georgia, too!

CORA   I's scared to death for de boy, William. I don't know what to do. De Colonel says he won't send him off to school no mo'. Says he's mo' sassy and impudent now than any nigger he ever seed. Bert never has been like you was, and de girls, quiet and sensible like you knowed you had to be. (*She sits down*) De Colonel say he's gonna make Bert stay here now and work on this plantation like de rest of his niggers. He's gonna show him what color he is. Like that time when he beat him for callin' him "papa." He say he's gwine to teach him his place and make de boy know where he belongs. Seems like me or you can't show him. Colonel Tom has to take him in hand, or these white folks'll kill him around here and then—oh, My God!

WILLIAM   A nigger's just got to know his place in de South, that's all, ain't he, ma?

CORA   Yes, son. That's all, I reckon.

WILLIAM   And ma brother's one damn fool nigger. Don't seems like he knows nothin'. He's gonna ruin us all round here. Makin' it bad for everybody.

CORA   Oh, Lawd, have mercy! (*Beginning to cry*) I don't know what to do. De way he's acting up can't go on. Way he's acting to de Colonel can't last. Somethin's gonna happen to ma chile. I had a bad dream last night, too, and I looked out and seed de moon all red with blood. I seed a path o' living blood across this house, I tell you, in my sleep. Oh, Lawd, have mercy! (*Sobbing*) Oh, Lawd, help me in ma troubles. (*The noise of the returning Ford is heard outside.* CORA *looks up, rises, and goes to the window.*) There's de chile now, William. Run out to de back door and tell him I wants to see him. Bring him in here where Sam and Livonia and de rest of 'em won't hear ever'thing we's sayin'. I got to talk to ma boy. He's ma baby boy, and he don't know de way.

> (*Exit* WILLIAM *through the door left.* CORA *is wiping her eyes and pulling herself together when the front door is flung open with a bang and* ROBERT *enters.*)

ROBERT   (*Running to his mother and hugging her teasingly*) Hello, ma! Your daughter got off, and I've come back to keep you company in the parlor! Bring out the cookies and lemonade. *Mister* Norwood's here!

CORA   (*Beginning to sob anew*) Take yo' hands off me, boy! Why don't you mind? Why don't you mind me?

ROBERT   (*Suddenly serious, backing away*) Why, mamma, what's the matter? Did I scare you? Your eyes are all wet! Has somebody been telling you 'bout this morning?

CORA   (*Not heeding his words*) Why don't you mind me, son? Ain't I told you and told you not to come in that front door, never? (*Suddenly angry*) Will somebody have to beat it into you? What's got wrong with you when you was away at that school? What am I gonna do?

ROBERT   (*Carelessly*) Oh, I knew that the Colonel wasn't here. I passed him and old man Higgins on the road down by the south patch. He wouldn't even look at me when I waved at him. (*Half playfully*) Anyhow, isn't this my old man's house? Ain't I his son and heir? (*Grandly, strutting around*) Am I not Mr. Norwood, Junior?

CORA   (*Utterly serious*) I believes you goin' crazy, Bert. I believes you wants to get us all killed or run away or something awful like that. I believes . . . (WILLIAM *enters left*)

WILLIAM   Where's Bert? He ain't come round back—— (*Seeing his brother in the room*) How'd you get in here?

ROBERT   (*Grinning*) Houses have front doors.

WILLIAM   Oh, usin' de front door like de white folks, heh? You gwine do that once too much.

ROBERT   Yes, like de white folks. What's a front door for, you rabbit-hearted coon?

WILLIAM   Rabbit-hearted coon's better'n a dead coon any day.

ROBERT   I wouldn't say so. Besides you and me's only half-coons, anyhow, big boy. And I'm gonna act like my white half, not my black half. Get me, kid?

WILLIAM   Well, you ain't gonna act like it long here in de middle o' Georgy. And you ain't gonna act like it when de Colonel's around, either.

ROBERT   Oh, no? My stay down here'll be short and sweet, boy, short and sweet. The old man won't send me away to college no more—so you think I'm gonna stick around and work in the fields? Like fun? I might stay here awhile and teach some o' you darkies to think like men, maybe—till it gets too much for the old Colonel—but no more bowing down to white folks for me—not Robert Norwood.

CORA   Hush, son!

ROBERT   Certainly not right on my own old man's plantation—Georgia or no Georgia.

WILLIAM   (*Scornfully*) I hears you.

ROBERT   *You* can do it if you want to, but I'm ashamed of you. I've been away from here six years. (*Boasting*) I've learned something, seen people in Atlanta, and Richmond, and Washington where the football team went—real colored people who don't have to take off their hats to white folks or let 'em go to bed with their sisters—like that young Higgins boy, asking me what night Sallie was comin' to town. A damn cracker! (*To* CORA) 'Scuse me, ma. (*Continuing*) Back here in these woods maybe Sam and Livonia and you and mama and everybody's got their places fixed for 'em, but not me. (*Seriously*) Nobody's gonna fix a place for me. I'm old man Norwood's son. Nobody fixed a place for him. (*Playfully again*) Look at me. I'm a 'fay boy. (*Pretends to shake his hair back*) See these gray eyes? I got the right to everything everybody else has. (*Punching his brother in the belly*), Don't talk to me, old slavery-time Uncle Tom.

WILLIAM   (*Resentfully*) I ain't playin', boy. (*Pushes younger brother back with some force*) I ain't playin' a-tall.

CORA   All right, chilluns, stop. Stop! And William, you take Billy and go on home. 'Vonia's got to get supper and she don't like no young-uns under her feet in de kitchen. I wants to talk to Bert in here now 'fore Colonel Tom gets back. (*Exit* WILLIAM *left.* CORA *continues to* BERT) Sit down, child, right here a minute, and listen.

ROBERT   (*Sitting down*) All right, ma.

CORA   Hard as I's worked and begged and humbled maself to get de Colonel to keep you chilluns in school, you comes home wid yo' head full o' stubbornness and yo' mouth full o' sass for me an' de white folks an' everybody. You know can't no colored boy here talk like you's been doin' to no white folks, let alone to de Colonel and that old devil of a Talbot. They ain't gonna stand fo' yo' sass. Not only you, but I 'spects we's all gwine to pay fo' it, every colored soul on this place. I was scared to death today fo' yo' sister, Sallie, scared de Colonel warn't gwine to let her go back to school, neither, 'count o' yo' doins, but he did, thank

Gawd—and then you come near makin' her miss de train. Did she have time to get her ticket and all?

ROBERT   Sure! Had to drive like sin to get there with her, though. I didn't mean to be late getting back here for her, ma, but I had a little run-in about them radio tubes in town.

CORA   (*Worried*)   What's that?

ROBERT   The tubes was smashed when I got 'em, and I had already made out my money order, so the woman in the post office wouldn't give the three dollars back to me. All I did was explain to her that we could send the tubes back —but she got hot because there were two or three white folks waiting behind me to get stamps, I guess. So she yells at me to move on and not give her any of my "educated nigger talk." So I said, "I'm going to finish showing you these tubes before I move on"—and then she screamed and called the mail clerk working in the back, and told him to throw me out. (*Boasting*)   He didn't do it by himself, though. Had to call all the white loafers out in the square to get me through that door.

CORA   (*Fearfully*)   Lawd have mercy!

ROBERT   Guess if I hadn't-a had the Ford then, they'd've beat me half-to-death, but when I saw how many crackers there was, I jumped in the car and beat it on away.

CORA   Thank God for that!

ROBERT   Not even a football man   (*Half-boasting*)   like me could tackle the whole junction. 'Bout a dozen colored guys standing around, too, and not one of 'em would help me—the dumb jiggaboos! They been telling me ever since I been here, (*Imitating darky talk*)   "You can't argue wid whut folks, man. You better stay out o' this Junction. You must ain't got no sense, nigger! You's a fool" . . . Maybe I am a fool, ma—but I didn't want to come back here nohow.

CORA   I's sorry I sent for you.

ROBERT   Besides you, there ain't nobody in this country but
a lot of evil white folks and cowardly niggers. (*Earnestly*)
I'm no nigger, anyhow, am I, ma? I'm half-white. The
Colonel's my father—the richest man in the county—
and I'm not going to take a lot of stuff from nobody if I
do have to stay here, not from the old man either. He
thinks I ought to be out there in the sun working, with
Talbot standing over me like I belonged in the chain gang.
Well, he's got another thought coming! (*Stubbornly*)
I'm a Norwood—not a field-hand nigger.

CORA   You means you ain't workin' no mo'?

ROBERT   (*Flaring*)   No, I'm not going to work in the fields.
What did he send me away to school for—just to come
back here and be his servant, or pick his hills of cotton?

CORA   He sent you away to de school because *I* asked him
and begged him, and got down on my knees to him, that's
why. (*Quietly*)   And now I just wants to make you see
some sense, if you can. I knows, honey, you reads in de
books and de papers, and you knows a lot more'n I do.
But, chile, you's in Georgy—and I don't see how it is you
don't know where you's at. This ain't up North—and even
up yonder where we hears it's so fine, yo' sister has to pass
for white to get along good.

ROBERT   (*Bitterly*)   I know it.

CORA   She ain't workin' in no hotel kitchen like de Colonel
thinks. She's in a office typewriting. And Sallie's studyin'
de typewriter, too, at de school, but yo' pappy don't know
it. I knows we ain't s'posed to study nothin' but cookin' and
hard workin' here in Georgy. That's all I ever done, or
knowed about. I been workin' on this very place all ma life
—even 'fore I come to live in this Big House. When de
Colonel's wife died, I come here, and borned you chilluns.
And de Colonel's been real good to me in his way. Let you

all sleep in this house with me when you was little, and sent you all off to school when you growed up. Ain't no white man in this county done that with his cullud chilluns before, far as I can know. But you—Robert, be awful, awful careful! When de Colonel comes back, in a few minutes, he wants to talk to you. Talk right to him, boy. Talk like you was colored, 'cause you ain't white.

ROBERT   (*Angrily*)   And I'm not black either. Look at me, mama. (*Rising and throwing up his arms*)   Don't I look like my father? Ain't I as light as he is? Ain't my eyes gray like his eyes are? (*The noise of a car is heard outside*) Ain't this our house?

CORA   That's him now. (*Agitated*)   Hurry, chile, and let's get out of this room. Come on through yonder to the kitchen. (*She starts toward the door left.*)   And I'll tell him you're here.

ROBERT   I don't want to run into the kitchen. Isn't this our house? (*As* CORA *crosses hurriedly left,* ROBERT *goes toward the front door*)   The Ford is parked out in front, anyway.

CORA   (*At the door left to the rear of the house*)   Robert! Robert! (*As* ROBERT *nears the front door,* COLONEL NOR-WOOD *enters, almost runs into the boy, stops at the threshold and stares unbelievingly at his son.* CORA *backs up against the door left.*)

NORWOOD   Get out of here! (*He points toward the door to rear of the house where* CORA *is standing*)

ROBERT   (*Half-smiling*)   Didn't you want to talk to me?

NORWOOD   Get out of here!

ROBERT   Not that way. (*The* COLONEL *raises his cane to strike the boy.* CORA *screams.* BERT *draws himself up to his full height, taller than the old man and looking very much like him, pale and proud. The man and the boy face each other.* NORWOOD *does not strike.*)

NORWOOD   (*In a hoarse whisper*) Get out of here. (*His hand is trembling as he points.*)

CORA   Robert! Come on, son, come on! Oh, my God, come on. (*Opening the door left*)

ROBERT   Not that way, ma. (ROBERT *walks proudly out the front door.* NORWOOD, *in an impotent rage, crosses the room to a small cabinet right, opens it nervously with a key from his pocket, takes out a pistol, and starts toward the front door.* CORA *overtakes him, seizes his arm, stops him.*)

CORA   He's our son, Tom. (*She sinks slowly to her knees, holding his body.*) Remember, he's our son.

CURTAIN

Act II

Scene 1

TIME   *After supper. Sunset.*
SETTING   *The same.*
ACTION   *As the curtain rises, the stage is empty. Through the windows the late afternoon sun makes two bright paths toward the footlights.* SAM, *carrying a tray bearing a whiskey bottle and a bowl of ice, enters left and crosses toward the library. He stoops at the door right, listens a moment, knocks, then opens the door and goes in. In a moment* SAM *returns. As he leaves the library, he is heard replying to a request of* NORWOOD'S.

SAM   Yes, sah, Colonel! Sho' will, sah! Right away, sah! Yes, sah, I'll tell him. (*He closes the door and crosses the stage muttering to himself.*) Six o'clock. Most nigh that now. Better tell Cora to get that boy right in here. Can't nobody else do nothin' with that fool Bert but Cora. (*He exits left. Can be heard calling*) Cora! You, Cora . . .

(*Again the stage is empty. Off stage, outside, the bark of a dog is heard, the sound of Negroes singing down the road, the cry of a child. The breeze moves the shadows of leaves and tree limbs across the sunlit paths from the windows. The door left opens and* CORA *enters, followed by* ROBERT.)

CORA   (*Softly to* ROBERT *behind her in the dining room*) It's all right, son. He ain't come out yet, but it's nearly six, and that's when he said he wanted you, but I was afraid maybe you was gonna be late. I sent for you to come up here to de house and eat supper with me in de kitchen. Where'd you eat yo' vittuals at, chile?

ROBERT   Down at Willie's house, ma. After the old man tried to hit me you still want me to hang around and eat up here?

CORA　　I wanted you to be here on time, honey, that's all. (*She is very nervous.*)　I kinder likes to have you eat with me sometimes, too, but you ain't et up here more'n once this summer. But this evenin' I just wanted you to be here when de Colonel sent word for you, 'cause we's done had enough trouble today.

ROBERT　　He's not here on time, himself, is he?

CORA　　He's in de library. Sam couldn't get him to eat no supper tonight, and I ain't seen him a-tall.

ROBERT　　Maybe he wants to see me in the library, then.

CORA　　You know he don't 'low no colored folks in there 'mongst his books and things 'cept Sam. Some o' his white friends goes in there, but none o' us.

ROBERT　　Maybe he wants to see *me* in there, though.

CORA　　Can't you never talk sense, Robert? This ain't no time for foolin' and jokin'. Nearly thirty years in this house and I ain't never been in there myself, not once, 'mongst de Colonel's papers. (*The clock strikes six.*)　Stand over yonder and wait till he comes out. I's gwine on upstairs now, so's he can talk to you. And don't aggravate him no mo' fo' God's sake. Agree to whatever he say. I's scared fo' you, chile, de way you been actin', and de fool tricks you done today, and de trouble about de post office besides. Don't aggravate him. Fo' yo' sake, honey, 'cause I loves you—and fo' all de po' colored folks on this place what has such a hard time when his humors get on him—agree to whatever he say, will you, Bert?

ROBERT　　All right, ma. (*Voice rising*) But he better not start to hit me again.

CORA　　Shs-ss-s! He'll hear you. He's right in there.

ROBERT　　(*Sullenly*) This was the day I ought to have started back to school—like my sister. I stayed my summer out here, didn't I? Why didn't he keep his promise to me? You said if I came home I could go back to college again.

CORA   Shs-ss-s! He'll be here now. Don't say nothin', chile. I's done all I could.

ROBERT   All right, ma.

CORA   (*Approaching the stairs*) I'll be in ma room, honey, where I can hear you when you goes out. I'll come down to de back door and see you 'fore you goes back to de shack. Don't aggravate him, chile.

> (*She ascends the stairs. The boy sits down sullenly, left, and stares at the door opposite from which his father must enter. The clock strikes the quarter after six. The shadows of the window curtains have lengthened on the carpet. The sunshine has deepened to a pale orange, and the light paths grow less distinct across the floor. The boy sits up straight in his chair. He looks at the library door. It opens.* NORWOOD *enters. He is bent and pale. He looks across the room and sees the boy. Suddenly he straightens up. The old commanding look comes into his face. He strides directly across the room toward his son. The boy, half afraid, half defiant, yet sure of himself, rises. Now that* ROBERT *is standing, the white man turns, goes back to a chair near the table, right, and seats himself. He takes out a cigar, cuts off the end and lights it, and in a voice of mixed condescension and contempt, he speaks to his son.* ROBERT *remains standing near the chair.*)

NORWOOD   I don't want to have to beat you another time as I did when you were a child. The next time I might not be able to control myself. I might kill you if I touched you again. I been runnin' this plantation for thirty-five years, and I never had to beat a Nigra as old as you are. I never had to beat one of Cora's children either—but you. The rest of 'em had sense 'nough to keep out of my sight, and to speak to me like they should . . . I don't have any trouble with my colored folks. Never have trouble. They do what

I say, or what Mr. Talbot says, and that's all there is to it. I give 'em a chance. If they turn in crops they get paid. If they're workin' for wages, they get paid. If they want to spend their money on licker, or buy an old car, or fix up their cabins, they can. Do what they choose long as they know their places and it don't hinder their work. And to Cora's young ones I give all the chances any colored folks ever had in these parts. More'n many a white child's had. I sent you all off to school. Let Bertha go on up North when she got grown and educated. Intend to let Sallie do the same. Gave your brother William that house he's living in when he got married, pay him for his work, help him out if he needs it. None of my darkies suffer. Sent you to college. Would have kept on, would have sent you back today, but I don't intend to pay for no darky, or white boy either if I had one, that acts the way you've been acting. And certainly for no black fool. Now I want to know what's wrong with you? I don't usually talk about what I'm going to do with anybody on this place. It's my habit to tell people *what to do*, not discuss it with 'em. But I want to know what's the matter with you—whether you're crazy or not. In that case, you'll have to be locked up. And if you aren't, you'll have to change your ways a damn sight or it won't be safe for you here, and you know it—venting your impudence on white women, parking the car in front of my door, driving like mad through the Junction, and going, everywhere, just as you please. Now, I'm going to let you talk to me, but I want you to talk right.

ROBERT   (*Still standing*) What do you mean, "talk right?"

NORWOOD   I mean talk like a nigger should to a white man.

ROBERT   Oh! But I'm not a nigger, Colonel Tom. I'm your son.

NORWOOD   (*Testily*) You're Cora's boy.

ROBERT   Women don't have children by themselves.

NORWOOD   Nigger women don't know the fathers. You're a
      bastard.

> (ROBERT *clenches his fist.* NORWOOD *turns toward the*
> *drawer where the pistol is, takes it out, and lays it on*
> *the table. The wind blows the lace curtains at the*
> *windows, and sweeps the shadows of falling leaves*
> *across the paths of sunlight on the floor.*)

ROBERT   I've heard that before. I've heard it from Negroes,
      and I've heard it from white folks. Now I hear it from
      you. (*Slowly*) You're talking about my mother.

NORWOOD   I'm talking about Cora, yes. Her children are
      bastards.

ROBERT   (*Quickly*) And you're their father. (*Angrily*)
      How come I look like you, if you're not my father?

NORWOOD   Don't shout at me, boy. I can hear you. (*Half-
      smiling*) How come your skin is yellow and your elbows
      rusty? How come they threw you out of the post office to-
      day for talking to a white woman? How come you're the
      crazy young buck you are?

ROBERT   They had no right to throw me out. I asked for my
      money back when I saw the broken tubes. Just as you had
      no right to raise that cane today when I was standing at
      the door of this house where *you* live, while *I* have to sleep
      in a shack down the road with the field hands. (*Slowly*)
      But my mother sleeps with you.

NORWOOD   You don't like it?

ROBERT   No, I don't like it.

NORWOOD   What can you do about it?

ROBERT   (*After a pause*) I'd like to kill all the white men
      in the world.

NORWOOD   (*Starting*) Niggers like you are hung to trees.

ROBERT   I'm not a nigger.

NORWOOD   You don't like your own race? (ROBERT *is silent*) Yet you don't like white folks either?

ROBERT   (*Defiantly*) You think I ought to?

NORWOOD   You evidently don't like me.

ROBERT   (*Boyishly*) I used to like you, when I first knew you were my father, when I was a little kid, before that time you beat me under the feet of your horses. (*Slowly*) I liked you until then.

NORWOOD   (*A little pleased*) So you did, heh? (*Fingering his pistol*) A pickaninny calling me "papa." I should've broken your young neck for that first time. I should've broken your head for you today, too—since I didn't then.

ROBERT   (*Laughing scornfully*) You should've broken my head?

NORWOOD   Should've gotten rid of you before this. But you was Cora's child. I tried to help you. (*Aggrieved*) I treated you decent, schooled you. Paid for it. But tonight you'll get the hell off this place and stay off. Get the hell out of this county. (*Suddenly furious*) Get out of this state. Don't let me lay eyes on you again. Get out of here now. Talbot and the storekeeper are coming up here this evening to talk cotton with me. I'll tell Talbot to *see* that you go. That's all. (NORWOOD *motions toward the door, left.*) Tell Sam to come in here when you go out. Tell him to make a light here.

ROBERT   (*Impudently*) *Ring* for Sam—I'm not going through the kitchen. (*He starts toward the front door*) I'm not your servant. You're not going to tell me what to do. You're not going to have Talbot run me off the place like a field hand you don't want to use any more.

NORWOOD   (*Springing between his son and the front door, pistol in hand*) You black bastard! (ROBERT *goes toward him calmly, grasps his father's arm and twists it until the gun falls to the floor. The older man bends backward in startled fury and pain.*)   Don't you dare put your . . .

ROBERT   (*Laughing*)   Why don't you shoot, papa? (*Louder*)   Why don't you shoot?

NORWOOD   (*Gasping as he struggles, fighting back*)   . . . black . . . hands . . . on . . . you . . .

ROBERT   (*Hysterically, as he takes his father by the throat*) Why don't you shoot, papa?   (NORWOOD's *hands claw the air helplessly.* ROBERT *chokes the struggling white man until his body grows limp*)   Why don't you shoot!   (*Laughing*)   Why don't you shoot? Huh? Why?

(CORA *appears at the top of the stairs, hearing the commotion. She screams.*)

CORA   Oh, my God!   (*She rushes down.* ROBERT *drops the body of his father at her feet in a path of flame from the setting sun.* CORA *starts and stares in horror.*)

ROBERT   (*Wildly*)   Why didn't he shoot, mama? He didn't want *me* to live. Why didn't he shoot?   (*Laughing*)   He was the boss. Telling me what to do. Why didn't he shoot, then? He was the white man.

CORA   (*Falling on the body*)   Colonel Tom! Colonel Tom! Tom! Tom!   (*Gazes across the corpse at her son*)   He's yo' father, Bert.

ROBERT   He's dead. The white man's dead. My father's dead.   (*Laughing*)   I'm living.

CORA   Tom! Tom! Tom!

ROBERT   Niggers are living. He's dead.   (*Picks up the pistol*)   This is what he wanted to kill me with, but he's dead. I can use it now. Use it on all the white men in the world, because they'll be coming looking for me now.   (*Stuffs the pistol into his shirt*)   They'll want me now.

CORA   (*Rising and running toward her boy*)   Quick, chile, out that way,   (*Pointing toward the front door*)   so they won't see you in de kitchen. Make for de swamp, honey. Cross de fields fo' de swamp. Go de crick way. In runnin' water, dogs can't smell no tracks. Hurry, chile!

ROBERT   Yes, mama. I can go out the front way now, easy. But if I see they gonna get me before I can reach the swamp, I'm coming back here, mama, and (*Proudly*) let them take me out of my father's house—if they can. (*Pats the gun under his shirt*) They're not going to string me up to some roadside tree for the crackers to laugh at.

CORA   (*Moaning aloud*) Oh, O-o-o! Hurry! Hurry, chile!

ROBERT   I'm going, ma. (*He opens the door. The sunset streams in like a river of blood*)

CORA   Run, chile!

ROBERT   Not out of my father's house. (*He exits slowly, tall and straight against the sun.*)

CORA   Fo' God's sake, hurry, chile! (*Glancing down the road*) Lawd have mercy! There's Talbot and de storekeeper in de drive. They sees my boy! (*Moaning*) They sees ma boy. (*Relieved*) But thank God, they's passin' him! (CORA *backs up against the wall in the vestibule. She stands as if petrified as* TALBOT *and the* STOREKEEPER *enter*)

TALBOT   Hello, Cora. What's the matter with you? Where's that damn fool boy o' your'n goin', coming out the front door like he owned the house? What's the matter with you, woman? Can't you talk? Can't you talk? Where's Norwood? Let's have some light in this dark place. (*He reaches behind the door and turns on the lights.* CORA *remains backed up against the wall, looking out into the twilight, watching* ROBERT *as he goes across the field*) Good God, Jim! Look at this! (*The* TWO WHITE MEN *stop in horror before the sight of* NORWOOD's *body on the floor.*)

STOREKEEPER   He's blue in the face. (*Bends over the body*) That nigger we saw walking out the door! (*Rising ex-*

citedly) That nigger bastard of Cora's . . . (*Stooping over the body again*) Why the Colonel's dead!

TALBOT   That nigger! (*Rushes toward the door*) He's running toward the swamp now . . . We'll get him . . . Telephone town—there, in the library. Telephone the sheriff. Get men, white men, after that nigger.

> (STOREKEEPER *rushes into the library. He can be heard talking excitedly on the phone.*)

STOREKEEPER   Sheriff! Sheriff! Is this the sheriff? I'm calling from Norwood's plantation. That nigger, Bert, has just killed Norwood—and run, headed for the swamp. Notify the gas station at the crossroads! Tell the boys at the sawmill to head him off at the creek. Warn everybody to be on the lookout. Call your deputies! Yes! Yes! Spread a dragnet. Get out the dogs. Meanwhile we'll start after him. (*He slams the phone down and comes back into the room.*) Cora, where's Norwood's car? In the barn? (CORA *does not answer.*)

TALBOT   Talk, you black bitch!

> (*She remains silent.* TALBOT *runs, yelling and talking, out into the yard, followed by the* STOREKEEPER. *Sounds of excited shouting outside, and the roar of a motor rushing down the drive. In the sky the twilight deepens into early night.* CORA *stands looking into the darkness.*)

CORA   My boy can't get to de swamp now. They's telephoned the white folks down that way. So he'll come back home now. Maybe he'll turn into de crick and follow de branch home directly. (*Protectively*) But they shan't get him. I'll make a place for to hide him. I'll make a place upstairs down under de floor, under ma bed. In a minute ma boy'll be runnin' from de white folks with their hounds and their ropes and their guns and everything they uses to kill po' colored folks with. (*Distressed*) Ma boy'll be out there

runnin'. (*Turning to the body on the floor*) Colonel
Tom, you hear me? Our boy, out there runnin'. (*Fiercely*)
You said he was ma boy—*ma* bastard boy. I heard you . . .
but he's yours too . . . but yonder in de dark runnin'—runnin' from yo' people, from white people. (*Pleadingly*)
Why don't you get up and stop 'em? He's *your* boy. His
eyes is gray—like your eyes. He's tall like you's tall. He's
proud like you's proud. And he's runnin'—runnin' from
po' white trash what ain't worth de little finger o' nobody
what's got your blood in 'em, Tom. (*Demandingly*)
Why don't you get up from there and stop 'em, Colonel
Tom? What's that you say? He ain't your chile? He's ma
bastard chile? My yellow bastard chile? (*Proudly*) Yes,
he's mine. But don't call him that. Don't you touch him.
Don't you put your white hands on him. You's beat him
enough, and cussed him enough. Don't you touch him now.
He *is* ma boy and no white folks gonna touch him now.
That's finished. I'm gonna make a place for him upstairs
under ma bed. (*Backs away from the body toward the
stairs*) He's ma chile. Don't you come in ma bedroom
while he's up there. Don't you come to my bed no mo'. I
calls you to help me now, and you just lays there. I calls you
for to wake up, and you just lays there. Whenever you
called me, in de night, I woke up. When you called for me
to love, I always reached out ma arms fo' you. I borned
you five chilluns and now one of 'em is out yonder in de
dark runnin' from yo' people. Our youngest boy out yonder in de dark runnin'. (*Accusingly*) He's runnin' from
you, too. You said he warn't your'n—he's just Cora's po'
little yellow bastard. But he *is* your'n, Colonel Tom.
(*Sadly*) And he's runnin' from you. You are out yonder
in de dark, (*Points toward the door*) runnin' our chile,
with de hounds and de gun in yo' hand, and Talbot's
followin' 'hind you with a rope to hang Robert with.
(*Confidently*) I been sleepin' with you too long, Colonel
Tom, not to know that this ain't you layin' down there with

yo' eyes shut on de floor. You can't fool me—you ain't never been so still like this before—you's out yonder runnin' ma boy through de fields in de dark, runnin' ma poor little helpless Bert through de fields in de dark to lynch him . . . Damn you, Colonel Norwood! (*Backing slowly up the stairs, staring at the rigid body below her*) Damn you, Thomas Norwood! God damn you!

CURTAIN

Scene 2

TIME   *One hour later. Night.*
SETTING   *The same.*
ACTION   *As the curtain rises, the* UNDERTAKER *is talking to* SAM *at the outer door. All through this act the approaching cries of the man hunt are heard.*

UNDERTAKER   Reckon there won't be no orders to bring his corpse back out here, Sam. None of us ain't seen Talbot or Mr. Higgins, but I'm sure they'll be having the funeral in town. The coroner told us to bring the body into the Junction. Ain't nothin' but niggers left out here now.

SAM   (*Very frightened*) Yes, sah! Yes, sah! You's right, sah! Nothin' but us niggers, sah!

UNDERTAKER   The Colonel didn't have no relatives far as you know, did he, Sam?

SAM   No, sah. Ain't had none. No, sah! You's right, sah!

UNDERTAKER   Well, you got everything o' his locked up around here, ain't you? Too bad there ain't no white folks about to look after the Colonel's stuff, but every white man that's able to walk's out with the posse. They'll have that young nigger swingin' before ten.

SAM   (*Trembling*) Yes, sah, yes, sah! I 'spects so. Yes, sah!

UNDERTAKER   Say, where's that woman the Colonel's been living with—where's that black housekeeper, Cora, that murderin' bastard's mother?

SAM   She here, sah! She's up in her room.

UNDERTAKER   (*Curiously*) I'd like to see how she looks. Get her down here. Say, how about a little drink before we start that ride back to town, for me and my partner out there with the body?

SAM   Cora got de keys to all de licker, sah!

UNDERTAKER   Well, get her down here then, double quick! (SAM *goes up the stairs. The* UNDERTAKER *leans in the front doorway talking to his partner outside in the wagon*) Bad business, a white man having saucy nigger children on his hands, and his black woman living in his own house.

VOICE OUTSIDE   Damn right, Charlie.

UNDERTAKER   Norwood didn't have a gang o' yellow gals, though, like Higgins and some o' these other big bugs. Just this one bitch far's I know, livin' with him damn near like a wife. Didn't even have much company out here. And they tell me ain't been a white woman stayed here over-night since his wife died when I was a baby. (SAM'S *shuffle is heard on the stairs*) Here comes a drink, I reckon, boy. You needn't get down off the ambulance. I'll have Sam bring it out there to you. (SAM *descends followed by* CORA *who comes down the stairs. She says nothing. The* UNDERTAKER *looks up grinning at* CORA) Well, so you're the Cora that's got these educated nigger children? Hum-m! Well, I guess you'll see one of 'em swinging full of bullet holes when you wake up in the morning. They'll probably hang him to that tree down here by the Colonel's gate—'cause they tell me he strutted right out the front gate past that tree after the murder. Or maybe they'll burn him. How'd you like to see him swinging there roasted in the morning when you wake up, girlie?

CORA   (*Calmly*)   Is that all you wanted to say to me?

UNDERTAKER   Don't get smart! Maybe you think there's nobody to boss you now. We gonna have a little drink before we go. Get out a bottle of rye.

CORA   I takes ma orders from Colonel Norwood, sir.

UNDERTAKER   Well, you'll take no more orders from him. He's dead out there in my wagon—so get along and get the bottle.

CORA   He's out yonder with de mob, not in your wagon.

UNDERTAKER   I tell you he's in my wagon!

CORA   He's out there with de mob.

UNDERTAKER   God damn! (*To his partner outside*)   I believe this black woman's gone crazy in here. (*To* CORA) Get the keys out for that licker, and be quick about it! (CORA *does not move.* SAM *looks from one to the other, frightened.*)

VOICE OUTSIDE   Aw, to hell with the licker, Charlie. Come on, let's start back to town. We want to get in on some of that excitement, too. They should've found that nigger by now—and I want to see 'em drag him out here.

UNDERTAKER   All right, Jim. (*To* CORA *and* SAM) Don't you all go to bed until you see that bonfire. You niggers are getting besides yourselves around Polk County. We'll burn a few more of you if you don't be careful. (*He exits, and the noise of the dead-wagon going down the road is heard.*)

SAM   Oh, Lawd, hab mercy on me! I prays, Lawd hab mercy! O, ma Lawd, ma Lawd, ma Lawd! Cora, is you a fool? *Is* you a fool? Why didn't you give de mens de licker, riled as these white folks is? In ma old age is I gonna be burnt by de crackers? Lawd, is I sinned? Lawd, what has I done? (*Suddenly stops moaning and becomes schemingly calm*)   I don't have to stay here tonight, does I? I done locked up de Colonel's library, and he can't be wantin' nothin'. No, ma Lawd, he won't want nothin' now. He's with Jesus—or with de devil, one. (*To* CORA) I's gwine on away from here. Sam's gwine in town to his chilluns' house, and I ain't gwine by no road either. I gwine through de holler where I don't have to pass no white folks.

CORA   Yes, Samuel, you go on. De Colonel can get his own drinks when he comes back tonight.

SAM   (*Bucking his eyes in astonishment at* CORA) Lawd God Jesus!

> (*He bolts out of the room as fast as his old legs will carry him.* CORA *comes down stairs, looks for a long moment out into the darkness, then closes the front door and draws the blinds. She looks down at the spot where the* COLONEL'S *body lay.*)

CORA   All de colored folks are runnin' from you tonight. Po' Colonel Tom, you too old now to be out with de mob. You got no business goin', but you had to go, I reckon. I 'members that time they hung Luke Jordon, you sent yo' dogs out to hunt him. The next day you killed all de dogs. You were kinder softhearted. Said you didn't like that kind of sport. Told me in bed one night you could hear them dogs howlin' in yo' sleep. But de time they burnt de courthouse when that po' little cullud boy was locked up in it cause they said he hugged a white girl, you was with 'em again. Said you had to go help 'em. Now you's out chasin' ma boy. (*As she stands at the window, she sees a passing figure.*) There goes yo' other woman, Colonel Tom, Livonia is runnin' from you too, now. She would've wanted you last night. Been wantin' you again ever since she got old and fat and you stopped layin' with her and put her in the kitchen to cook. Don't think I don't know, Colonel Tom. Don't think I don't remember them nights when you used to sleep in that cabin down by de spring. I knew 'Vonia was there with you. I ain't no fool, Colonel Tom.

But she ain't bore you no chilluns. I'm de one that bore 'em. (*Musing*) White mens, and colored womens, and little bastard chilluns—that's de old way of de South—but it's ending now. Three of your yellow brothers yo' father had by Aunt Sallie Deal—what had to come and do your laundry to make her livin'—you got colored relatives scattered all over this county. Them de ways o' de South— mixtries, mixtries. (WILLIAM *enters left, silently, as his mother talks. She is sitting in a chair now. Without looking up*) Is that you, William?

WILLIAM   Yes, ma, it's me.

CORA   Is you runnin' from him, too?

WILLIAM   (*Hesitatingly*) Well, ma, you see . . . don't you think kinder . . . well, I reckon I ought to take Libby and ma babies on down to de church house with Reverend Martin and them, or else get 'long to town if I can hitch up them mules. They's scared to be out here, my wife and her ma. All de folks done gone from de houses down yonder by de branch, and you can hear de hounds a bayin' off yonder by de swamp, and cars is tearin' up that road, and de white folks is yellin' and hollerin' and carryin' on somethin' terrible over toward de brook. I done told Robert 'bout his foolishness. They's gonna hang him sure. Don't you think you better be comin' with us, ma. That is, do you want to? 'Course we can go by ourselves, and maybe you wants to stay here and take care o' de big house. I don't want to leave you, ma, but I . . . I . . .

CORA   Yo' brother'll be back, son, then I won't be by myself.

WILLIAM   (*Bewildered by his mother's sureness*) I thought Bert went . . . I thought he run . . . I thought . . .

CORA   No, honey. He went, but they ain't gonna get him out there. I sees him comin' back here now, to be with me. I's gwine to guard him 'till he can get away.

WILLIAM   Then de white folks'll come here, too.

CORA   Yes, de Colonel'll come back here sure. (*The deep baying of the hounds is heard at a distance through the night.*) Colonel Tom will come after his son.

WILLIAM   My God, ma! Come with us to town.

CORA   Go on, William, go on! Don't wait for them to get back. You never was much like neither one o' them—neither de Colonel or Bert—you's mo' like de field hands. Too much o' ma blood in you, I guess. You never liked Bert much, neither, and you always was afraid of de Colonel. Go on, son, and hide yo' wife and her ma and your chilluns. Ain't nothin' gonna hurt you. You never did go against nobody. Neither did I, till tonight. Tried to live right and not hurt a soul, white or colored. (*Addressing space*) I tried to live right, Lord. (*Angrily*) Tried to live right, Lord. (*Throws out her arms resentfully as if to say, "and this is what you give me."*) What's de matter, Lawd, you ain't with me?

(*The hounds are heard howling again.*)

WILLIAM   I'm gone, ma. (*He exits fearfully as his mother talks.*)

CORA   (*Bending over the spot on the floor where the* COLONEL *has lain. She calls*) Colonel Tom! Colonel Tom! Colonel Tom! Look! Bertha and Sallie and William and Bert, all your chilluns, runnin' from you, and you layin' on de floor there, dead! (*Pointing*) Out yonder with the mob, dead. And when you come home, upstairs in my bed on top of my body, dead. (*Goes to the window, returns, sits down, and begins to speak as if remembering a far-off dream.*) Colonel Thomas Norwood! I'm just poor Cora Lewis, Colonel Norwood. Little black Cora Lewis, Colonel Norwood. I'm just fifteen years old. Thirty years ago, you put your hands on me to feel my breasts, and you say, "You a pretty little piece of flesh, ain't you? Black and sweet, ain't you?" And I lift up ma face, and you pull me to you, and we laid down under the trees that night, and I wonder if your wife'll know when you go back up the road into the big house. And I wonder if my mama'll know it, when I go back to our cabin. Mama said she nursed you when you was a baby, just like she nursed me. And I loved you in the dark, down there under that tree by de gate, afraid of you and proud of you, feelin' your gray eyes lookin' at me in de dark. Then I cried and cried and told ma mother about it, but she didn't take it hard like I thought she'd take it. She said fine white mens like de young Colonel always took good care o' their colored womens. She said it was better than marryin' some black field hand and workin' all your life in de cotton and cane. Better even than havin' a job like ma had, takin' care o' de white chilluns. Takin' care o' you, Colonel Tom. (*As* CORA *speaks the sound of the approaching mob gradually grows louder and louder. Auto horns, the howling of dogs, the far-off shouts of men, full of malignant force and power, increase in volume.*) And I was happy because I liked you, 'cause you was tall and proud, 'cause you said I was sweet to you and called me purty. And when yo' wife died—de Mrs. Norwood (*Scornfully*) that never bore you any chilluns, the pale beautiful Mrs. Norwood that was like a slender pine tree in de winter frost . . . I knowed you wanted me. I was full with child by you then—William, it was—our first boy. And ma mammy said, go up there and keep de house for Colonel Tom, sweep de floors and make de beds, and by and by, you won't have to sweep de floors and make no beds. And what ma mammy said was right. It all come true. Sam and Rusus and 'Vonia and Lucy did de waitin' on you and me, and de washin' and de cleanin' and de cookin'. And all I did was a little sewin' now and then, and a little preservin' in de summer and a little makin' of pies and sweet cakes and things you like to eat on Christmas. And de years went by. And I was always ready for you when you come to me in de night. And we had them chilluns, your chilluns and mine, Tom Norwood, all of 'em! William, born dark like me, dumb like me, and then Baby John what died; then Bertha, white and smart like you; and then Bert with your eyes and your ways and your temper, and mighty nigh your color; then Sallie, nearly white, too, and smart, and purty. But Bert was yo' chile! He was always yo' child . . . Good-looking, and kind, and headstrong, and strange, and stubborn, and proud like you, and de one I could love most 'cause he needed de most lovin'. And he wanted to call you "papa," and I tried to teach him no, but he did it anyhow and *(Sternly)* you beat him, Colonel Thomas Norwood. And he growed up with de beatin' in his heart, and your eyes in his head, and your ways, and your pride. And this summer he looked like you that time I first knowed you down by de road under them trees, young and fiery and proud. There was no touchin' Bert, just like there was no touchin' you. I could only love him, like I loved you. I could only love him. But I couldn't talk to him, because he hated you. He had your ways—and you beat him! After you beat that chile, then you died, Colonel Norwood. You died here in this house, and you been living dead a long time. You lived dead. *(Her voice rises above the nearing sounds of the mob.)* And when I said this evenin', "Get up! Why don't you help me?" You'd done been dead a long time—a long time before you laid down on this floor, here, with the breath choked out o' you—and Bert standin' over you living, living, living. That's why you hated him. And you want to kill him. Always, you wanted to kill him. Out there with de hounds and de torches and de cars and de guns, you want to kill ma boy. But you won't kill him! He's comin' home first. He's comin' home to me. He's comin' home! *(Outside the noise is tremendous now, the lights of autos flash on the window curtains, there are shouts and cries.* CORA *sits, tense, in the middle of the room.)* He's comin' home!

A MAN'S VOICE   (*Outside*)   He's somewhere on this lot.

ANOTHER VOICE   Don't shoot, men. We want to get him alive.

VOICE   Close in on him. He must be in them bushes by the
house.

FIRST VOICE   Porch! Porch! Porch! There he is yonder—running to the door!

> (*Suddenly shots are heard. The door bursts open and*
> ROBERT *enters, firing back into the darkness. The shots
> are returned by the mob, breaking the windows.
> Flares, lights, voices, curses, screams.*)

VOICES   Nigger! Nigger! Nigger! Get the nigger!

> (CORA *rushes toward the door and bolts it after her
> son's entrance.*)

CORA   (*Leaning against the door*)   I was waiting for you,
honey. Yo' hiding place is all ready, upstairs, under ma
bed, under de floor. I sawed a place there fo' you. They
can't find you there. Hurry—before yo' father comes.

ROBERT   (*Panting*)   No time to hide, ma. They're at the
door now. They'll be coming up the back way, too.
(*Sounds of knocking and the breaking of glass*)   They'll
be coming in the windows. They'll be coming in everywhere. And only one bullet left, ma. It's for me.

CORA   Yes, it's fo' you, chile. Save it. Go upstairs in mama's
room. Lay on ma bed and rest.

ROBERT   (*Going slowly toward the stairs with the pistol in
his hand*)   Goodnight, ma. I'm awful tired of running,
ma. They been chasing me for hours.

CORA   Goodnight, son.

> (CORA *follows him to the foot of the steps. The door
> begins to give at the forcing of the mob. As* ROBERT
> *disappears above, it bursts open. A great crowd of
> white men pour into the room with guns, ropes, clubs,*

flashlights, and knives. CORA *turns on the stairs, facing them quietly.* TALBOT, *the leader of the mob, stops.*)

TALBOT   Be careful, men. He's armed. (*To* CORA) Where is that yellow bastard of yours—upstairs?

CORA   Yes, he's going to sleep. Be quiet, you all. Wait. (*She bars the way with outspread arms.*)

TALBOT   (*Harshly*) Wait, hell! Come on, boys, let's go. (*A single shot is heard upstairs.*) What's that?

CORA   (*Calmly*) My boy . . . is gone . . . to sleep!

(TALBOT *and some of the men rush up the stairway,* CORA *makes a final gesture of love toward the room above. Yelling and shouting, through all the doors and windows, a great crowd pours into the room. The roar of the mob fills the house, the whole night, the whole world. Suddenly* TALBOT *returns at the top of the steps and a hush falls over the crowd.*)

TALBOT   Too late, men. We're just a little too late.

(*A sigh of disappointment rises from the mob.* TALBOT *comes down the stairs, walks up to* CORA *and slaps her once across the face. She does not move. It is as though no human hand can touch her again.*)

CURTAIN

NATIVE SON

A Revised Dramatization (1968)
By PAUL GREEN

The Original Dramatization (1941)
By PAUL GREEN and RICHARD WRIGHT from

Richard Wright's Novel of the Same Name

"In their big house I was all trembling and afraid."
—Bigger Thomas

PAUL GREEN is one of the pioneers of the folk drama movement in America, which he developed over the last thirty years at the University of North Carolina. No other White writer has written as large a corpus of dramatic work on the life of both Black and White in the South. His early plays like *The No Count Boy*, *White Dresses*, and *In Abraham's Bosom* (for which he won the Pulitzer Prize in 1926–1927) were among the first plays produced by amateur Negro theatres in the 1930's. Lately Green has been the chief developer of symphonic drama (outdoor historical musical plays). Among this genre have been *The Lost Colony*, *The Common Glory*, *The Founders*, and *Wilderness Road*.

In 1940 Paul Green was approached to dramatize Richard Wright's shattering novel, *Native Son*. In regard to this dramatization, which was produced and directed by Orson Welles at the St. James Theatre on March 24, 1941, to resounding success, Green has written:

> I read the novel and finally decided I would tackle it. I made three stipulations—one being that I would have freedom to invent new characters and make editorial story changes where necessary, another being that I could make the Communist slant in the book comic when I felt like it, and last, that Richard Wright come and be with me during my dramatizing work—this last being necessary I felt for discussion purposes as I went along. The agreement was made, and Wright came up from Mexico and stayed here in Chapel Hill some four weeks. He didn't write any of the dramatization but he was of great help in that I could check matters with him. He was of such help that I suggested we sign the dramatization together. His agent suggested that since I had done the dramatization and Wright had done the novel, the billing should be "by Paul Green and Richard Wright."[1]

In 1968 Wright's widow suggested to Green that he do a revision of the earlier adaptation of *Native Son*. He responded

---

[1] Paul Green to William Brasmer, March 5, 1969.

to the suggestion and produced the revision which has its initial publication here. The revision proved to be a moving experience for Green:

> Last night I reread it and checked the corrections. Golly, what a pitiful story. My heart aches for poor Bigger Thomas, the lost one, and for Mary Dalton, lost likewise, and for dear suffering Clara Mears. The revised script seems to me to make the story really fit into the present crooked and awry niche of the times.[2]

Whether the updating of the story has been entirely successful may be a point of contention for some readers. No one will deny the drama's power, however, nor its convincing evocation of Bigger's tragic plight. "Poor Bigger Thomas," yes. Victimized at first by the injustice of unequal opportunity and material squalor, he ends up at last becoming the victim of circumstances brought about ironically by the rich Mary Dalton, who had wanted to help him fight for genuine "freedom."

---

2 Paul Green to William Brasmer, March 17, 1969.

NATIVE SON

Characters

(In the order of their appearance)

DAVID A. BUCKLEY   *a State's attorney, about forty*

BIGGER THOMAS   *a Negro youth, nineteen or twenty*

HANNAH THOMAS   *his mother, fifty-five*

VERA THOMAS   *his sister, sixteen*

BUDDY THOMAS   *his brother, twelve*

MARY EMMET   *a social worker, about twenty-five*

JACK HENSON
"G. H." RANKIN   } *cronies of Bigger and about his age*
GUS MITCHELL

CLARA MEARS   *Bigger's sweetheart, twenty*

ERNIE JONES   *a cafe and nightclub owner, forty*

HENRY G. DALTON   *an American millionaire, about fifty-five*

ELLEN DALTON   *his wife, about fifty*

PEGGY CALLAHAN   *the Irish cook and maid for the Daltons,
forty*

JEFF BRITTEN   *a private detective, about forty*

MARY DALTON   *the Dalton daughter, about twenty-one or
twenty-two*

JAN ERLONE   *a labor leader, twenty-eight*

NEWSPAPERMAN JED   *about thirty-five*

OTHER NEWSPAPERMEN   *of different ages*

THREE POLICEMEN   *mostly young men*

EDWARD MAX   *a lawyer, sixty or more*

JUDGE ALVIN C. HANLEY   *fifty*

TWO MILITAMEN   *twenty-one*

THE SHERIFF   *forty-five*

THE CLERK   *thirty-five*

COURT STENOGRAPHER   *thirty*

74

SCENES

TIME *The present*

PLACE *Somewhere in a huge American city.*

To be produced without intermission.

PROLOGUE

The theatre audience is separated from the orchestra pit by a wooden railing. The floor of the pit is raised a little above the auditorium floor—denoting the courtroom—and two tables are at the right and left, surrounded by chairs. In the center of the pit a few steps lead up to the stage floor level above. The house lights dim slowly down. The front curtain rises and we see only a flat black backdrop at the rear. After a moment David A. Buckley, the state's attorney, appears, standing on the stage floor at the left. He is a slender, narrow-shouldered and well-dressed man of forty or so with a round florid face, and is as intense as he is humorless. As he reaches his position, the lights from overhead right wash quickly down on him and the house lights go entirely out. The pit now is in darkness.

This is the first publication of the revised dramatization. The text printed here is from the typescript copy (New York: Samuel French, 1968).

BUCKLEY   (*Speaking clearly and emphatically in the air.*)
In connection with this case we have heard criticism of
the American nation and its methods of government. That
government is not on trial here today. This criminal is on
trial.   (*He gestures to the left.*)   I deplore that in these
crucial times the viperous issue of race and class hatred
have been dragged forward in order to excuse a brutal
and perverted murder. I shall not lower the dignity of
this court nor weaken the righteousness of the people's
cause at this time by deigning to answer or discuss these
incompetent, irrelevant and immaterial arguments.   (*Far
away the chimes of a great clock ring and the huge black
backdrop curtain slowly rises. Buckley goes on.*)   The law
of this land is strong and gracious enough to allow all of
us to exist in peace and not tremble for fear that at any
moment some half-human fiend may climb through the
windows of our homes to rape and murder our wives, our
sweethearts and our daughters. We are waiting to hear
that jungle law does not prevail in this great city. We want
to know that we need not load our guns and sharpen our
knives to protect ourselves. And, your Honor, there is no
better way of erasing such fears and ending such thinking
than by imposing the penalty of death upon this miserable
human being, Bigger Thomas.   (*His long forefinger spears
the darkness, and the lights fade quickly out from him.
Somewhere an alarm clock rings.*)

Scene 1

SETTING   *A small poverty-stricken room in an apartment
house in the crowded Black Belt of a great American city.
A door at the right leads into a hallway, and at the right
center is a pallet of quilts upon which two of the Thomas
family, Bigger and Buddy, sleep. Farther back and at the
right is a rusty iron bed upon which Vera and Hannah
sleep, and at the center rear is a small dresser with a dull
and splotched mirror. At the left rear, screened from view*

*by a cheap chintz curtain, is a corner nook with a gas stove,
a sink, and shelves for groceries. A dropleaf table, covered
with an oil-cloth, is against the wall at the left front. There
are a couple of chairs, a box and a chest about the room.
The plastered walls are cracked and show the lathing here
and there. A few crayon likenesses of dead relatives are on
the wall—Bigger's father, his grandfather and grandmother.
And in clear dominance above the one bed at the right rear
is a large colored lithograph of Jesus Christ hanging on the
cross, with the motto—"I am the Resurrection and the Life."
A flower pot on the sill of the window at the left center
with a single red geranium is the room's one pretense to
beauty. As the curtain rises the family is getting dressed
and preparing breakfast. The muffled form of Bigger
Thomas lies bundled under a quilt on the pallet. Far away
in the distance the chimes of a great clock are heard ringing. Hannah, the middle-aged careworn mother, still wearing her flannel nightgown is busy at the stove. She strikes
a match and lights the stove.*

HANNAH   Bigger—Bigger! Vera! You children hurry up.
That old clock done struck the half-past. Hear me, Vera?

VERA   Yes, Ma. (VERA *is a slender brown-skinned girl of
sixteen or more dressed in a pink cotton nightgown.*)

HANNAH   And you too, Buddy. I got a big washing on my
hands today. (*Buddy, a dark sober little fellow of ten or
twelve, is standing by the stove buttoning his shirt with one
hand and warming the other at the gas flame. He is shivering and shaking from the morning chill.*)

BUDDY   Yes'm.

HANNAH   And, Vera, you got to git to that sewing class.
(BUDDY *sneezes.*)   Yeh, look at that boy, caught cold
again sleeping on that old floor. Told you to sleep with me
and Vera at the bed foot. (HANNAH *is now fastening her
skirt which she has pulled up under her nightgown.*)   Turn
your head, son, so we can get our clothes on.
(*Silently* BUDDY *turns and looks toward the pallet
where* BIGGER *lies, buttoning his shirt the while. The*

sleeping BIGGER *turns muttering over under his quilt and stuffs a pillow against his head.*)

VERA   Ma wants you to get up too, Bigger. Somebody'll stumble on you lying there. (*She pulls her dress over her head and slips her cotton nightgown off underneath it.* HANNAH *looks toward the pallet and sighs as she lets her nightgown drop.*)

HANNAH   Get the milk from the hall, Buddy.

BUDDY   Yes'm. (*He quickly pulls on his little old coat, his lips blubbering from the cold.* HANNAH *lays her nightgown aside, pushes the table out from the wall and begins setting a few dishes on it.* BUDDY *goes out as she calls after him.*)

HANNAH   Take the empty bottle. Every time I got to tell you. (*He turns back, picks up a bottle by the door and disappears.*) And, Vera, spread up the bed. (*She begins singing her shrill morning song as she works.*)

> Life is like a mountain railroad
> With an engineer that's brave—
> We must make the run successful
> From the cradle to the grave.

BIGGER   (*Muttering from his pallet.*) How the hell can a man sleep with all this racket?

VERA   (*A little testily.*) Sleep—who'd want to sleep when the rest of us got to work so hard?

BIGGER   (*Growling.*) Yeah, start right in soon's I git my eyes open! (*He covers his head with the quilt again.*)

HANNAH   Leave him alone, Vera.

VERA   It's the truth, Ma. He ought to be up looking for that job.

HANNAH   Well, he's got his application in down at the employment agency.

VERA   But he ought to get out—*hunt* for work—maybe ask that truck man to take him back, and we can have something for Christmas.

BIGGER (*Sitting suddenly up.*) And him sassing at me?

(BIGGER *is a dark muscular young fellow of twenty or so, with deepset eyes and sensitive heavy face. He is dressed in rumpled trousers, shirt and socks.*)

VERA Thought it was you sassing at him?

BIGGER You go to—

HANNAH Maybe you'd better get up, son.

BIGGER Might as well—all the tongues clanging like fire bells. (HANNAH *goes out.* BIGGER *rises and stands over his shoes, kicks one into place with his foot, and then rams his right foot down halfway into it. He stomps against the side of the wall to get the shoe on. A pot clatters to the floor behind the curtain, bang-a-lang-lang.*) These old shoes wet from that snow four days ago. I was looking for a job then.

VERA (*Who is now putting things on the table.*) Well, knocking the house down won't dry 'em. (BIGGER *stomps his left foot against the wall to get his other shoe on.* BUDDY *enters at the right with a bottle of milk.* BIGGER *lights a cigarette.*)

BUDDY (*Coming up to the table and helping* VERA.) Goody, peaches to go with them cornflakes!

VERA And we better go slow on 'em too. That surplus food got to last till Saturday. (BUDDY *ducks into the alcove and out again with a couple of glasses and pours the milk.* BIGGER *stands smoking and staring before him.* HANNAH *returns, still singing her song.*)

HANNAH

> Watch the curves, the fills, the tunnels,
> Never falter, never fail,
> Keep your hand upon the throttle
> And your eyes upon the rail.

(*She hands her towel to Vera who takes it and goes out at the right.* BUDDY *strains at the can of peaches with a large pocket knife.* HANNAH *starts working busily again at the breakfast.*)

Gimme that knife! And get away from this table until you
done washed yourself—Go on! Vera's got the towel.
(BUDDY *shies away and goes out.* HANNAH *appraises the*
knife an instant in her hand.)   Why any human being
wants to have around a knife big as this I don't see. Why
you give it to him, Bigger?

BIGGER   (*Mumbling.*)   He wanted to tote it a little bit.
(HANNAH *opens the can.* BIGGER *now sits bent over in a*
chair still smoking and idly turning the pages of a movie
magazine spread on the floor before him. She looks across
at him.)

HANNAH   Bigger, try for one time to roll up that pallet. No
telling when Miss Emmet might come by.

BIGGER   (*Still lazily reading.*)   That old case worker ain't
studying 'bout us.

HANNAH   She got us on welfare, she done that.   (VERA
comes in again. BIGGER *rises and rushes out at the right,*
bumping into somebody in the hall. A flooding high-
pitched woman's voice fills the air with a splatter of
words.)

VOICE   Heigh—you! Yeh, look at you, just look at you—a-
tromping and a-scrouging. I'm ahead of you and you
knows it! Git back in there and wait your turn, boy. Git
back!   (BIGGER *turns back and stands sheepishly in the*
door.)

VERA   (*With a biting little laugh.*)   Reckon Sister Temple
told him his manners.

BIGGER   (*Wrathfully.*)   All right now, and what's so funny
about that old woman with the toilet trots?   (BUDDY *re-*
enters.)

BUDDY   Here's yo' towel, Bigger.   (BIGGER *grabs the towel,*
balls it up and hurls it across the room, then goes over to
the chest, sits down and resumes his magazine. VERA *and*

BUDDY *help their mother at the table, passing in and out of the alcove with a few dishes and food.*)

VERA   (*Coming from the stove.*)   And that's another thing he ain't got—no respect.

HANNAH   Sister Temple lives with her Lord.

BIGGER   And her epsom salts. Eats it like oatmeal. Jack says so.

VERA   Yeh, and that Jack's breaking his grandma's heart like you're breaking Ma's.

BIGGER   I wish you'd stop being so cruddy, dirting up where you don't belong.

HANNAH   (*Opening a box of cornflakes.*)   That's no way to speak to your own sister, son, and she getting to be a young lady now.   (BIGGER *flaps his magazine over irritatedly.*)

VERA   If you was the kind of man Ma always hoped you'd be, you'd not have to wait for your turn to go to the bathroom. You'd be up early and get there first. But no—you'd rather hang around Ernie's place with Jack and that lowlife gang and let us live on relief.

HANNAH   Hush, Vera.

BIGGER   Yeh, hush—always hush.   (*Muttering.*)   Relief didn't say more'n forty people have to use the same bathroom every morning—lining up like women to see Snotty Sinatra—   (*With sudden viciousness as he flings his arm around.*)   It's the way the damned white folks built these rat nests.

VERA   Now don't start cussing the white folks again. We won't listen to it.

HANNAH   They what keep us alive right this minute.   (*He gets up and strides into the hall.* HANNAH *wags her head dolefully.*)   Now here we go again. Said to myself last night, we was gonna quit fussing at him. Lying in bed there thinking about it, I said so. Don't do no good.

VERA   How can we help it and seem like some strange devil growing in him all the time. Used to he was smart at school, helped about. Now— (*Her voice filled with angry earnestness.*) He gets more like a stranger to us every day. He ain't never got a smile for anybody. And there's that Clara woman he runs with. Here I try to make myself respectable and be something, and he—

HANNAH   Oh, Lord, I don't know. (*Calling contritely.*) Come on back, son. Le's try to eat in peace, Vera.

BUDDY   (*Piping up.*) Bigger says we ain't got nothing to smile about, says that's what's wrong with the niggers— with the Negroes—always smiling, and nothing to smile about. (*He leans over, smells the peaches, and wrinkles his nose in delight.*)

HANNAH   Yeh, he say a lot he hadn't ought to. If the white folks ever hear him—

VERA   And some these days they're gonna hear him—

HANNAH   Bigger needs God in him, that's what. I've prayed, and Sister Temple's prayed, and Reverend Hammond's put up special prayers for him. Yeh, God's what he needs, po' boy.

BIGGER   (*Who has reappeared in the door.*) God! (*Flinging out a gesture, his voice rising mockingly.*) Yeh, you got Him hanging on the wall there—the white folk's God!

VERA   Yeh, every morning he gets up like something mad at the world.

HANNAH   (*With a touch of piteousness as she looks fervently at the picture on the wall, her lips moving audibly, quoting.*) "I am the Resurrection and the Life." Your pa knowed that, son, your pa lived by it.

BIGGER   And he died by it. Down in East St. Louis— (*Half chanting.*) They hung his head on the thorny cross, the red blood trickled down.

VERA   (*Quickly*) Come on, le's eat breakfast.

HANNAH   And this ain't the way to start the day off.

BIGGER   Way you start every day—when I'm around.

BUDDY   (*Uncertainly.*) Yeh, let's eat, everybody. (*They sit to the table.* HANNAH *lifts the family Bible from the top of the chest and opens it. Suddenly there comes a thin, dry, rattling sound in the wall at the rear. They all sit listening an instant.* BUDDY *calls out.*) There's that rat again. I hear him.

BIGGER   Yeah, that's old man Dalton, all right. (*Hacking a hunk of bread off from the loaf and buttering it.*) Stick his head out this time, I'm gonna scrush it for him.

HANNAH   (*Reading.*) "I have trodden the winepress alone; and of people there was none with me: for I will tread them in mine anger, and trample them in my fury; and their blood shall be sprinkled upon my garments, and I will stain—" (*The noise in the wall is heard again as* BIGGER *sits alert.*) "—all my raiment. For the day of vengeance is in my heart, and the year of my redeemer is come—And I will tread down the people in mine anger, and make them drunk in my fury, and I will bring down their strength to the earth." Blessed be the name of the Lord. (*The noise in the wall is heard still again.*)

BUDDY   (*Whispering.*) That's him, all right.

HANNAH   (*Closing the Bible.*) Bow your heads. (BUDDY *and* VERA *bow their heads.* BIGGER *sits munching his bread and staring moodily before him.* HANNAH'S *words rise in deep humility.*) Lord our Father in Heaven, we thank Thee for the food You have prepared for the nourishment of our humble bodies. We thank Thee for the many blessings of Thy loving grace and mercy. Guide our poor feet in the path of righteousness for Your sake. Bless this home, this food, these children You gave me. Help me to raise them up for a pride and witness to their Lord. And Thine

be the power and the glory forever and ever—Amen.
(*They all begin eating,* HANNAH *lifting her gaze again to
Jesus on the wall. Suddenly* BIGGER *springs out of his chair
with a shout.*)

BIGGER   There he go! (*He lunges across the room, flings
himself over the bed and begins jabbing in the corner with
his foot. Then, springing back, he seizes an old baseball bat
from the floor.* BUDDY *grabs the bread knife and hops up
as* VERA *and* HANNAH *jump to their feet.*) He's our meat
this time. We got his hole stopped up.!

VERA   (*With a long squealing wail.*) Where is he, Ma?

BIGGER   (*Creeping towards the trunk.*) The sonofabitch,
I see his shiny eye. (*There is a knock on the door, but no
one heeds it.* BIGGER *lunges behind the trunk and strikes a
shattering blow against the floor.* BUDDY *rushes across the
room and peers under the bed.* BIGGER *creeps forward, his
whole body tensely alive.*)

BUDDY   (*Pointing.*) Yonder—yonder—

BIGGER   (*Bending down.*) Jesus, look at them teeth! (*He
grabs the end of the bed with one hand and swings it
around into the room.*) He's behind that box now. (*His
voice is charged with a harsh intensity. Again there is a
knock at the door.*)

VERA   (*Half-weeping.*) Let him go, Bigger! Let him go!

HANNAH   (*Piteously.*) Unstop the hole, let him out.

BIGGER   Gimme that flat iron, quick! (BUDDY *rushes over
to the alcove and hands him the flat iron.* BIGGER *takes aim,
and hurls it into the corner.*)

BUDDY   (*Jumping up and down excitedly.*) You hit him,
you hit him! (*The door opens silently and a young white
woman, carrying a black portfolio in her hands, stands in
the doorway. She is alert and business-like and looks inquiringly about the scene before her. Now* BIGGER *creeps*

toward the kitchen nook. HANNAH *and* VERA *have their arms about each other, watching him breathlessly.* BIGGER *stands waiting, poised, his bat raised.*)

BIGGER   (*His feet weaving to the right and left.*)   Yeah, there you sit on your hind legs and gnashing them tushes at me—I'm gonna beat your brains out—Wheeooh! (*With a yell he jumps forward and strikes with flailing, lightning blows along the curtain edge on the floor.*)

HANNAH   Bigger, Bigger!

BIGGER   (*Lifting the rat up and holding it by the tail, a murmuring chant running from his lips.*)   I got you, old man Dalton, got you that time. Yeh, you creep in the nighttime, you creep in the daytime, slipping around and devouring. I done told you yo' time would come—it's come. I put out your light, yeh, mashed you into a mushy, bloody pudding. You dead now—dead, dead, dead, dead—

VERA   Stop him, Ma! (*The woman in the door now stands a bit shaken in spite of herself.*)   Look, Ma!

HANNAH   (*Moaning.*)   Mercy sake, Bigger. Here's Miss Emmet.

BIGGER   Try to run now—try to bite me—just try it.

BUDDY   Yeh, just try to bite me.

BIGGER   You black, fat, slimy, ratty, greasy— (*His words gradually die out as he looks up and sees* MISS EMMET. *She comes on into the room.*)

HANNAH   Bigger, take that thing right out of here!

MISS EMMET   I came a little early—before you got to work.

BUDDY   We just killed a rat. Yessum. (*With a touch of boyish pride.*)   Bigger done it. Ain't he a big one?

BIGGER   (*Softly.*)   That scutter could cut your throat—the biggest one we ever killed. (*Holding him up.*)   See him, Miss Emmet? More'n a foot long.

MISS EMMET   Yes, I see it. (*Shuddering.*) Better throw
it away.

BIGGER   (*Feeling him.*) See how fat he is—feeding on garbage. They get more to eat than we do. Yeh, old Dalton,
you're going to the incinerator and there ain't no coming
back. Rubber-tired buggy, rubber-tired hack— (*He
shakes the rat at* VERA *and she squeals.*)

MISS EMMET   (*A bit sharply.*) Why do you call it Dalton,
Bigger?

BIGGER   Just call 'em that.

BUDDY   Yessum. Last week us killed another rat in here—
we calls 'em "Old Man Dalton"—the big man what owns
all the houses round here.

HANNAH   I said to him, "Anyhow, Bigger, you might leastwise say 'Mr. Dalton.' " (*A small smile passes around*
MISS EMMET'S *lips.*) Sit down, ma'am.

MISS EMMET   Yes, considering Mr. Dalton's kindness to the
people of your race. And especially Mrs. Dalton. (*She sits
down, opens her portfolio and takes out her papers.*)

BIGGER   (*Softly.*) Kind—

MISS EMMET   Yes, kind. Think of all he does for the Negro
people—that new recreation hall, with the ping-pong tables and—

BIGGER   Ping-pong tables. What good are they to a man
that's burning down? Yes, ma'm.

HANNAH   (*Sternly.*) Bigger!

BUDDY   Gimme heah, Bigger.

BIGGER   (*Now beginning to grow silent again, the excitement having died in him.*) Okay. (*He hands the rat to*
BUDDY *who takes it proudly and goes out.* BIGGER *sits down
on the chest, finishing a hunk of buttered bread.*)

HANNAH   (*Watching* MISS EMMET *eagerly, holding her cup of coffee in her hand.*) Don't mind him, ma'm. I pray the Lord you got some good news for us, ma'am.

MISS EMMET   I hope so.

HANNAH   Bless you! I knowed you'd help us.

MISS EMMET   Just a final question or two, Bigger, about your application. As head of the house— (*She takes out her ballpoint pen.* VERA *leaves the table and goes over to the mirror.*)

BIGGER   (*With a harsh little laugh.*) We ain't got nothin' but this one room, and there ain't no head to it.

MISS EMMET   But as soon as we place you in a job, Bigger, you'll feel differently about things.

BIGGER   (*Fumbling with the movie magazine.*) What kind of job I going to get?

MISS EMMET   Mr. Dalton is interested in placing his jobless tenants. He is one of our leaders in the local merit employment program. Yes, he is.

BIGGER   (*With the faintest touch of a snicker.*) Yessum.

HANNAH   (*Happily.*) Hear that, Bigger? (*She sets her coffee cup down and wipes her hands on her apron.* BUDDY *reappears and goes back to his bowl of cornflakes.*)

MISS EMMET   (*As she looks at her wrist watch.*) There's an opening with Mr. Dalton's family itself—the job of chauffeur. You might get that place. According to the record here, you are a first-rate driver.

BUDDY   He sure can drive. (*Snapping his fingers.*) She's gone from here. Hot dog!

MISS EMMET   But we must supply Mr. Dalton with all the facts. Here under previous history you failed to mention that matter of the reform school, Bigger.

BIGGER   (*With a growl.*)   Yeh, yeh—I knowed they was gonna find that out. Jesus! You white folks know everything!

MISS EMMET   When did it happen? The case history must be complete.

VERA   Go ahead, Bigger. Tell the lady.

BIGGER   You tell her, Ma. I done forgot them things.

HANNAH   It was a year ago last June, ma'am. That old no' count Gus Mitchell fellow told on him.   (*Eagerly.*)   But please, Miss Emmet—

MISS EMMET   (*Writing.*)   Three months term—Metropolitan Home for the Detention of Juvenile Delinquents—theft—taking of three automobile tires from a colored garage—Is that right?

BIGGER   (*With a faint touch of mockery.*)   Yessum, that must be about right.   (MISS EMMET *writes and then holds out her pen.*)

MISS EMMET   Please sign there.

BIGGER   (*With apparent reluctance as he takes the pen.*)   I done signed that paper once.

MISS EMMET   Yes, but this is added material and we must follow the Washington rules.

BIGGER   Sure if the big man in Washington say so. He the boss.   (*With a flourish, he writes his name.*)

MISS EMMET   (*Taking the blank.*)   I'll send Mr. Dalton a confidential report recommending you, Bigger. In fact I'll take it down to his office this morning.

HANNAH   (*Joy breaking over her face.*)   God bless you, ma'am. I been praying to hear something, and now to know that Bigger gonna have a good job—   (*Touching her hands together evangelically.*)   Bless the Lord, bless the Lord. Bigger will make a new start—From now on he will, ma'am. Won't you, son?   (BIGGER *is silent.*)

BUDDY   (*With fervent admiration.*)   You gonna drive Mr. Dalton's big car, Bigger. (*Suddenly putting his hands up on the steering wheel of an imaginary car and driving it around the room.*)   Swoos-s-h-h, look out, everybody— old cannonball coming round the bend. (*He bumps into* MISS EMMET *who stands up with a little gentle laugh.*)

HANNAH   Look out, boy, you 'bout to run over the lady!

BIGGER   (*Flinging up his hand and grinning as he adopts the attitude of a traffic cop, at the same time blowing a sharp whistle through his teeth.*)   Heigh, what you mean running through that red light? Pull up heah and lemme see your license, boy. (*He scuffs* BUDDY'S *hair a bit in spontaneous friendliness; then his face grows heavy again.*)   But, pshaw, I ain't gonna get that job.

MISS EMMET   Now goodbye, Mrs. Thomas. Goodbye, Bigger. You'll hear as soon as I contact Mr. Dalton. Keep your head up— (*She smiles wanly at them and goes out.*)

HANNAH   (*Following her to the door.*)   Bless you, ma'am, bless you—whole soul and body— (*She closes the door and turns happily about the room.*)   And my prayers are being answered. I knowed they would be. (*She turns to* VERA *and hugs her. Offstage we hear* MISS EMMET'S *knock on a door.*)

SISTER TEMPLE'S VOICE   (*Off scene.*)   Good morning, Miss Emmet. Well, bless your heart.

MISS EMMET'S VOICE   Good morning, Mrs. Temple. How are you?

SISTER TEMPLE'S VOICE   Well, I'll tell you, ma'am— (*The distant door closes.* HANNAH *begins piling the household wash rapidly into a sheet.*)

VERA   (*Coming by* BIGGER *and stopping—with deep earnestness.*)   Maybe this is the real break. We all so glad, Bigger. And we can quit living in one room like pigs.

BIGGER   Aw cut it out.

VERA   Goodbye, Ma. (*She goes by her mother, gives her a little pecking kiss, and then turning gives* BIGGER'S *arm an affectionate squeeze.*)   And you'll help me pay for my domestic science, won't you, Bigger?

HANNAH   Sure he will.

VERA   Yes. Come on, Buddy, time you was out selling your Saddy papers.

HANNAH   (*Jubilantly.*)   Ain't it the truth? And let's all hustle.   (BIGGER *is now sitting at the table idly marking across the movie magazine with a pencil.*)

BUDDY   (*Putting on his overcoat and cap.*)   'Bye, Ma. (*Standing in front of* BIGGER.)   You lemme ride in that Cadillac sometime?

BIGGER   (*Spreading out an imaginary document in front of him and beginning to write gravely.*)   Have to examine the archives of the Commitment Home first. How the hell I know what you been doing on the sly?

BUDDY   (*His face crinkling into a smile.*)   Bigger, you sure a case. Look, Ma, Bigger's smiling.

BIGGER   Hell, I ain't smiling none.   (BUDDY *scampers out after* VERA.)

HANNAH   (*Laying a coin on the table by him.*)   Here, son, take this last fifty cents. I trust you now. Run down there to the corner and get me two bars of that hard soap, a bottle of bluing, and a box of starch, and a can of Red Devil lye, and make a B-line back to the basement. Sister Temple and me will be needing it for the work.   (BIGGER *continues to scrawl with his pencil.*)   Hear me?

BIGGER   Yeh.

HANNAH   (*Turning to him, her voice affectionate and serious.*)   Bigger, that good white lady is right. From this time forth you begin to be the real head of the house. She gonna get you that job. I ain't gonna be with you always, trying to make a home for you children. And Vera and Buddy has got to have protection. Hear me, son? (*She lifts the bundled sheet of clothes over her shoulder.*)

BIGGER   Uhm—

HANNAH   I'll be too old to work soon. (*Laying a hand gently on his shoulder.*) And someday yet you'll believe like me—my boy—believe in Him— (*She indicates the calendar on the wall, then bends over, touches him lightly on the hair with her lips and goes silently and suddenly out. For an instant he sits stock still. His hand goes up into the air, as if to feel the top of his head where she kissed him, and then comes down on the table in a clenched fist. He looks upward at the picture of Christ on the wall. He begins to study it closely, and gradually a wry twisting smile slides around his lips.*)

BIGGER   (*Reading the motto quotingly.*) "I am the Resurrection and the Life"—Uhm— (*He gets sharply up and puts on his old leather coat and cap. The chimes begin to ring again. He stands listening.*) They ringing your bells, Lord, high in the white man's tower! (*As if irritated by some inner thought he slaps the coin down on the table.*) Heads I do, tails I don't. (*Disgustedly.*) Heads. (*He gives a little laugh, shakes his shoulders and spits angrily at the stove. A signal whistle from the street below comes up outside the window at the left. It is repeated. He stands in indecision a moment and then goes over and looks out and down. Finally he raises his hand in a sort of fascist salute and waves it across the pane.*) Okay, be right with you, Jack! (*He turns back toward the bed, pulls forth a wooden packing box from underneath it and unlocks it. He takes out a pistol and crams it into his blouse.* HANNAH *comes suddenly in, still carrying the sheet of clothes slung over her shoulder.*)

HANNAH   (*To herself.*) Seem like my mind failing away. Forgot my washboard again. (*Queryingly.*) What you up to, boy? (*Without answering* BIGGER *kicks the box back under the bed and goes quickly out. Something in his actions disturbs* HANNAH. *She gazes worriedly after him and then hurries to the door and calls.*) Bigger! (*More loudly.*) Bigger! Come back here, boy! (*But there is no answer. Slowly and heavily she turns into the room again to get her washboard. The scene fades out as the chimes continue to ring.*)

Scene 2

The chimes give way to an incoming roll of city traffic din. This din continues for a while. The scene opens on a street and sidewalk in front of Ernie's Kitchen shack. At the right front the gullet of a narrow alleyway leads back into the shadows. And at the opening of the alleyway sits a garbage can, looking like a squat molar in its mouth, across which is a staring label saying "Help Keep Our City Clean." The entrance to Ernie's place of business is through a door in the center with windows on either side. Adjoining the "shack" is an empty building with a boarded-up window on which are posters announcing the candidacy of two men for the office of State's attorney. Their names written in large letters respectively are David A. Buckley and Edward Max. Max is somewhat elderly, genial, heavy-shouldered and announced to be "The people's choice." At the left front is a hydrant and near it a steel lamppost topped above with the usual globular glass. The sounds of a busy thoroughfare are heard off at the left—a streetcar clanging, automobile horns, now and then a tremulous roar of a heavy truck, and once or twice the siren of a squad or ambulance car—a great wash of droning distant sound. Jack Henson, a young Negro about Bigger's age, is sitting on an ash can at the left, his head bent over, his cap pulled down and his coat collar turned up to warm him in the splotch of winter sun. He is waiting for Bigger. Presently Bigger enters.

BIGGER   Hiya, Jack.

JACK   How you doing, Bigger?

BIGGER   (*Looking at his watch.*)   Time G. H. was here.

JACK   They'll be here. Everything's jake.   (*Softly as he stands up.*)   Passed by old Blum's while ago—he was setting back in there like a crab.

BIGGER   (*Looking carefully about him.*)   Yeh, I seen him. Back to the door—bent over by the cash register working in his books. How much you think we get?

JACK   Hundred-fifty bucks anyhow. It's a cinch.

BIGGER   Cinch—and a white man?   (*He chuckles ironically.*)

JACK   Getting up into big time, boy.   (*He laughs.*)

BIGGER   Uhm—Twenty minutes till. Gimme a cigarette, Jack. I done smoked out.

JACK   (*Peering at him.*)   Twenty minutes till—   (*Narrowly.*)   —and ain't no gun in it.   (*He pulls out a package of cigarettes.*)   This is my second pack already.

BIGGER   (*Taking a cigarette.*)   Who said a gun? Gus?

JACK   Nobody. Somebody get killed—then the hot seat. (*Whistling.*)   Jesus. No!

BIGGER   (*Staring at him.*)   That Gus Mitchell—old tongue wags at both ends. He keep mo' out of trouble just wagging one end.   (*He lights up his cigarette and holds the match for* JACK.)

JACK   Gus got mighty sharp eyes, though.   (*After a few draws.*)   Gosh, you shake like an old woman. And what your hands doing sweating so?

BIGGER   (*Throwing down the match.*)   Hell, light it yourself.   (JACK *lights up.* CLARA MEARS, *an attractive, frank-faced Negro girl, comes in at the right, carrying a package under one arm. She smiles brightly over at* BIGGER *and stops.*)

CLARA   Thought maybe I'd find you here.

BIGGER   Smart girl—

CLARA   Missed you last night, honey.

BIGGER   I was busy.

CLARA   Gonna see you tonight?

BIGGER   Maybe.

CLARA   The Rhinelanders got a house full of company for Christmas—but I'll get off early somehow. They's a swell picture on. Wanted to tell you. (*Looking at her wrist watch and then up at the sun.*) Gee, I got to hurry. (*Giving* BIGGER's *arm a farewell squeeze.*) It's a date.

BIGGER   (*Still nonchalantly.*) Okay. (*She gazes deep into his face and then hurries out at the left.*)

JACK   Uck, that gal loves the very ground you walk on. Lady-killer!

BIGGER   It don't matter.

JACK   Uh?

BIGGER   Love 'em and leave 'em.

JACK   Not Clara.

BIGGER   Huh?

JACK   Nothing. (*They suck their cigarettes in silence a moment and stare off before them.* BIGGER *runs his fingers around inside his collar and twists his head.*) Kinder warm today—for December.

BIGGER   Yeh.

JACK   Be glad when summer comes and them sweet old watermelons start rolling up from the South.

BIGGER   (*Sharply.*) Summer or winter—all the same. (*He pulls out his dollar watch again.*)

JACK   Yeh, all the same. Quit looking at that old watch—time never pass. (*He chuckles.*)

BIGGER   Now what? (*He spits.*)

JACK   Gus say he don't want you in on the job either—Too nervous, he say.

BIGGER   The lousy runt!

JACK   Say you too hair-trigger. Now keep your shirt on and quit that spitting. There he come. (JACK *straightens up and stares off as* GUS *comes briskly into the scene from the left. He is a small-sized young Negro and wears his cap turned round like a baseball catcher. As he enters, he cups his right hand to his mouth as though holding an imaginary telephone. He grins as he bows.*)

GUS   Hello-hello.

JACK   (*Responding quickly and pantomiming.*) Yello— Yes—uhm—old Gus boy—

GUS   Who's that speaking?

JACK   Why—er—this the president of the United States speaking, yessir.

GUS   Thought so. Oh, yes, Mr. President. What's on your mind?

JACK   I'm calling a cabinet meeting this afternoon at three o'clock and as secretary of state you must be there.

BIGGER   (*Satirically.*) Hah-hah.

GUS   Well, now, Mr. President, I'm pretty busy. The atom bomb is 'bout to fall in Asia, and I'm thinking of sending them Chinese another note.

JACK   Forget the Chinks. Looks like we might declare war on old Castro any minute.

BIGGER   (*Pantomiming like the others.*) Hello, Mr. President. I just cut in from my private line and heard what you said. You better wait about that war business. The nee-groes is raising sand all over the country, rising up with Black Power. You better put 'em down first. Yes sir, put the nee-groes down first.

JACK   Oh, if it's about the Nigras, Mr. Goldberg, we'll wait on the war. We'd like for you to be with us, too, this evening. Out of your rich experience, sir—.

BIGGER   I'll be right there, sir. In a crisis like this we Republicans and Democrats got to pull together. We're first and foremost Americans. And the civil rights quarrel needs a strong hand—

GUS   Reckon we can do without you, Mr. Goldberg. (*They bow in sudden and rich physical laughter, slapping their thighs, their knees easy and bent.* ERNIE *comes to the rear door and stands looking out. He is a stoutish phlegmatic Negro of fifty or more.*)

ERNIE   'Bout time to open up here, and how you 'speck me to have any customers and you all boys wallowing all over the pavement?

BIGGER   Aw, go suck something.

ERNIE   (*Angrily.*)   And I don't want your back-talk, Bigger Thomas. Cut out the monkey-shines and move on.

BIGGER   Three o'clock our zero hour—ten minutes and we go.

ERNIE   Ten minutes then, 'fore I call a cop. (*He turns back into the shadow.*)   You're up to devilment, I know you. (*He disappears.*)

BIGGER   (*Muttering.*)   Sonofabitch! (*Turning toward* GUS *and staring at him with hard bright eyes.*) So you don't want Mr. Goldberg in on the deal—meaning me, hunh?

GUS   Aw, I was just joking, Bigger.

BIGGER   You wanter live and keep doing well, so drop the joking. (*Stirring restlessly about.*)   But, hell, I ain't against no war. I'd just soon fight as stand here waiting all day.

JACK   Fight who?

BIGGER   Hell, anybody. I'd just soon take a gun and pop off a few of these white folks—old Blum too.

GUS   (*To* JACK.)   Hah, I told you. He dreams about guns all the time.

BIGGER   Damn right. Jack, you know where them white folks live?

JACK   Oh, yeh, they live everywhere.

BIGGER   No, they don't. (*Doubling his fist and striking his solar-plexus.*)   Right down here in my guts is where they live. Every time I see one of 'em it feels like I wanta vomit him up.

JACK   Hum—

BIGGER   When I think of 'em feels like something—something bad gonna happen.

GUS   Yeh, but it don't do no good to feel that way.

BIGGER   Ha, you ain't never felt nothing. Right now old Blum's gnawing round my liver here.

JACK   (*Softly.*)   Yeh, and in your lungs and throat too—like fire. We gonna spew him out in a few minutes now.

BIGGER   Sometime you can hardly breathe. You know what —sometime—   (*With sudden anger.*)   Where's G. H.? Eight minutes to nine. Goddammit, I'm ready for old Blum!

JACK   Christ, don't talk so loud. Ernie'll hear you. We got five minutes yet. (*They are silent for a moment.* BIGGER *tilts back his face and the sun shines full upon it.* JACK *stares up at the sky and sneezes twice.*)

GUS   That's a sign o' bad luck too.

BIGGER   (*Yelling.*)   Go to hell!

GUS   (*Doggedly.*)   Grandmammy allus said so—double sneezes, evil scizes.

BIGGER   Superstition—you niggers—signs, wonders—Look up there—the white man's sign.

JACK   What?

BIGGER   (*Dramatically.*) That airplane—writing on the sky—like a little finger— (*They all three look up.*) He so high up he looks like a little bird.

GUS   (*Waving his hands.*) Sailing and looping and zooming—

JACK   And that white smoke coming out of his tail—

BIGGER   Like toothpaste from a tube—like a plume, like a coil of white lead—little river 'crost the fields of heaven. (*He walks restlessly about again.*)

JACK   (*Reading—afar off.*) "Use Speed Gasoline"—

BIGGER   (*Exultantly.*) Speed! That's what them white boys got!

GUS   (*Whispering.*) Daredevils—

BIGGER   Go on, boys, fly them planes, fly 'em to the end of the world, fly 'em smack into the sun! I'm with you. Goddam! (*He stares up, the sunlight on his face.*)

GUS   (*Unable to let well enough alone, doffing his cap in a mock bow to* BIGGER.) Yessir! If you wasn't *black* and if you had some *money* and if you was *educated* so you could pass the exam to that *aviation* school, you might could be with 'em.

BIGGER   (*Fiercely.*) Yeh, keep on, keep on.

JACK   (*Flexing his hands as though holding onto controls and making the sound of an airplane motor.*) Thrr-hu-hu-hu-hu—

GUS   Wish I had wings for to fly.

BIGGER   (*Satirically.*) God's gonna give us all some wings— in the judgment day. (*He joins* JACK *in the roar of the plane, primping his lips.* GUS *also joins in, and for a mo-*

ment the sound of the motor goes on uninterruptedly. G. H., *a very black heavy-set young Negro comes in at the left. He lifts one hand in a mocking salute, holding his nose with the other.* BIGGER *sees him and barks out an order.*) You pilot!

G. H.   (*Falling in with the game.*) Yessuh.

BIGGER   Give her the stick and pull right over there. (*He bends over, squinting, as if peering down through glasses from a great height.*) Uhm, uhm, look at that great crowd down there on Michigan Avenue doing their Christmas shopping. Hah, hah, hah, peace on earth!

JACK   Yessuh. (*Making the rat-tat-tat of a machine gun.*) Rat-tat-tat-tat-tat-tat, rat-tat-tat-tat-tat—

BIGGER   Look at 'em fall— (*Speaking in a half singsong croon as he turns with growing excitement about him—exultantly.*) Like kingpens—like broomstraw in the fire—Now we gonna atom bomb that Tribune tower. (*He leads off with the zooming roar of an airplane throttle opened at full speed. The others join in.* BIGGER *cries out wildly.*) Turn it loose! (*He makes a kicking motion downward with his foot, and then in a high whine depicts the passage of the bombs earthward. They all make the "boom" of the explosion together.*)

GUS   (*Bent over, staring down.*) Lawd, look at the smoke!

JACK   A mushroom cloud—going up—up, going up!

GUS   A direct hit, Major.

BIGGER   Up, up till it hide the throne of God. (*Loudly.*) And the fires—like red flowers blooming in the night—things flying through the air—houses—people—streetcars—chunks of sidewalk and pavements. Goddam!

GUS   Better dodge them brickbats flying up here—uh-uh! (*He slaps the side of his face.*) Something hit me.

BIGGER   Uh-unh, it stinks. Must be a piece of old Mayor Kelly's tail. Throw it overboard. Whoom—Tracer bullets.

(*Yelling.*)   Look out! There come the fighter planes!
(*Frantically pulling his pistol.*)   Cold steel! Watch the
turn—Put it through the navel.   (*The three boys look at
him and then spring back in fear, their playful spirit suddenly gone.*)

G. H.   Great God!

GUS   (*Pointing.*)   Look, he's got a gun! I knowed it.   (BIG-
GER *continues to aim about him. The others mumble in
half fear.*)

BIGGER   (*Hunching out his shoulder and running at* JACK
who dodges him.)   Crash him! Crash him!

GUS   (*Throwing out his hands.*)   Put up that gun, fool!

BIGGER   (*Whirling and leveling the gun at* GUS.)   Ride into
'em or I'll shoot your lights out.   (*He gives a high wild
laugh.*)

G. H.   Bigger, for Christ's sake! Somebody'll see you!

GUS   I told you he's crazy! Now just look at him!—

BIGGER   (*Advancing upon* GUS *with gun leveled.*)   You sonofabitch, don't you call me crazy!—

GUS   (*Backing away toward the other two boys, who stare
at him silently.*)   He's yellow. He's scared to rob a white
man, that how come he brung that gun.   (*He moves behind* JACK.)   I told you to leave him out of it.   (BIGGER
puts up his gun and suddenly shoots out his hand, seizes
GUS *by the collar and bangs his head against the wall.*)

BIGGER   (*His face working in violent rage, as he pulls his
knife.*)   I don't need no gun. Yellow, hunh?   (*Pushing the
knife against* GUS's *stomach.*)   Take it back.

JACK   That ain't no way to play, Bigger.

BIGGER   Who the hell said I was playing?

GUS   Please, Bigger, I just joking. Oh, you hurt me.

BIGGER   (*His lips snarled back over his teeth.*)   Want me to
cut your belly button out?

G. H.   Aw, leave him alone, Bigger.

BIGGER   Put your hands up. Way up! (GUS *swallows and stretches his hands high along the wall. He stares out with wide frightened eyes, and sweat begins to trickle down his temples. His lips hang open and loose.*)   Shut them liver lips.

GUS   (*In a tense whisper.*)   Bigger!

BIGGER   (*Pressing the point of the knife deeper against his belly.*)   Take it back. Say "I'm a lying sonofabitch."

GUS   (*With a moan.*)   Quit!

BIGGER   Say it, say it.

G. H.   (*Staring horrified at him.*)   For Christ's sake, Bigger!

BIGGER   Take it back. Say it.   (GUS *begins to slump down along the wall.* BIGGER *jabs him slightly. He straightens up quickly with a howl.*)   Say, "I'm a lying sonofabitch."

GUS   I'm—I'm a lying sonofabitch.   (*His arm falls down and his head slumps forward.* BIGGER *releases him.*)

BIGGER   Next time you whimper on me I'm gonna kill you. Now scat.   (*Hissing.*)   You ain't gonna be in on robbing old Blum. I'll take your share of the haul.   (*He starts at* GUS *again, who gazes wildly around him a moment and then flies out of the scene at the right. The noise of the city rolls in across the scene as they are silent.*)   Goddammit, somebody say something!

JACK   (*Watching him.*)   Don't cuss at us.

BIGGER   I am cussing at you. Come on, will you!

G. H.   (*Angrily.*)   Aw, lay off.   (*Somewhere from a tower a clock booms three times. They listen, stock still.*)

BIGGER   All right, zero hour.

G. H.   I ain't going nowhere—now.

BIGGER   Hundred fifty bucks waiting in that cash drawer. (*They eye him in cold silence.*)   Goddammit, you scared.

JACK   Yeh, we was gonna walk in quiet, put a piece of little hard stick against old Blum's back—"Hand over your money," we say, and then back out. Now you bring along a gun and a knife—maybe kill somebody and put us in the 'lectric chair. (*Laughing harshly.*) Who's scared? (*He pulls a sort of wooden peg from his pocket and throws it into the alley.*)

BIGGER   (*Laughing hysterically.*) So you all turn against me—eigh? I knowed you bastards was scared! I'll do it by myself—just watch. And when I do, don't nobody even speak to me, don't ask me for time to die, you hear? (ERNIE *comes to the door.*)

ERNIE   Bigger, get away from here.

BIGGER   (*Whirling on him and jerking out his knife.*) Make me!

ERNIE   I'll fix you this time— (*He turns around and reaches up as if to lift a hidden weapon down from above the door. But* BIGGER *springs forward, grabs him and jerks him out to the sidewalk. With a swipe of his knife he cuts off a piece of* ERNIE'S *coat and holds it up, yelling.*)

BIGGER   This is a sample of the cloth! Wanta see a sample of the flesh?

ERNIE   (*Gasping.*) I'll get my gun—I'll shoot you—

G. H.   Come on. Let's get away from here. (BUDDY *comes running into the scene carrying a bundle of papers under his arm and an envelope in his hand. He stops for an instant at the edge of the scene and then hurries forward.*)

BUDDY   Bigger—I come by the house—that lady sent a message for you. (BIGGER *stares at Ernie and chuckles, at the same time reaching out and taking the letter from* BUDDY. BUDDY *looks off, then springs away out at the left calling.*) Paper, mister, paper!

BIGGER   You all keep quiet whilst I reads my mail. (*He*

*backs off a few steps and opens the letter with a rip of his
knife. The others watch him.*)   Good Gordon gin! Old
man Dalton wants to see me at my convenience—immediately if not sooner. (*Shouting out at them.*)   Damn all of
you now—you can all go to hell! I'm gonna be driving for a
millionaire, and don't you speak to me no more, none of
you. Hear me? That little old trifling stick-up job! See I
laughs at it. (*He laughs and spits.*)   See, I spit in your
slimy faces too—you bunch of yellow cowards.

JACK   (*Placatingly, as he edges forward.*)   Is it a job for
real, Bigger?

BIGGER   And when I go riding by in that Cadillac, tip your
hats at me—you'd better—yeh, you had. (ERNIE *has been
edging back into the door.*)   Yeh, get your gun, Ernie.
I ain't afraid of it—I'm finished with all you cheesy little
punks. I'm on my way now— (*He makes an upward gesture, then feeling in his coat pocket, pulls out a coin and
scornfully throws it at them.*)   Here, take this fifty cents
and buy you some hash. (*He turns and goes quickly out
at the left.*)

ERNIE   (*Sarcastically.*)   On his way—

JACK   Take more'n a job to cure what ails him.

G. H.   (*Picking up the piece of money.*)   Come on, let's get
something to drink.

JACK   Yeh. And a dime for some canned music.

G. H.   Old rock and roll take the pressure off. (*They disappear into the diner. We hear* G. H. *deposit a coin in the
juke box.*)

ERNIE   (*Staring off in the direction* BIGGER *has gone.*)   That
fool's gonna kill somebody yet. (*He mops his forehead.*)
Or somebody's gonna kill him. (*He turns and goes into
the diner. The boys are heard clapping their hands as the
automatic phonograph begins playing a drum-beaten blues
song. The scene fades out as the song continues.*)

Scene 3

The following morning. As the rock and roll music fades away, the curtain rises on the sun-filled spotless Dalton break-fast room. To the left is an archway which leads into the dining room and to the right a door that leads to a hall. A wide triple window at the rear gives a view beyond of the Dalton private grounds. The table in the center of the room is decorated with a vase of gorgeous yellow chrysanthemums, and by the window is a large bird cage with three or four rest-less parakeets captive in it. When the curtain rises Mr. and Mrs. Dalton are seated at the table and Peggy is making toast on an electric toaster at the right. A portable tea wagon with plates and hot dishes is just behind her. Peggy is the Irish cook and maid. She is about forty years old and wears a blue dress with white apron, collar and cap—the typical maid's uniform. Mr. Dalton is holding an application form in one hand and a coffee cup in the other. He is about fifty-five or sixty and wears glasses. Mrs. Dalton is a middle-aged, thin, almost ascetic woman, dressed in flowing white with a knitted shawl draped loosely about her shoulders. She holds a white pet cat in the crook of her arm and one pallid hand fumbles at the food in front of her. Her eyes are staring and blinkless. Bigger, dressed as usual in his old black leather jacket, is standing before Mr. Dalton with his cap in his hand. Miss Emmet stands nearby, and out in the alcove Jeff Britten, Mr. Dalton's private detective, sits reading a newspaper. He is a muscular, dapper moustached little man of middle age.

DALTON   (*Reading in a hurried slurring tone.*)   Twenty years of age—grammar school education—poor student but learns quickly when he applies himself— (*He glances at* BIGGER.)   Well, at least they say you've got native intelli-gence, Bigger. Counted as head of the house—color com-plex—father slain in a race riot in East St. Louis when applicant was five years old. (*He looks up again, clearing his throat.*)   Quite a lot of background factors, Miss Em-met. (MISS EMMET *nods.*)   Right, Ellen? Hmn—knows how—

MRS. DALTON   (*Quietly.*) Yes. (*As* DALTON *reads on* BIG-
GER *now and then lifts his slumbrous eyes and gives* MRS.
DALTON'S *sightless face a somewhat awed and inquiring
look.*)

DALTON   Knows how to obey orders but of unstable equilib-
rium as to disposition. (*Chuckling.*) Never mind all
these words, Bigger—part of the new social philosophy the
government and the president believe in. What kind of
car did you drive last?

MISS EMMET   (*As* BIGGER *is silent.*) Tell him, Bigger.

BIGGER   A truck, sir.

BRITTEN   (*Calling out.*) What?

BIGGER   A truck, sir.

BRITTEN   Got your license?

BIGGER   Yessuh.

MISS EMMET   Show it to Mr. Dalton. (BIGGER *hands the
license to* MR. DALTON.)

BIGGER   I can drive most any kind, sir. I can handle a Cadillac
right off.

DALTON   Well, I have a Buick. (*He hands the license back
to* BIGGER.)

BIGGER   Yessuh.

DALTON   Simplicity—homely virtues—they are important.
(BIGGER *looks at him.*) Now about that reform school
business, Bigger. Just forget it. I was a boy myself once
and God knows I got into plenty of jams.

MRS. DALTON   (*Softly.*) But you weren't colored, Henry.
There's a difference.

DALTON   (*A little impatiently.*) I know, I know, Ellen,
that's why I'm telling him to forget it.

BRITTEN   (*Rising and calling out.*) We'd better get started,
Mr. Dalton.

DALTON   (*Rising also.*) Yes, Britten. (*To* MRS. DALTON.)
They're threatening a rent strike over on Prairie Avenue.

BRITTEN   Left-wingers behind it, Mrs. Dalton. But we'll
take care of them radicals all right. Oh, yes.

DALTON   More of that Edward Max's work. Britten's trailing right after him.

BRITTEN   And we'll see he never becomes solicitor—we'll
see to that.

DALTON   And that squirt of a labor leader—Jan Erlone—

BRITTEN   We've got an eye on him too.

DALTON   Good. Peggy, suppose you show Bigger around.
Let him try his hand at the furnace. He suits me all right,
Ellen. (*To* MISS EMMET.)   I always leave the final decision in these matters to Mrs. Dalton. (MISS EMMET *nods
again.*)

MRS. DALTON   (*As* DALTON *starts to leave.*)   The flowers,
Henry.

DALTON   Huh? Oh, yes. (*A buzzer sounds, and* PEGGY *steps
by* BIGGER *toward the dining room.* DALTON *calls out.*)   No,
you don't, Peggy. Mary will have her breakfast downstairs
here.

PEGGY   (*Stopping.*)   Yes, sir.

DALTON   No more of this breakfast in bed business. I've told
her. (*He takes his overcoat and cane from* BRITTEN *who
has picked them up from a chair.*)

MRS. DALTON   But she was out late last night, Henry, at the
university.

DALTON   She can get up just the same. (*He bends to kiss*
MRS. DALTON *on the forehead.*) Oh—the flowers. You
wanted me to take them down to be entered.

MRS. DALTON   Yes, I'll show you. (*She rises and goes out at
the right, followed by* DALTON *and* MISS EMMET. PEGGY *be-*

gins to clean up the table. BRITTEN *strolls forward from the alcove. He comes over to* BIGGER *and takes hold of his jacket sleeve.*)

BRITTEN   Where'd you get that jacket, boy?

BIGGER   (*Trembling.*)   From the welfare, suh.

BRITTEN   Hmn. (*Chuckling.*)   I'm Mr. Dalton's private detective. Asking questions is my business. (*He turns and goes out after* DALTON. *The buzzer sounds again, more insistently this time.*)

PEGGY   I know— in my soft heart I want to answer it. But Mr. Dalton's right. We got to be firm with Miss Mary. Want one of my rolls?

BIGGER   No'm—no'm—I ain't hungry.

PEGGY   (*Deftly buttering a roll and sticking it out at him.*) Take it. (*He takes it with a slow hand and bites into it.*) Good?

BIGGER   Yes ma'am. Sure—mighty good.

PEGGY   That's one thing I can pride myself on—my bread. I always say everybody in the world's got at least one talent —it's up to him to find it and be happy. Mine's cooking and I evermore like to do it. (*Staring at* BIGGER *an instant.*)   Well, you've got a talent, too. That's the way the Lord made us. Of course maybe it's a little harder for you colored people to find yours on account of—well, but don't *you* get discouraged. Mrs. Dalton will help you. (*The sound of an automatic furnace turning itself on in a great windy draught comes up from the basement below.* BIGGER *stands listening to it.*)   That's the furnace—works by machinery. A big thing it is—has to be big to warm this old house. That'll be one of your duties—to keep it stoked up and the ashes cleaned out.

BIGGER   Yes'm. I can learn machinery easy.

PEGGY   Maybe that's your gift. I believe you're going to fit here. (*Still working at her duties.*)   Before I forget it—

Miss Mary's going to Detroit tomorrow to visit her grand-mother. You'll have to come early to drive her to the LaSalle Street station.

BIGGER   Yes'm.

PEGGY   That'll be one of your jobs too—looking after Miss Mary. You haven't seen her yet—she's gone a little wild lately, she has—but to me she's still a baby and always will be. Green used to watch after her—bring her home at night when she was out late. You'll have to do that. (BIG-GER *looks around at her.*)   She ain't a bit like her father and mother. Runs around with all sorts of people—a crazy bunch of radicals and poets and long-haired folks. That labor defender Jan Erlone is a friend of hers—old Edward Max too—and they all the time working against her own father. But she's good-hearted—she'll learn better—she'll marry and settle down some of these days. And when she does, it'll be a load off my mind. And don't you pay no attention to them friends of hers. Keep to your job.

BIGGER   Yes'm.

PEGGY   Now Mrs. Dalton—you'll like her. She's wonderful. She's had a hard life too. Trouble. There's been talk about it, but that's none of my business.

BIGGER   She—she can't see, can she?

PEGGY   (*Pouring herself a cup of coffee and drinking from it.*)   She's blind. Went blind years ago when her second child was born. It died. She's been blind ever since. Queer. The doctors can't explain it. But she's good. Wonderful heart. And deep too. Knows things. Sees through people. Never talks much, but she loves people and tries to do something for them. Loves that cat and her piano and her flowers. (*She sets her cup down and wipes her hands on her apron.* MRS. DALTON *comes feeling her way in from the right dressed as before and still carrying the white cat.* BIGGER *springs around clattering the dishes on the table.*)

MRS. DALTON   Have you told the young man his duties, Peggy?

PEGGY   Part of 'em, ma'am. I ain't spoke about the flowers yet.

MRS. DALTON   Yes, that's another thing, Bigger. You are expected to water the plants every morning. Peggy will show you. And now I want to talk to you a bit. (PEGGY *rolls the tea-wagon off with the dishes.* MRS. DALTON *makes her way along the table and sits down. She takes one of the blooms from the vase on the table and strokes it against her cheek.*) Flowers are wonderful creatures, Bigger. Each with soul of its own. I hope you will learn to love them while you are here.

BIGGER   (*In almost mumbling incoherence.*) Yessum. (*He looks about him and nervously lifts a glass of water from the table. He drinks and watches* MRS. DALTON *over the rim.*)

MRS. DALTON   And now I want to congratulate you. We've decided to engage you. This is your new start. The path of life lies before you white and clean. I am sure you have lived in confusion and uncertainty. You have drifted. Now you are one of us—a member of the family now—and we'll do all in our power to help you find your way in this new life.

BIGGER   (*Spasmodically.*) Thanky, ma'am, thanky. Yessum.

MRS. DALTON   (*Her face tilted up as if drinking in the sunlight that pours through the window.*) Bigger, you hate white people, don't you?

BIGGER   Uck! (*The glass of water drops from his hand and crashes to the floor.*) Oh— (*He bends down in a scramble to pick up the glass, but his eyes remain on her face. His hands feel blindly among the splinters, gathering them. He stands up again, his knees bent a little, as though standing before a source of blasting judgment.*)

MRS. DALTON   Never mind the glass. It's unimportant. I think I understand why you hate white people.

BIGGER   No'm I don't hate 'em. You got me wrong, ma'am. (*He backs abruptly into the wall and stops.*)

MRS. DALTON   And if you have a gun, Bigger, I hope you'll bring it to me.

BIGGER   (*Terrified.*)   No'm I ain't got no gun, and no knife neither.

MRS. DALTON   (*Quietly, gently.*)   Perhaps you are lying now, but you'll learn to tell the truth. I'll be waiting, Bigger. Bring your gun and knife to me. You won't need them here. We are your friends.

BIGGER   (*Harshly.*)   I ain't got no gun, I tell you, and I ain't got no knife.   (MRS. DALTON'S *frail hand has gone up into the air as if to stop him. It drops now back into her lap and lies still. She heaves a sigh.*)

MRS. DALTON   Bigger, I have known what fear is. But I am afraid no longer. I have dedicated my life to wiping out fear. We must wipe it out of you. For fear produces hate and hate produces death and destruction. That is the woeful lesson of this pitiful tragic warlike world. And if we as individuals cannot win a victory over ourselves, how can we expect the nations to?

BIGGER   (*Whispering, but watching her as if fascinated.*) Yessum.

MRS. DALTON   (*Rising.*)   Now, that's all. You have the job. Your pay will be thirty-five dollars a week, which will go to your mother to help support the home. There will be ten dollars more for yourself, and something extra for Christmas. You will have every second Sunday off. Is that clear?

BIGGER   (*Still in a whisper.*)   Yessum.

MRS. DALTON   (*Turning.*)   And if anything ever bothers

you, come to me and we'll talk it over. We have a lot of books in the library. You can read any you like.

BIGGER   No'm. Yessum.

MRS. DALTON   Remember, you don't have to read them. And now, I will tell Peggy to show you the rest of the routine. (*She turns and moves slowly out at the left, stroking her face with the chrysanthemum bloom as she goes.* BIGGER *stares after her. The door closes, and he gazes about him as if in a dream.*)

BIGGER   (*His thoughts gradually rising into a murmur.*) Uhm—she's queer—like a ghost. Makes me feel all weak inside, like the eye of judgment looking at me. (*He sinks down in a chair, his face perplexed and heavy.* MARY DALTON *enters from the left, dressed in a flowing red robe, opened at the bosom. Her hair is touseled, and she is puffing a cigarette. She is a slender pale-faced girl of some twenty-two or -three, with wide, restless dark eyes. Her lips are rouged heavily and her finger nails done to a deep vermillion. Her whole appearance denotes boredom and weary childlike disillusionment. She comes on over to the table, then stops and glances at* BIGGER *who has sprung up.*)

MARY   (*Quenching her cigarette in a coffee cup.*) Keep your seat, I'm not going to hurt you. (BIGGER *stands with down-cast eyes saying nothing.* MARY *pours herself a cup of coffee, pulls a little tin box from her pocket and puts a couple of aspirin tablets into her mouth. She gazes over at* BIGGER *as she gulps from her cup.*) What's your name?

BIGGER   Bigger—Bigger Thomas, ma'am.

MARY   Funny name—where'd you get it?

BIGGER   (*Without looking up.*) They just gave it to me, ma'am, I reckon.

MARY   (*Sitting down and picking idly at a roll.*) Our new chauffeur, huh?

BIGGER   Yessum.

MARY   Do you belong to a union?

BIGGER   No'm—no'm, I ain't never fooled with them things, no, ma'am.

MARY   I'll take you to see Jan Erlone. Better join a union or Father'll exploit your shirt off. My name is Mary Dalton. I'm the pampered daughter and heiress to all the Dalton millions. And I've got a helluva hangover.

BIGGER   (*Uncertainly.*) Yessum.

MARY   Guess they've already told you about me though— how lazy I am and all—Peggy has, bless her sweet dumb soul. Has Mother hired you?

BIGGER   Yessum.

MARY   Well, don't take the job. (*Now* BIGGER *looks up at her.*) I mean it. You'd better keep away from us—from Mother. She'll try to give you a serious ambitious soul, fill you with a yen to be something in this world. And you've got no chance to be it. None of you downtrodden people have got any chance in a capitalistic world. So don't try it.

BIGGER   No'm—I— (*His voice dies out.*)

MARY   I'm what you might call a rebel—I'm against my parents. We carry on an endless warfare in this house. Mother usually has the last say-so, she and Peggy. They made a law-abiding punk out of Green. But with you— (*She stares at him with her cryptic dark eyes.*) What the Negro race needs is a hell-raising leader, not a philosopher of non-violence.

BIGGER   (*Swallowing.*) Yessum.

MARY   (*Mockingly.*) "Yessum, yessum"—the subservience of the defeated. You must meet Jan Erlone and the labor folks. We're having a celebration down at headquarters tonight. You'll drive me down there—

BIGGER   Got to—got to stick to my job.

MARY   That's your job—to take me where I want to go. (*As if quoting.*) There is a new spirit abroad in the world, Bigger. People have lost their trust in the old leaders. The old security is gone. Upheavals are ripping this terrestrial ball to pieces. Young people don't know where to turn any more. They can't hope or plan any more. Can't think ahead for the next month because they don't know whether there'll be a next month or not. Everywhere we are searching for something to live for—to dream for—to fight for. We have been betrayed, Bigger. And we alone can save ourselves—the young people, the laboring people. And in the great struggle—all are brothers, black, white, yellow or red. (BIGGER *blinks helplessly at her. She strikes the the table a blow with her little fist and rises.* BIGGER *backs away from her vehemence.*) Don't think I'm crazy. Father and mother are. And tonight remember—at Ernie's place—Edward Max will tell you. He's a great man, Bigger. He sees the truth. Father and Mother are the blind ones. They think they can keep the old order going. But they can't—can't, I tell you. We'll kill it—all of us will kill it. There'll be a new day—freedom, self-expression for you and your people, for me and others like me. Understand?

BIGGER   I dunno—Yes'm.

MARY   And you won't be like Green—hand out fawning for favor, creeping up the back way. No, you won't. Who knows you might be a leader among your race. And I'd have a hand in it. Mother's spoiled and worthless daughter would have a hand in it. (*With a laugh she throws her coffee cup against the wall and breaks it.*) And tonight we'll go down there. You'll meet people in another world—the world of the future.

BIGGER   No'm. Got to stick to my job.

MARY   (*With a kicking motion of her foot.*) Your job is to do what I tell you! (PEGGY *comes in at the left.*)

PEGGY   Did something break, Miss Mary?

MARY   I dropped my cup.

PEGGY   (*Sighing.*)   Is your head better?

MARY   No.

PEGGY   I'll get you a hot pad.

MARY   No, thank you.

PEGGY   I wanted to bring your breakfast up, honey, but Mr.
Dalton—

MARY   (*Yelling.*)   Go away and let me alone!

PEGGY   (*After a moment quietly.*)   Come with me, Bigger,
and I'll show you about the furnace.

BIGGER   Yessum. (*In the distance* MRS. DALTON *begins playing Mendelssohn's "Spring Song" on the piano.* MARY
shudders.)

PEGGY   And the flowers.

BIGGER   Yessum. (*He follows her abjectly out. The piano
continues to play.* MARY *lights a cigarette and stands smoking, gazing before her.*)

MARY   (*Mockingly in the air.*)   Yassum—yassum. (*The
piano continues to play. The scene fades out.*)

Scene 4

*The upstairs bedroom of Mary Dalton, that night. When the
curtain rises, the piano stops playing. At the left front is a
door opening into the hall, and to the left, and set at an angle
from the audience, is Mary's bed draped in ghostly white and
raised like a dais or bier. At the center rear is a filmy cur-
tained window, and to the right of that, a huge oblong mirror,
so tilted that its depths are discernible, but only a vague blur
of images is reflected in it. In front of the mirror is a deli-
cately-patterned chaise lounge and stool. An entrance to the
dressing-room is at the right front. The walls of the bedroom*

are cold and dead, and the whole scene is bathed in the snowy city's pallid light which glimmers through the window. Bigger's voice is heard in the hall off-scene.

BIGGER'S VOICE   (*In hushed anxiety.*)   Please, Miss Dalton. Please, stand up and walk. Is this your room?

MARY'S VOICE   (*Stiff-lipped and almost mechanical.*)   A great celebration, Bigger. God, I'm drunk!

BIGGER'S VOICE   (*Tense and pleading.*)   Sh-sh—   (MARY *appears in the door, her hat awry, her hair hanging down, her eyes set in a frozen stare and her face mask-like and dead. She has some pamphlets in her right hand.*)

MARY   And you're drunk, too, Bigger.   (*Jerking at him with her left hand.*)   It's a victory, Bigger. Hooray for the rent strike. Hooray for our side!

BIGGER   For Christ sake!   (*In a sort of moan.*)   I don't want to go in there, ma'am. This ain't my job, Miss Dalton.

MARY   It is your job—to see me home—safe home.   (*She pulls* BIGGER *on into the room. His head is lowered, his face somewhat averted from her. On his left arm he carries* MARY'S *red handbag, hung by its handle. He is dressed in his chauffeur's uniform, his cap off.*)   The people are strong, Bigger—you and me—thousands like us—Poor father—Gimme a drink. Why don't you give me a drink?   (*She reaches for the handbag.*)

BIGGER   No'm.

MARY   (*Rocking her head from right to left—mockingly.*)   Yessum—yessum—   (BIGGER *lifts his arm horizontally before him, the purse hanging obediently down.* MARY *fumbles it open and pulls out a little bottle. She unstops the bottle and waves it under her nose, then takes a little drink.*)   My father—a landlord that walks like a man—a gentleman of the old school—the old school—and it's the *new* school, Bigger. I hear the bells ringing for the scholars to come in—all over the world. And we had a big celebration. Such dancing, such wine!

BIGGER   (*Moaning again.*)   Lemme go, Miss Mary. (*Suddenly his head snaps about him as if hearing an enemy in the dark.*)   I got to go—ain't my job—got to get out of here.

MARY   And poor mother—a suffering ghost, Bigger—long, long ago when a child she got a terrible fright. A hungry colored man broke into her bedroom. But you don't frighten me. I frighten you now—see, it's all reversed. Crazy world, ain't it? Know what I am?

BIGGER   This your room, Miss Mary. They kill me—kill me they find me in here!

MARY   (*Insistently.*)   Know what I am?

BIGGER   (*Peeping furtively out from beneath his brows.*)   I dunno—no'm—I dunno.

MARY   I'm what the Chinese Reds call "the penitent rich"— I feed the poor—   (*Her hands go out as if scattering largess to a begging world, and she strews the pamphlets about the room.*)   And I'm drunk—and I'm dead—drunk and dead—inside I am—   (*Shaking her head.*)   You the priest and I'm the sinner—I want to talk—Trouble with the world, Bigger—nobody to talk to—mother and father —they talk—talk up to God in the sky—I talk down— way, way down to you at the bottom—   (*With wild, emotional impulsiveness.*)   Oh, I wish I was black—honest I do—black like you—down there with you—to start all over again—a new life—   (*She puts out her hand towards him. He shivers and stands helpless before her. She touches his hair.*)   Your hair is hard. Like little black wires—I know—it has to be hard—tough—to stand it—   (*She touches his cheek.*)

BIGGER   (*In a whispering scream.*)   No—no! (*The air of his lungs hisses through his lips and dies as it were in an echoing supplication. His face glistens more brightly with the sweat that drenches it. He spits emptily.)*

MARY   *(Looking at her hand.)* See, not shoe polish—it don't come off. *(Now touching her own cheek and gazing at her crooked, spread-out little fingers.)* And it don't stain the white—see. And behind it like mine your blood is red. *(Wagging her head hopelessly.)* There's a difference and there's not a difference—outside there's a difference—inside no difference— *(Half singing.)* A rose by any other name—Bigger, speak to me. *(And now his eyes are lifted, gazing burningly at her like two live coals.)* Bigger, what are you thinking—what are you feeling? *(She begins to weep noiselessly.)*

BIGGER   *(Moaning, twisting his shoulders as if in the grip of some overpowering, aching pain.)* You cut me—tear into me— *(Gasping.)* Open me like a can—see all my guts— *(Whining.)* Lemme go—

MARY   *(With eager lisping.)* Yes, that's what I want—to break through and find you—find somebody—I'm lost. *(She sags heavily down, about to fall.)*

BIGGER   *(Gasping, his lips tortured and twisted.)* Have nothing to do with you—ain't gonna touch you—bitch— *(As he speaks, she falls suddenly into his arms.)* Ain't my job—ain't my job—

MARY   Your arms—hard, too strong—hurt—make me feel safe—and hurt—in the deep black jungle—I want to suffer—nothing to frighten me—home—at the bottom—begin all over again—home—take me home. *(A melody rising from her motionless doll-like lips.)* "Swing low, sweet chariot, coming for to carry me home—" My mother sings it.

BIGGER   Shut up!

MARY   Mother! *(Her eyes blare wide with fear.)* Let me go! Let me—

BIGGER   Turn her loose—Turn her loose! (*But still his arms, as if against his will, hold to her.*)

MARY   (*Now staring at him coldly.*) Who are you? (*Lifting a weak hand, she strikes him blindly in the face.*)

BIGGER   Hit me! Hit me!

MARY   Stop— (*Shrieking.*) Stop it! (*She wiggles like a rubber thing queerly alive, and the breath goes out of her. Her head falls back. She lies still and limp in his arms. For a moment* BIGGER *does not move. Spellbound he gazes at her face, his lips open and breathless.*)

BIGGER   I lost too—like you—dunno where to go—nothing but darkness to carry me home. (*He jerks his face away from hers and lowers her feet to the floor, but the upper part of her body hangs over his arm. He looks frantically about him, then eases and half-drags her to the bed, the handbag still hanging on his arm. He flings her roughly on it, then steps back, gazing at her. Her dress has flown up, revealing her long silk-stockinged legs and thighs. He pulls the dress down. A sob rises into his throat. Dropping on his knees by the bed, he buries his face in the silken coverlet, kissing the glowing fold of her dress.*) Miss Mary—Mary —Mary—Mary—Name like the mother of Jesus—Jesus hanging on the wall—and I call to you—help me—save me—pleas'm, speak to me—this here Bigger begging you now— (*With his head still bowed, his hands go up and onto her reclining figure. His fumbling fingers feel along her body and on to her white and delicate throat.*) And you sweet and soft and—lost—and they ain't nothing I can do—nothing— (*Whispering, as his head flies up again.*) Gotta get away—get away quick! (*But still his hands caress her pallid throat. Now as if from some interminable distance deep in the muffled house comes the sound of* MRS. DALTON'S *gentle voice.*)

MRS. DALTON'S VOICE   (*Off-scene.*) Mary!—Where are you, Mary?— (BIGGER *springs up terrified, rooted to his*

tracks. The door at the left swings open and the blur of
MRS. DALTON's *tall form stands there in its white dressing
gown. And now, as if the calling voice had penetrated into*
MARY's *deep unconsciousness, the bed heaves and a murmur rises from it.* BIGGER's *whole body grows taut, caught
in a flooding horror of fear. He stares at* MRS. DALTON *with
wide eyes, and as she moves farther into the room, he backs
noiselessly around the bed from her, the palms of his hands
outstretched as if in piteous supplication before her unsee-
ing vision, and his lips making a gaping, soundless cry. For
an instant the scene is silent.* MRS. DALTON *clasps her long
fingers in front of her and stands listening down at the bed.
She speaks in her normal voice.*) Mary? (BIGGER *remains
across the bed from* MRS. DALTON, *his face tilted and his
eyes glued in awe upon the white figure. One of his hands
is half-raised, the fingers weakly open as if an object he
had been holding had just dropped from them.* MRS. DAL-
TON *calls again.*) Mary, are you asleep? (*There is no
answer from the bed. The white figure turns slowly and
seems to look about the room.* BIGGER *shrinks back into the
shadows as if unable to face the blinding condemnation of
that sightless face.* MRS. DALTON *feels toward the bed and
then, as if touching* MARY *through the air itself, suddenly
draws back.*) You've been drinking. You reek of liquor.
(BIGGER *carries his right hand to his mouth as if about to
scream. The white figure now sits sorrowfully down on the
edge of the bed, her head dropped woefully over. Her hand
goes out and rests lovingly and piteously on* MARY's *brow.
Her voice is like a whisper coming from the bottom of a
deep empty well.*) My poor child—why do I fail you?
Sleep—sleep then. (*Rising, she fumbles for the coverlet,
spreads it over* MARY's *feet and turns back toward the door.
A low sigh of relief passes through* BIGGER's *lips.* MRS. DAL-
TON *wheels about.*) What is it? (*The sleeping figure lifts
a hand and mumbles as if waking up. Quick as a flash and
with an instinctive action* BIGGER *picks up a pillow and*

pushes it down against MARY'S *face. Her white little hands
flash up in the gloom clawing helplessly at his arms. But he
holds the pillow against her, heedless of her struggle, his
face turned watchfully towards* MRS. DALTON. *She takes a
step back towards the bed, then stops—in alarm.*)   Mary
—are you ill?   (MARY'S *form on the bed heaves, and there
is a sound of a heavy breath. Her legs begin to thrash about,
and with his other hand* BIGGER *holds them still. A quick,
muscular tautness in* BIGGER'S *entire body indicates the
enormous strength with which he is holding the pillow and
controlling* MARY'S *movements. The white hands continue
to clutch futilely at his wrists.* MRS. DALTON'S *voice calls
out sharply.*)   What is it, Mary?   (*Listening and then
speaking softly.*)   It's nothing.—She's sleeping.   (*The
white hands have fallen limp by the pillow now.*)   Good
night, Mary, I'll call you early for your train.   (*She moves
silently from the room. The door closes behind her with a
loud sound. For a moment the scene is silent, then with a
deep, short gasp of relieved tension,* BIGGER *falls to the
floor, catching the weight of his body upon his hands and
knees. His chest heaves in and out as though he had just
completed a hard footrace. Gradually, his breathing subsides. He stands slowly up, looking at the door, his body re-
laxed now, the burden of fear gone from him. Then he
looks toward the bed, his whole attitude changing, his body
becoming taut again. He takes a step forward, then stops
uncertainly. He stares at the white form and brings his
hand in a bewildered gesture to his forehead. He looks
downward in a deep tense study, his face now devoid of
that former hard concentration, but beginning to be trou-
bled by the stillness in the bed. He moves forward, bends,
and stares apprehensively down at* MARY'S *face. Slowly his
right hand goes up into the air, the fingers sensitively
poised, until again he assumes the same position in which
he was standing and looking when the white blur of* MRS.
DALTON *first roused him. Convulsively his hands beat the
sides of his head with two fists. He still stares anxiously at*

MARY'S *face, as though a dreadful knowledge were on the threshold of his consciousness, an awful fact about to blast and devastate him much as fiery lightning might strike a helpless tree. His right hand moves timidly toward* MARY *and touches her, then is jerked quickly away. He touches her head again now, gently rolls it from side to side, then puts his hands behind him as if they had suffered some strange and sudden burn or hurt.*)

BIGGER   (*In a whimper.*) Naw—naw— (*For a moment he stands looking at the still form, as though it had in some manner deeply offended him. Once more he places his hand upon* MARY'S *head. This time it remains there and his body does not move. He mumbles frenziedly.*) She's still —still as death—Naw—naw—naw— (*He is silent for an instant, then whispers.*) She's dead—I smothered her. (*He takes a quick step back.*) I didn't, I tell you, I didn't. Wake up, wake up. (*His voice takes on a note of pleading.*) Miss Dalton, Miss Mary—Oh, Lord have mercy! (*Listening.*) Somebody coming—They'll come and find me here. (*For a second he stands bent over, then straightens up suddenly. He turns, walks swiftly to the door, opens it, and looks out into the darkness. All is quiet. He walks back to the center of the room and stands looking at the bed. He mumbles piteously.*) Like a little flower— scrushed and broken— (*Rubbing his eyes with his fists as if trying to wake himself.*) Naw—naw—naw— I didn't go to do it—I didn't go to do it— (*In a clear sober, deep voice, as if all his faculties were suddenly alive.*) I got to get out of here—I got to run off now, right now. (*He shakes his head bewilderedly, still speaking in a deep, sober voice.*) Naw—they'll say I done it—I'm black and they'll say I done it—I can't run off—they'll know—they'll say— they'll catch me. (*Again he bends over the bed.*) I didn't go to do it. You know I didn't. It was your fault—your fault. I'm just working here. I didn't want to come here. You know I didn't. I was scared—I didn't want to come to your room—you were too drunk to walk—you made me come— (*His voice dies out of him in a sob, and he is silent. Far away a clock booms the hour. Slowly his body straightens with intent and purpose.*) Seem like that clock winding itself up to wake the world and tell what I done. Got to hide her—get her away from here—so they'll never know—can't tell what happened— (*He stops, trembling violently, then looking back over his shoulder at the door, slides his hands under* MARY'S *body and lifts her in his arms. He turns undecidedly about and sees the mirror. There confronting him is the huge image of himself, a black animal giant, holding* MARY *in his arms. He starts back with a low hoarse cry.*) Who you! Don't you look at me—don't say I done it. I didn't, I tell you. (*For a moment the image in the mirror holds him fascinated. He hugs* MARY *to him as if to protect her and himself. Gradually he looks down at her—mumbling.*) She's cold—cold —she's cold now— (*Then suddenly and vehemently to the image in the mirror, as the hum of the furnace switching itself on is heard below.*) I didn't rape her—they'll say I did—I'll hide her—they'll never know—I'll hide her— (*His voice dies to an indistinguishable whisper.*) Naw, ain't nothing happened. Just a dream—all quick-like —a dream—I been dreaming. (*With a smothered shriek.*) It ain't no dream—it's happened! Cold—cold—she's growing cold. (*Listening to the furnace draft.*) Yeh, everything cold around me—like a great tomb. That furnace needs tending, boy— (*He jerks his head up again, as if struck by a smashing thought.*) Furnace fire—hot— hot as hell fire—like the Hebrew children standing in it— and it burn 'em—purify 'em—eat 'em down in its redhot throat—and there ain't no trace—they gone—wiped away —nobody to know—nobody to see— (*With a moaning cry he rushes through the door with the body of* MARY *in his arms, the handbag still hanging on his arm. The sound of the furnace draft grows louder and continues. The scene fades out.*)

Scene 5

The sound of the furnace draft dissolves gradually into the metallic tingling of a telephone. The curtain rises on the Dalton study. It is the afternoon of the same day. At the right of the room are bookshelves, and at the left a fireplace in which some logs are burning. At the left front a door leads to the hall. A large flat-topped desk is in the rear center, and across the back is a glass partition looking into a fairy-land of flowers and plants in the conservatory, with a door to the right leading into it. The conservatory is bathed in golden artificial sunlight. On a table near the partition is a large vase of luxurious roses.

Dalton is standing by the desk using the telephone. Mrs. Dalton is sitting in a chair, bolt upright, listening.

DALTON   No, she's not here. (*He pauses, then hangs up the receiver and turns to* MRS. DALTON.) Well, that's final. She didn't go to Detroit, Ellen.

MRS. DALTON   (*With a tremor in her voice.*) Mary had been drinking again last night, Henry. When I came into her room—I—

DALTON   Yes, yes—maybe that Erlone fellow knows something. She was out with him.

MRS. DALTON   He's been down at the station waiting to see her off, he says. He called up—

DALTON   Well, Britten is a smart detective. He ought to be back any minute with some news. (PEGGY *comes in with a tray at the right front. Her face shows signs of recent weeping.*)

PEGGY   Here's your tea, Mrs. Dalton.

MRS. DALTON   (*With a gesture.*) No thank you, Peggy.

PEGGY   But you must keep up your strength, Mrs. Dalton.

MRS. DALTON   No, thank you.

PEGGY   Mr. Jan Erlone just phoned again—said he was coming right over. He seems worried too. (*She turns and hurriedly goes out, meeting* BRITTEN *in the doorway. She stops.* BRITTEN *comes on in. He goes over to the fireplace and shakes a bit of snow from his hat and coat.*)

BRITTEN   Snow's pouring down, all right—regular blizzard for old Santa Claus. Well, Mr. Dalton, looks like Buckley better get busy. That labor crowd's talking up this fellow Edward Max.

DALTON   I know, I know—What did you find out at the station, Britten?

BRITTEN   Nothing. Absolutely nothing. (*A sob breaks from* PEGGY. *She goes out.*)   Mmm—I don't understand that car sitting out there, the window open—must have been there for hours—snow four inches deep on the top—I measured it. Your chauffeur says he brought Miss Dalton home about two-thirty.

MRS. DALTON   About two-thirty this morning. I heard the clock strike. Later I went to her room.

BRITTEN   Ahm—By the way, that colored boy Thomas—is he all right?

DALTON   He seems all right.

BRITTEN   Yeh, he does—dumb-like. Seems to know his place.

DALTON   We have his complete record. I talked to him. I'm sure he's all right. (PEGGY *comes in again and listens. While they are talking,* BIGGER *slowly enters the conservatory at the rear. He has a watering can in his hand and goes about quietly and methodically watering the flowers. But even in his nonchalant and detached manner, we sense that he is straining every sense and nerve to hear the words of the group in the study.*)

BRITTEN   (*To* PEGGY.)   And what do you think of this colored boy?

PEGGY   He's just like all colored boys to me.

BRITTEN   Is he polite? Does he pull off his cap when he comes into the house?

PEGGY   Yes, sir.

BRITTEN   Does he seem to be acting at any time? I mean, does he appear like he's more ignorant than he really is?

PEGGY   I don't know, Mr. Britten.

BRITTEN   I'd like to talk to him again.

PEGGY   (*Gesturing toward the rear glass door of the conservatory.*)   He's out there.

BRITTEN   (*In a loud voice.*)   Come in here, boy! (BIGGER *turns, opens the glass door and comes slowly through, still carrying the watering pot in his hand.* BRITTEN *turns to him and shouts.*)   I want to ask you some more questions!

BIGGER   (*Blinking and starting back, then stopping.*)   Yes-suh.

BRITTEN   What time do you say you took Miss Dalton from here last night?

BIGGER   About eight-thirty, suh.

BRITTEN   You drove her to her night class at the University? (BIGGER *hangs his head and makes no answer.*)   Open your mouth and talk, boy. (*He puts out a placating hand to the* DALTONS. *They wait.*)

BIGGER   Well, Mister, you see—I'm just working here.

BRITTEN   You told me that before. You drove her to school, didn't you? (BIGGER *still makes no answer.*)   I asked you a question, boy!

BIGGER   (*His eyes strangely alert and yet his face impassive.*) No, suh. I didn't drive her to school.

BRITTEN   Where did you drive her?

BIGGER   Well, suh, she told me after I got as far as the Park to turn around and take her to the Loop.

DALTON   (*His lips parted in surprise.*)   She didn't go to
    school?

BIGGER   No, suh.

BRITTEN   Huh?

DALTON   Why didn't you tell me this before, Bigger?

BIGGER   (*Quietly.*)   She told me not to, suh.

BRITTEN   Where did you take her then?

BIGGER   To the Loop.

BRITTEN   Whereabouts in the Loop?

BIGGER   To Lake Street.

BRITTEN   Do you remember the number?

BIGGER   Sixteen, I think, suh.

BRITTEN   (*Rubbing his chin.*)   That's a good boy—Uhm—
    Sixteen Lake Street then?

BIGGER   Yessuh.

BRITTEN   (*Kindly.*)   Say, boy, your water is pouring out on
    the floor.

BIGGER   Thank you, suh. Yessuh!   (*He jerks the watering
    can up straight and hugs it in front of him.*)

BRITTEN   How long was she in this place—number Sixteen?

BIGGER   'Bout half an hour, I reckon, suh.

BRITTEN   Then what happened?

BIGGER   (*Quietly as before.*)   Then they came out.

BRITTEN   They?

BIGGER   Her and this—this Mr. Jan.

BRITTEN   Jan Erlone?

DALTON   Jan Erlone—that's a friend of hers—

BRITTEN   (*He looks triumphantly around him.*)   And then
    you drove 'em to—?

BIGGER   He wanted to drive and she told me to let him.

BRITTEN   And where did they go?

BIGGER   To the speaking—to hear that man—Mr. Max—

BRITTEN   Ah-hah—Erlone's one of Max's crowd—Hear that, Mr. Dalton?—And then where did you go?

BIGGER   Mr. Jan drove to Ernie's Kitchen Shack.

BRITTEN   And how long did they stay there?

BIGGER   Well, we must have stayed—

BRITTEN   We?

BIGGER   You see, Mister, I did what they told me. I was only working for 'em.

BRITTEN   And then what did you do?

BIGGER   They kept worrying me until I went in and had a drink with 'em.

BRITTEN   (*With a placating gesture toward* MRS. DALTON.) A drink, eh? So they were drinking—

BIGGER   Farewell party and Christmas and all—yessuh.

BRITTEN   And then you brought them home here?

BIGGER   Yessuh.

MRS. DALTON   (*In sad, but firm graciousness.*)   How intoxicated was Miss Dalton, Bigger?

BIGGER   (*Not looking at her.*)   She—she couldn't hardly stand up—up—ma'am.

BRITTEN   And he—this Erlone—he helped her to her room? Huh? (PEGGY *bows her head in her apron.*)

DALTON   That's all right, Bigger. Go ahead and tell us.

BIGGER   Yessuh.

BRITTEN   She had passed out, huh?

BIGGER   Well, yes, suh. I 'spect you'd call it that.

BRITTEN   (*Conclusively.*)   And they told you to leave the car outside, huh?

BIGGER   Yes, suh, he told me to leave the car. And I could go on home, get my things, and come back this morning.

BRITTEN   How was this Erlone acting? Drunk, eh?

BIGGER   Yes, suh, I guess he was drunk. (*Suddenly* BRITTEN *takes from his pocket a small batch of pamphlets and holds them under* BIGGER'S *nose.*)

BRITTEN   Where did you get these pamphlets?

BIGGER   I ain't never seen them things before.

BRITTEN   Oh, yeah? I got 'em out of your overcoat pocket— in the basement. Is that your coat?

BIGGER   Yessuh.

BRITTEN   Is that the coat you were wearing last night?

BIGGER   Yessuh.

BRITTEN   Then where did you get them?

BIGGER   Miss Dalton, she gave 'em to me, I reckon, but I didn't read 'em—

BRITTEN   What unit are you in?

BIGGER   (*Backing away.*)   Suh?

BRITTEN   (*Savagely.*)   Come on, Comrade. Tell me what unit you are in? (BIGGER *stares at him in speechless amazement.*)   Who's your organizer?

BIGGER   I don't know what you mean, suh!

DALTON   Britten, he doesn't know anything about that.

BRITTEN   Didn't you know this Erlone before you came to work here?

BIGGER   Naw, suh, naw, suh—You got me wrong, suh. I ain't never fooled around with them long hair folks. The ones at the meeting last night was the first ones I ever met, so help me God. (*Now* BRITTEN *comes pushing nearer to*

BIGGER *till he has forced him back against the wall at the right. He looks him squarely in the eye, then grabs him by the collar and rams his head against the wall.*)

BRITTEN   Come on, gimme the facts. Tell me about Miss Dalton and that Erlone. What did he do to her?

BIGGER   Naw, suh, I ain't—I don't know—Naw, suh.

DALTON   (*Sternly.*)   That's enough, Britten.

BRITTEN   Okay. I guess he's all right.   (*Smiling kindly at* BIGGER.)   Just playing a little, son.   (BIGGER *gulps and stares at him.*)   If you say he's okay, then he's okay with me, Mr. Dalton.   (*To* BIGGER.)   You say Erlone told you to leave the car in the drive and then he helped Miss Dalton up to the steps.

BIGGER   Yes, suh.

BRITTEN   And did he go away?

BIGGER   He helped her up the steps, suh, and—uh, she was just about passed out.

BRITTEN   And he went with her into the house?

BIGGER   Yes, suh—   (*He suddenly stops and stares toward the door at the left front.* JAN ERLONE *enters. His manner is nervous and agitated, and his face is pale.* ERLONE *is somewhat of the unwashed intellectual type, carelessly dressed and in need of a haircut.*)

ERLONE   What are you telling these people, Bigger Thomas?

BRITTEN   Oh, so you walked right in?

ERLONE   (*Ignoring him.*)   What's all this about? Have you heard anything from Mary—Miss Dalton?

BRITTEN   (*Savagely.*)   You're just in time to tell us.   (ERLONE *stares at* BIGGER *who straightens up and gazes before him.*)

ERLONE   (*To the others.*)   What's happened? Tell me.

BRITTEN   Take it easy. You got plenty of time. I know your
kind—you like to rush in and have things your way.   (*He
turns to* BIGGER.)   Bigger, is this the man that came home
with Miss Dalton last night?   (ERLONE *blinks. He stares at*
BRITTEN, *then at* BIGGER.)

BIGGER   (*Without flinching.*)   Yes, suh.   (ERLONE *stares at*
BIGGER *again with wide incredulous eyes.*)

ERLONE   You didn't bring me here, Bigger. Why do you
tell them that?   (*Crossing to* MRS. DALTON.)   Mrs. Dalton, I'm worried too. That's why I'm here. What is this?
(*To* BRITTEN.)   What are you making this man lie for?

BRITTEN   Where is Miss Dalton, Erlone?

ERLONE   She was supposed to go to Detroit this morning, to
see her grandmother.

BRITTEN   We know that. But she didn't go. Did you see Miss
Dalton last night?

ERLONE   (*Hesitating.*)   No.

BRITTEN   But you were with her and with this Negro boy—
at Ernie's Kitchen Shack.

ERLONE   All right then, I saw her. So what?

BRITTEN   (*Sarcastically.*)   So you saw her. Where is she
now?

ERLONE   If she's not in Detroit, I don't know where she is.

BRITTEN   You and Miss Dalton were drunk last night.

ERLONE   Oh, come on! We weren't drunk. We just had a
little to drink.

BRITTEN   You brought her home about two in the morning.

ERLONE   (*After a pause.*)   No.   (BIGGER *is seen to take a
quick step backward and his hand reaches for the knob of
the glass door.*)

DALTON   Mr. Erlone, we know my daughter was drunk last
night when you brought her here. She was too drunk to

leave here by herself. We know that. Now do you know where she is?

ERLONE   (*Stammering.*) I—I didn't come here last night.

BRITTEN   But you were with her and she was drunk. Do you mean you left her in that condition?

ERLONE   (*Hesitating and swallowing.*) Well, I came as far as the door with her. I had to go to a meeting. I took the trolley back. Had to hurry. (*He turns to* BIGGER.) Bigger, what are you telling these people? (BIGGER *makes no answer.*)

MRS. DALTON   (*In an agitated voice.*) I'll see you in my room, Henry—please. (PEGGY *comes over to her, helps her up and assists her from the room. Just before she leaves,* MRS. DALTON *turns and looks toward* ERLONE *with her sightless eyes. Then lowering her head, she goes away with* PEGGY.)

ERLONE   (*Beseechingly around him.*) Bigger, didn't you get Miss Dalton home safely? What's happened to her? (BIGGER *gazes stonily at him and does not answer.* ERLONE *seems to read a strange and ultimate antagonism in* BIGGER'S *face, for he gradually lowers his head and stares at the floor.*)

BRITTEN   (*Chuckling.*) So Bigger brought her home and you didn't?

ERLONE   Yes.

BRITTEN   You're a liar, Erlone. First you say you didn't see her, then you did. Then you didn't bring her home, then you did. Then again you didn't—Come on, what's your game?

ERLONE   (*In a low desolate voice as he stares about him.*) I was trying to protect her.

BRITTEN   You're trying to protect yourself and making a damn poor job of it.

ERLONE   I didn't come here, I tell you.

BRITTEN   You got Miss Dalton drunk, Erlone—you brought
her here early this morning. You told the boy to leave the
car out in the driveway. You went inside and went upstairs with her, and now she's disappeared. Where is she?
(ERLONE *looks at him with bewildered eyes.*)

ERLONE   Listen, I told you all I know.

DALTON   (*Stepping forward.*)   Erlone, you and I don't
agree on certain things—civic matters, politics. Let's forget our differences. I want to know where my daughter is.

ERLONE   I tell you I don't know, Mr. Dalton.   (DALTON
throws up his hands in futile, desperate anger.)

DALTON   We'll see you upstairs later, Britten.   (*He goes
out.*)

BRITTEN   (*Blocking the way to the door and glaring at* ER-
LONE *as he yells.*)   Get over there, you!   (ERLONE *backs
away from his menacing look.*)   Now listen to me, you
goddam Communist!—

ERLONE   I tell you I don't know where she is!

BRITTEN   All right. You don't know now—eh? But you will
know, and you'll know damn soon. The FBI and Edgar
Hoover have a way of handling your kind—   (*He turns to
go as* PEGGY *appears in the door.*)

PEGGY   Mr. Dalton said please come up, Mr. Britten. And
you better look after the furnace, Bigger. It needs tending—

BRITTEN   Okay. That's all I got to say now, Erlone.   (*He
follows* PEGGY *out. For a moment* ERLONE *looks down at the
floor.* BIGGER *watches him with steady, smoldering eyes. In
the street outside, a chorus begins singing a Christmas
carol. Slowly* BIGGER's *hand goes up and slides into his coat
and rests there. Presently* ERLONE *looks up.*)

ERLONE   Bigger.

BIGGER   (*In a low humming voice.*)   Go on away from here,
Mr. Jan. Go on way.

ERLONE   What's all this about, Bigger? Why did you tell
those lies? I haven't done anything to you, have I? Where's
Mary?

BIGGER   (*Mumbling.*)   I don't want to talk to you.

ERLONE   (*Desperately.*)   But what have I done to you?

BIGGER   I don't want to talk to you.   (*With a sharp cry.*)
Get out!

ERLONE   Listen, Bigger. If these people are bothering you,
just tell me. Don't be scared. We are used to this sort of
persecution. Mr. Max will help you in your rights. He
knows their crooked law. Listen, now. Tell me about it.
Come on, we'll go out and get a cup of coffee and talk it
over. (ERLONE *comes toward him.* BIGGER *suddenly whips
out his gun, and* ERLONE *stops with white face.*)   For God's
sake, man, what are you doing!

BIGGER   I don't need you—that Mr. Max neither—
(*Hoarsely.*)   Get out!

ERLONE   I haven't bothered you. Don't—

BIGGER   (*His voice tense and hysterical.*)   Leave me alone.

ERLONE   (*Backing away from him.*)   For Christ's sake,
man!

BIGGER   (*His voice rising almost to a scream.*)   Get away
from here! Now! Now!   (ERLONE *backs farther away,
then turns and goes rapidly out at the right front, looking
back over his shoulder with hurt and helpless eyes. For a
moment* BIGGER *stands still, then slowly his hand replaces
the pistol in his coat. In the basement below, the windy
draft of the furnace begins blowing. He jerks his head up
with a shudder, listening. Gradually a low moaning sound
rises from his lips. For a moment he remains so, then wheel-
ing quickly, he goes into the conservatory and passes out*

of sight through the flowers at the right rear, leaving the watering pot sitting on the floor. The music of the carol singers comes in more strongly from the street and continues. The scene fades out.)

Scene 6

The curtain rises on Clara Mears' one-room kitchenette apartment down in the racial ghetto of the great city. A bed is at the left rear, a window by it, and a dresser at the right front next to the door. In the right rear are a sink and little table. It is night, a few hours later. Clara is standing in front of her mirror arranging her hair. She is partly dressed. Bigger is sitting on the edge of the bed dressed only in his trousers. His naked shoulders are hunched over.

CLARA   (*Glancing over at* BIGGER'S *coat hanging on the chair at the left.*)   Look, puddles of water dripped all over the floor from your coat.   (*She moves the chair and coat over near the radiator, then goes back to the mirror. The carol singing dies away.*)

BIGGER   (*Muttering.*)   Yeh, like a little brown doll talking about wet coat and puddles on the floor. Rain and snow, they don't matter.   (*He flings out a clenched fist and bangs the railing of the bed.* CLARA *turns toward him questioningly.*)

CLARA   Bigger, what's wrong with you?

BIGGER   (*Musingly.*)   She asks me what's wrong—yeh, what's wrong?

CLARA   You *ain't* yourself tonight.

BIGGER   All right, I ain't. I'm different then.

CLARA   (*Tripping swiftly over and dropping on her knees by him.*)   Bigger, honey, don't be like that. You hurt me. Don't stay way off from me. All the time I loved you in my arms there, seemed like your mind was full of something different. I felt your hands feeling at me but not you—not you.

BIGGER   You done had all you want from me in the bed, and now I better go.

CLARA   (*Impulsively grabbing his hand and kissing it.*) Please, Bigger, I don't mean to make you mad. I want to satisfy you—make you happy—that's all I want. You know that. I ain't got nothing in this world but you.

BIGGER   Cut it out!

CLARA   I know everybody tries to turn you against me—say I ain't good for you—but I could be. I could make a home for you. I could—

BIGGER   (*Growling.*) Yeh—*if.* This whole world is one great big if. (*He turns and seizes her roughly by the shoulders, his voice a mixture of anguished cruelty and bitter love.*) Goddam it, you know why I come here—'cause I can't help it. I wish I could help it—*now* I wish I could— (*Springing up.*) And I can. I don't need you no more. I'm gonna be free of you. You drag me down—you tangle up in my feet like a vine—keep me from running free. I got to go. (*But lowering his head, he sinks down on the bed again.*) Sometimes I do love you, maybe, then you start holding me too tight, pulling at me, trying to suck me on down like a swamp.

CLARA   (*Half weeping.*) I don't—I don't—

BIGGER   Then I get mad, freeze on you, feel like slamming the door in your damn face, leave you out in the cold. Then I hate myself and I hate you for making me hate myself. Then it's your little soft baby-talk fumbling around my heart and then we get some likker and end up by kissing and biting and going to bed. Goddam, I hate it! I hate it! Wish it was different. *Now* I do.

CLARA   (*Echoing.*) Why you keep saying "now" all the time!

BIGGER   'Cause things come to me clear now, like watching the sun rise over the skyscrapers. Like the folks say you feel, maybe, when you been baptised. Like Ma in her dreams seeing God riding in the clouds on high. Yeh, from way up high I can look down and see things. A light busting in front of me like a big rocket showing up everything in no-man's land. (*His voice dies in his throat and he stares unseeingly in front of him.* CLARA's *inquiring, begging eyes are fastened on his face. He breaks into hoarse, raucous laughter and pounds his knees with his fists.*)

CLARA   (*Whispering.*) Why you laughing like that? (*She shudders.*)

BIGGER   I'm laughing—laughing at everybody—everybody in the whole damn world. Laughing at you.

CLARA   (*Piteously.*) Please, Bigger.

BIGGER   Feel like I'm living in a strange country, nobody there but me. Feel dizzy, like I'm gonna fall down from a million miles in the air, and my skin seems on fire when I think of it—like my hair gonna rise up straight on my head—like I'm sailing out in space all by myself like a star. Then I come back to you and feel your arms around me. Goddammit take 'em 'way.

CLARA   (*Her lips quivering.*) And they'd always be around you, Bigger—they would. (*Frantically.*) But you talk wild, drunk-like—

BIGGER   (*Gesturing.*) That little old bottle of whiskey? Didn't even feel it.

CLARA   Lie down and sleep now. I'll fix you a good supper. You tired. Your po' face tight and drawn and yo' eyes all full of blood. (*She rises and stands by his side.*)

BIGGER   (*His arm clutching around her as though suddenly doubting everything.*) You love me, Clara?

CLARA   (*Her body yielding instinctively to him.*) You know that. Yes, yes! (*She bends down and kisses him fiercely and awkwardly on the lips.*)   And it ain't things you give me. That ninety dollars there don't matter. There it is on the dresser. It don't matter at all. I give it back. (*She steps over, takes some bills from the dresser top and stuffs them into one of the coat's pockets. She draws her hand away with an exclamation.*)   Something hard in your coat, Bigger! You got a gun. (*Gasping.*)   Is that why you got all that money. You robbed somebody?

BIGGER   I ain't, I tell you. Well, maybe they give me something in advance on my job.

CLARA   Who? (*Looking at him sharply.*)   Old white gal I seen you eating with, down at Ernie's last night?

BIGGER   Maybe.

CLARA   (*In fierce jealousy.*)   She's crazy. Her face say she's crazy.

BIGGER   (*Sharply.*)   Aw, don't worry 'bout her.

CLARA   (*Anxiously.*)   Leave her alone, honey. She'll get you in trouble.

BIGGER   Nunh-unh.

CLARA   Say, Bigger, where is this you working—this Dalton place?

BIGGER   (*Sharply.*)   How come you want to know that?

CLARA   I just like to know, honey! How come you don't want to talk none?

BIGGER   Over there on Drexel . . .

CLARA   That's where them rich folks live. . . That's where they had that kidnaping last year.

BIGGER   Huh?

CLARA   Kidnap that little girl—and killed her—and tried to get money from her folks?

BIGGER   (*Staring off.*)   Tried to get money. Yeh, yeh, I remember. (*Springing up.*)   Money! Goddammit. Everybody talking about it—papers with headlines, telephones ringing. Yeh, let 'em ring—ringing all over America, asking, asking about Bigger. The bells ringing, the sirens and the ambulances beating their gongs, and Bigger's name on the hot wires of the world.

CLARA   Bigger! Bigger! (*In sharp and unbelieving reproof.*) There's something wrong, make you talk like that.

BIGGER   (*Turning to her and speaking almost kindly, as he touches her face affectionately.*) Yeh, Clara, plenty wrong. I tell you now, and you stay with me?

CLARA   What is it, Bigger?

BIGGER   (*Shouting.*) You stay with me, I say!

CLARA   Yes, anything, Bigger. I stay with you.

BIGGER   Sit down. (*She sinks obediently to the bed.*) Listen, now. I'm a fool to tell you, but I got to tell you. (*Queerly.*) Got to tell somebody. I don't know what's gonna happen, Clara. (*Suddenly matter-of-factly.*) Maybe I got to get out of town soon.

CLARA   What you done? I warned you 'bout Gus and that Jack.

BIGGER   Right now, it come to me, you help me, you and me together—nobody won't know—we be safe then, money make us safe.

CLARA   (*Her eyes wide and still.*) What you talking about?

BIGGER   (*Rising and beginning to pace the floor.*) Listen. This gal where I work—this Dalton gal—she's crazy. Crazier'n hell, see? Father's a rich man—millionaire— (*Gasping.*) Millionaire! (*Shooting his words out again.*) And she's done run off—Always hanging around with them Commies—maybe done run off with one of 'em.

CLARA   I told you.

BIGGER   Nobody don't know where she's gone. So last night I took—naw, she give me money to hush my mouth. See?

Never mind it's yours now. They throw money around everywhere. They don't care none. Just pay in advance maybe.

CLARA   I don't care none, either, Bigger. It ain't the money.

BIGGER   (*Shouting.*) Shut your damn mouth. (*Pulling the back of his hand nervously across his lips.*) They don't know where she is—so, they sit worrying. All day they been worrying. The old man pacing the floor like me now. (*A harsh laugh breaking from him.*) But I'm walking different. See? Different. And that blind woman—holds them white flower hands together, with that white cat in 'em, and crying out, "Where's my daughter?" and that fat detective slob trompling about mashing things down. "Where is she?" they saying. They don't know. I know.

CLARA   (*Crying out.*) Bigger, what have you done?

BIGGER   And what they thinking? I tell you. Think she's kidnaped. Yeh, them communists got her. I heard 'em say so. Gonna ask for money, see?—plenty. They pay the money—pay it to you and me. We cash in, 'cause nobody else is trying to. See?

CLARA   We can't do that.

BIGGER   (*Shouting again.*) We going to do it!

CLARA   (*Pleadingly.*) But she'll show up, Bigger. She'll come back.

BIGGER   (*Waving his hand excitedly.*) Don't worry about that. Yeh, money. They got plenty of dough. They won't miss it. Then you and me—we's free. Goddammit, free! you hear me? Free like them. How come they free? money —money— (*Suddenly sitting down and turning excitedly and close to her.*) One them old empty buildings over there—I'll hide in it. Yeh, 36 Place and Michigan—door open all the time. I'll write 'em a letter.

CLARA   (*Weeping.*) They'll get us for it. The white folks never stop looking—

BIGGER   But looking for the wrong baby. And this is one
time the black folks is going to be smarter than the white.

CLARA   But you know where the girl is. She'll show up.

BIGGER   She won't.

CLARA   How you know?

BIGGER   She just won't.

CLARA   Bigger, you ain't done nothing to that girl, have you?

BIGGER   (*Throwing back his hand.*)   Say that again and
I'll slap you through the floor. Yeh, I'll get the pencil and
paper— (*Springing up and moving toward the dresser.*)
Write them a letter—print it. Think they sharp, huh? We
see. We see. (*He rummages in the dresser.* CLARA *gazes
helplessly at him, words beginning to break through her
dying sobs.*)

CLARA   Bigger, what you doing? What you doing to me? All
my life's been full of hard work, work every day long as I
can remember. Tired enough to drop, I begun to get
drunk to sleep. And then I found you. I was happy. All
the time I been hoping the way would come clear for you
and me. And it will someday. Don't do it, Bigger, don't
do it.

BIGGER   (*Unheedingly.*)   Here she is. (*He gets the paper
and pencil. Looking about him for a place to write, he
drops down on the floor and spreads the sheet out, biting
the pencil ruminatively the while.*)

CLARA   I wish one of us had died before we was born—God
knows I do. All you ever caused me was trouble—just plain
black trouble. I been a fool—just a blind, dumb, black,
drunk fool. And I'll go on being a fool 'cause I love you—
love you clean down to hell—ain't never had nobody but
you—nobody in my arms but you, close against me but
you— (*She moves unsteadily over and stands behind him.*

Falling down on her knees, she lays her face against the back of his neck, her arms around him.)

BIGGER   Shut up, now. I got to write. No, I'll print it. Yeh, I'll sign the note "Red." They're all scared of Reds. (*Exultantly.*)   Won't ever think we done it. Don't think we got guts enough. (*Excitedly.*)   We got guts, ain't we, Clara? Guts to do anything. (*Writing.*)   "Dear Sir." Ha! ha! Naw, just "Sir." (*Cocking his head.*)   Look at that word. A few more of them and the whole world turn upside-down, and we done it. Big headlines in the papers, police running around like chickens with their heads cut off—and all the time we stay back watching, waiting to pick up the dough where they put it. (*His voice rising to a croon.*)   Twenty years, up and down the dark alleys, like a rat. Nobody hear us — (CLARA *slides further down on the floor beside him, her face buried protectively and protectedly against him.*)   —nobody hear you, nobody pay any attention to you, and the white folks walking high and mighty don't even know we're alive. Now they cut the pigeon wing the way we say—yeh, we call the figgers, we pull the strings.

CLARA   (*Moaning.*)   Bigger, Bigger! (*She falls sobbing on the floor.*)

BIGGER   (*His head raised, staring off, his face alight with his vision.*)   Like bars falling away—like doors swinging open and walls falling down. And all the big cars and all the big buildings, and the finery and the marching up and down, and the big churches and the bells ringing and the millionaires walking in and out bowing low before their God. Hah, hah! It ain't God now, it's Bigger. Bigger Thomas, that's my name! (CLARA's *sobs break hopelessly through the room.* BIGGER *bends his head and begins to write.*) "Sir: —We got your daughter—say nothing—the ransom is—" (*From a church somewhere across the street a*

Negro song service has begun. It continues for a moment. The scene fades out.)

Scene 7

The song service dies away, and the curtain comes up on the basement of the Dalton home, the next night. The walls of the scene are painted a solid, glistening gray; the ceiling is high and crossed by the tubes of many white asbestos-covered pipes. To the left rear is a huge squat iron furnace, with the dull baleful eye of the fire showing through its isinglass door and reflecting on the wall. Behind it is the jutting angle of the coal bin. At the center rear are steps leading up to the kitchen pantry above. At the center right a door leads to the outside. To the left near the stairs are trunks, boxes, and piles of old newspapers, and on the opposite side of the stairs clothes are hanging to dry.

When the curtain rises, Bigger is seen standing by the furnace, motionless and looking intently before him. He starts in terror as the door at the upper center rear opens and Britten stands looking down into the reddish gloom.

BRITTEN   That you, Bigger?

BIGGER   Oh— (*He whirls and backs quickly to the wall, his hands groping for an ax that hangs there within reach. He comes to himself quickly.*)   Yessuh—yessuh.

BRITTEN   (*Descending the stairs.*)   Fixing the furnace?

BIGGER   (*Still gripping the ax in his right hand.*)   Yessuh.

BRITTEN   (*With a little laugh.*)   What—with the ax?

BIGGER   (*In confusion.*)   No suh—no, suh—Huh—I— (*He breaks off, hangs the ax back on the wall and picks up the shovel.*)

BRITTEN   You sure jumped like the devil was after you. (*Coming over to the furnace.*)   Yeh, I reckon you are a little on edge. Doggone it, I'm nervous as a cat myself with all this "Who shot John" around here.   (BIGGER *still stands with the shovel in his hand, watching his movements.* BRIT-TEN *opens the big door of the furnace and stoops to gaze inside.* BIGGER *quickly gets behind him with the shovel and slowly raises it.* BRITTEN *clangs the door shut and straightens up.*) No wonder the house is freezing upstairs—a gorm of ashes is banked up in there.

BIGGER   (*Lowering the shovel and backing away, his eyes fastened intently upon* BRITTEN'S *face.*)   Yessuh, I'm gonna fix it right away.

BRITTEN   (*As a pounding begins on the door at the right.*) What's that? Just listen to 'em. Damn newspapermen again. (*The pounding continues.*) Say, Bigger, did you lock that gate to the driveway? (*Before* BIGGER *can answer, the door at the right opens and several newspapermen crowd their way in, some of them with cameras.* BRITTEN *tries to stop them.*)   You can't come in. Get out and stay out.

VOICE   We're in, Mr. Britten. (*One of the newspapermen is a lean lynx-eyed horse-trader type of man with an old dark felt hat set back on his head. He is about 35.* BIGGER *backs slowly away to the wall at the left and stands alert in the shadow. As the scene progresses, the newspaperman who is called* JED *begins to study him.*)

BRITTEN   Now, listen here, boys. This is Mr. Dalton's home, and Mr. Dalton's got no statement to make.

VOICES   What's the dope? Come on, Britten, what's going on?

BRITTEN   Nothing! (*The first newspaperman pushes forward, a cigarette in his mouth and snow on his old hat and coat.* BRITTEN *growls at him.*)   So Mr. Jed the snooper is in my hair again, fouling up the premises.

NEWSPAPERMAN JED   (*Grinning.*) Yeh, looking for a louse, and you remember I often find him.

BRITTEN   Go off and die, you buzzard.

NEWSPAPERMAN JED   An inclusive word.

BRITTEN   Nuts to you.

NEWSPAPERMAN JED   As the monkey said. (*He begins to wander aimlessly about the scene, now and then cutting his eye at the nervous, trembling* BIGGER.)

VOICE   (*To* BRITTEN.) How about that Beatnik you picked up?

SECOND VOICE   Jan Erlone?

THIRD VOICE   Was the girl sleeping with him?

VOICE   He says he didn't even come here that night. Says he's got witnesses. Says you had him arrested because of his politics.

BRITTEN   (*Shouting.*) I don't know a thing, I tell you! (*The reporters have their pads and pencils out. They crowd around* BRITTEN, *shooting questions at him.*)

VOICES   When was Miss Dalton seen last? Can we get a picture of her room? Is the girl really missing? Or is this a publicity stunt, Britten? (*A flash bulb goes off in* BRITTEN's *face. He blinks and backs away.*)

BRITTEN   Hey, steady, boys.

VOICE   What's the matter?

BRITTEN   I only work here. For Christ's sake, give me a break. (*Another flash bulb explodes in his face.*)

VOICE   Mr. Dalton won't see us. So you talk. (BRITTEN *shakes his head vehemently.*)

ANOTHER VOICE,   Maybe this boy'll talk.

BRITTEN   He don't know a damn thing.

VOICE   Say, Mac, what do you think?

BIGGER   (*In a hard, cold voice.*) My name ain't Mac.

VOICE   That's the Thomas boy. Bigger Thomas.

VOICE   I'd like to ask you a few questions, Mr. Thomas. (BIGGER *makes no reply.*)

BRITTEN   He's dumb. He don't know nothing.

VOICE   Get a shot of him.   (*A bulb goes off in* BIGGER'S *face.* BIGGER *dodges, throwing his hands before his eyes.*)

BRITTEN   (*Helplessly.*)   Cut it out, will you? Listen, boys— they're worried about the girl—Mrs. Dalton's ill. The whole house is upset—   (*A newspaperman walks over to* BIGGER *and slips something into his hand.*)

VOICE   Come on, boy. Give us a break.

BRITTEN   (*Hurrying forward.*)   No, none of that.   (*He snatches the money from* BIGGER'S *fingers and returns it to the newspaperman.*)   Take your damn money back. (BIGGER *inches away from them, his head lowered. The door at the upper center opens and* MR. DALTON—*old, weary, and shaken—stands framed in the light, the red shadows flickering across his wan features. He holds a white piece of paper tremblingly in his hand. The talk stops, and photographers begin hastily getting their cameras ready.*)

DALTON   Gentlemen—   (*They all watch him, waiting, as he descends the steps.* BRITTEN *moves to his side with the protection of the law. Several flash bulbs now blind the scene as* DALTON *lifts his hand, emphasizing his words.*) Please, gentlemen—just a moment.   (*After a pause.*)   I am ready to make a statement now.   (*His voice fails, then goes on.*)   I want you to listen carefully—   (*Trying to control his emotion.*)   The way you gentlemen handle this will mean life or death to someone—someone very dear to me.   (*The bulbs flash again, making* DALTON *blink and lose the train of his thought. Pencils are already flying over their pads.* MRS. DALTON, *dressed in white and holding the white cat in her arms, appears in the doorway. She descends the stairs and stops. One photographer is on his knees, pointing his camera upwards.* PEGGY'S *face also comes timidly into the doorway, looking down.* BIGGER *remains silent by the wall, his right hand going now and then to his lips in a nervous gesture.*)

DALTON   Gentlemen, I have just phoned the police and requested that Mr. Jan Erlone be released immediately. I
want it known and understood publicly that I have no
charges to prefer against him. It is of the utmost importance that this be understood. I hope your papers will
carry the story. Further, I want to announce publicly that
I apologize for his arrest and inconvenience. Gentlemen,
our daughter, Mary Dalton— (*His voice chokes.*) —has
been kidnaped. (*There is a commotion in the basement.*
BRITTEN *confirms the news with a sage nod of his head as
if he knew it all the time.*)

VOICE   How do you know, Mr. Dalton?

VOICE   When did it happen?

DALTON   (*Recovering himself.*)   We think it happened
early Sunday morning.

VOICE   How much are they asking?

DALTON   Twenty-five thousand dollars.

VOICE   Have you any idea who they are?

DALTON   We know nothing.

VOICE   Have you received any word from her, Mr. Dalton?

DALTON   No, not directly, but we *have* heard from the kid-
napers.

VOICE   Is that the letter there?

DALTON   Yes, this is it.

VOICE   Did it come through the mail? How did you get it?

DALTON   Someone left it under the door.

VOICE   When?

DALTON   About an hour ago, we think.

VOICE   Can we see the letter?

DALTON   The instructions for the delivery of the money are
here, and I have been cautioned not to make them public.

But you can say in your papers that thcse instructions will be followed, and I shall pay the ransom.

VOICE   How is the note signed? (*There is silence.*)

DALTON   It's signed "Red."

VOICES   Red! Do you know who it is? What does that mean?

DALTON   No.

VOICE   Do you think some Communist or Black Muslim person did it, Mr. Dalton?

DALTON   I don't know. I am not positively blaming anybody. If my daughter is returned, I'll ask no questions of anyone. Now, that's all, gentlemen—all! (*With a final wave of his hand, he turns and follows* MRS. DALTON *up the steps. A babble of noise breaks out among the newspapermen.*)

VOICES   (*Swirling around the confused* BRITTEN.) Get a shot of Miss Dalton's room. Climb a tree if you have to. And play up the blind mother and the cat. Try to get her to pose among her flowers. (*The newspapermen begin rushing out of the basement at the right.* BRITTEN *stands guarding the entrance up the stairs at the rear.*) Hell, this is bigger than the Jenkins child. Do you believe it? What do you think? (*And now the newspapermen have all scrambled out except* NEWSPAPERMAN JED, *who stands gazing with apparent idleness at* BIGGER'S *form in the shadow. He turns and strolls over toward the door at the right as if leaving, whistling aimlessly, through his teeth as he goes.* BRITTEN *mops his forehead and hurries up the stairs and out at the rear.* BIGGER *comes tremblingly forward and stands in front of the furnace, gazing at the red, gleaming light. And now we see that* NEWSPAPERMAN JED *has stopped in the shadow at the right and is looking back at* BIGGER. PEGGY *comes swiftly down the steps.*)

PEGGY   Bigger!

BIGGER   Huh? (*Whirling again.*)

PEGGY   For goodness sake, get the fire going!

BIGGER   Yessum.

PEGGY   Now! Mrs. Dalton's had to wear her shawl all day to keep warm. (*She picks up the shovel and hands it to him.*) Go ahead. It won't bite you— (*At the tone of her voice* NEWSPAPERMAN JED *looks around.*) I'll have your supper ready soon.

BIGGER   (*Taking the shovel mechanically.*) Yessum. (*She goes hurriedly up the stairs.* BIGGER *stands holding the shovel in his hand. He bends down, reaches out to open the door, then takes his hand away and backs off. The lean figure of* NEWSPAPERMAN JED *comes strolling back out of the shadows at the right.*)

NEWSPAPERMAN JED   What's the trouble, boy? (BIGGER *springs around, the shovel flying instinctively up in the air as if about to strike something.*)

BIGGER   (*Dropping the shovel swiftly down, its edge hitting the top of his foot.*) Nothing, suh—Nothing, suh. (*His foot, as though a separate and painful part of him, lifts itself up from the floor and wiggles in its shoe, then grows still again.*)

NEWSPAPERMAN JED   Awful nervous, huh?

BIGGER   Naw, suh. Naw, suh, I ain't nervous.

NEWSPAPERMAN JED   Have a cigarette.

BIGGER   Nawsuh, nawsuh.

NEWSPAPERMAN JED   (*Pulling one out and lighting it, then holding the package out to* BIGGER.) Don't smoke?

BIGGER   Yessuh. (*He takes one of the cigarettes, his hand trembling in spite of itself.*)

NEWSPAPERMAN JED   Here, let me light it for you. (*He strikes a match, and holds it for* BIGGER, *staring keenly at his face.*) Sort of warm, ain't you?

BIGGER   Naw, suh. Yessuh.

NEWSPAPERMAN JED   You're sweating a lot. And I'm freezing. You're supposed to tend the furnace, ain't you?

BIGGER   Yessuh.

NEWSPAPERMAN JED   (*Staring at him.*)   Then why don't
you do it?

BIGGER   (*Without moving.*)   Yessuh.

NEWSPAPERMAN JED   Sit down, son. I want to talk with you
a little. (*He pulls a couple of chairs out from the rear, sits
in one, and motions* BIGGER *to the other.* BIGGER *sinks
quietly down, breathing heavily. He sucks the smoke of the
cigarette deep into his lungs, and as if through that action
gaining control of himself, lifts his face and looks directly
at his questioner.*)

BIGGER   (*In a clear hard voice.*)   How come you want to
talk to me?

NEWSPAPERMAN JED   Just a few questions. You know anything connected with this story is news. Say, what do you
think of private property?

BIGGER   Suh? Naw, suh, I don't own no property.

NEWSPAPERMAN JED   (*Soothingly.*)   Sure, sure. (*Puffing
on his cigarette, his eyes crinkling into a gentle smile.*)
Tell me, what do *you* think of Miss Dalton? I've heard she
was sort of wild.

BIGGER   (*Quickly.*)   Nawsuh, nawsuh. She was a mighty
fine lady.

NEWSPAPERMAN JED   (*Coolly, blowing a ring of smoke.*)
Why do you she *was?*

BIGGER   I—uh—I mean she was fine to me.

NEWSPAPERMAN JED   Yes, the Daltons are mighty fine folks.
(*As though veering off from the subject.*)   What did old
Edward Max talk about at that meeting the other night?

BIGGER   Suh?

NEWSPAPERMAN JED   Some of his radical ideas? What did
he say to you—well, about the rich and the poor?

BIGGER   Well, suh, he told me that some day there'd be no more rich folks and no more poor folks, if folks could get together in the new society—

NEWSPAPERMAN JED   Here's hoping, son—especially about the poor.

BIGGER   And he said that black men are beginning to have a chance—chance at good jobs like anybody else—and stand up high and equal—be free.

NEWSPAPERMAN JED   And no more second-class citizenship? No more riots and burnings?

BIGGER   Yessuh, no more of that. All—all for the good now. But we must still keep working.

NEWSPAPERMAN JED   For the new day—uh?

BIGGER   Yessuh, for the new day.

NEWSPAPERMAN JED   And what did the girl, Miss Dalton, say?

BIGGER   She said so too.

NEWSPAPERMAN JED   And what did he say to you about white women?

BIGGER   Nothing, suh, nothing.

NEWSPAPERMAN JED   (*Sighing.*)   Too bad! You know, Bigger, such things as this ought to be a warning to this country. Here was a happy family, living in peace, loving their neighbor, with one daughter—a beautiful daughter— You agree with that, don't you, Bigger?

BIGGER   Yessuh.

NEWSPAPERMAN JED   Yes, it's a warning to us. You might say she was a martyr, died to help us to see the error of our ways. We've got to learn to treat people better in this country—raise up the oppressed, give them a chance, as the President of the do-gooders say. Get rid of the slums. From what I've heard, Mary Dalton thought like that, too.

(BIGGER *now and then gives him a queer, questioning, baffled look.*) What do you think has happened to her?

BIGGER   I don't know, suh.

NEWSPAPERMAN JED   Look, that cigarette's burning your fingers. (BIGGER *drops it like a hot coal. He is offered another but shakes his head.*) They must have killed her, don't you think?

BIGGER   (*Spasmodically.*) They must've done it, suh.

NEWSPAPERMAN JED   Who?

BIGGER   Them radicals—them reds.

NEWSPAPERMAN JED   And then write a note signing their name to it? You don't think you'd do that, do you, Bigger? (*His voice is low and cool and insinuating.*)

BIGGER   Nawsuh, nawsuh.

NEWSPAPERMAN JED   (*Hunching his chair confidentially up toward* BIGGER.) Just suppose you had killed her, Bigger—

BIGGER   (*Wildly.*) Nawsuh, I didn't do it. I didn't do it!

NEWSPAPERMAN JED   Aw, take it easy. Just suppose I had killed her, then. Now that we both agree she's dead. Well, what would I do? (*He rises slowly out of his chair, pushes his hands into his pockets, and begins walking slowly back and forth in a weaving semicircle around* BIGGER, *his hat tilted back on his head as usual.*) Let me see. Yes, I need money. I'd write a ransom note, collect that and skedaddle before they found out she'd been murdered. Wouldn't you do it that way, Bigger?

BIGGER   Nawsuh.

NEWSPAPERMAN JED   What would you do?

BIGGER   I didn't do it.

NEWSPAPERMAN JED   I'm just imagining. Where were we? Oh, she's murdered. So now, we've got to dispose of the body—no traces—nobody ever to know. Well, what about a trunk—ship it off somewhere? Nunh-unh, that wouldn't do. In four days the smell. What about weights—sink her to the bottom of the lake? Nunh-unh, they always rise to the surface. Bury her? No, that's too difficult. Somebody see you digging. What is it that wipes away all traces, Bigger.

BIGGER   Dunno, suh.

NEWSPAPERMAN JED   I'll tell you—fire. (*Whirling and snapping his fingers.*)   Yeh, that's what I'd do—I'd burn the body up. Wouldn't you, Bigger? (*With sudden loudness.*)   Go ahead and shake the ashes down, like the woman said! (BIGGER's *head sinks lower still, his shoulders shaking. With a click the thermostat turns the furnace fan on. There is a deep, blowing draft of sound.* BIGGER *springs out of his chair.* NEWSPAPERMAN JED *looks at him wonderingly.*)   Come on, now. Shake 'em down. (*Flipping a coin in his hand.*)   Bet you two bits you won't. (BIGGER *bends puppet-like down and reaches for the shovel.* NEWSPAPERMAN JED *steps briskly over and lifts down the ax, and weighs it idly in his hand.* BIGGER *turns slowly around.* NEWSPAPERMAN JED *smiles at him.*)   This is a good ax, Bigger. Old Kelly. I used to chop with one like this when I was a kid, back on the farm. And I was good at trapping in the winter too—used to catch a lot— (*Snapping.*)   In my trap! (*And now in desperation,* BIGGER *turns fiercely back to the furnace, flings open the door and plunges the shovel into the blinding bank of glowing, red-hot ashes. A puff of dust sails out and settles about the room. Then flinging the shovel down, he hysterically seizes the upright grate handle and shakes it with a great clatter.*)   Hell of a lot of ashes in there, boy!

BIGGER   (*Breathing deeply.*)   It's all fixed now. Draws fine —everything be warmed up now. (*Yelling at the ceiling above him.*)   Miss Peggy, the furnace okay now! Listen at her sing! (*Making a puffing noise with his lips.*) She's putting on the steam now! Going to town. Goddam, Goddam! (*He begins whistling cheerily.*)

NEWSPAPERMAN JED   (*Hanging the ax on the wall behind him and strolling over again.*) Sing on, boy, sounds mighty good.

BIGGER   (*Joy breaking in his voice.*) Yessuh, and I can do old rock and roll if I'm pushed. Listen to that old coal crackle on down! The old valve creeping up—soon be popping off. Hear them drivers roll. (BRITTEN *comes hurriedly down the steps at the rear.*)

BRITTEN   What's going on here? Hell of a time to be singing. (NEWSPAPERMAN JED *is now standing by the pile of ashes, idly stirring them with the toe of his shoe.*)

NEWSPAPERMAN JED   He's a croon-baby. Come on, baby, sing us some more.

BIGGER   Got to clean up now. (*He grabs a broom from behind the furnace and goes to work.* NEWSPAPERMAN JED *bends down and picks something out of the ashes.*)

BRITTEN   So you're still here, huh?

NEWSPAPERMAN JED   Yeh, just poking around—looking for my story.

BRITTEN   (*Sarcastically.*) Ain't found it, I reckon.

NEWSPAPERMAN JED   Maybe—according to deduction—

BRITTEN   Hell of a note. We just called up the jail and that Erlone fellow won't leave. He's raising hell—

NEWSPAPERMAN JED   Says this Bigger boy's been lying, don't he? (*He stares at a tiny object he holds between his fingers.* BIGGER *stops stock-still, staring at the Newspaperman, caught again suddenly in the grip of his fear.*)

BRITTEN   How'd you know? That's just what he said.

NEWSPAPERMAN JED   (*Holding his hand out toward* BRITTEN.) Here's a platinum earring, Britten. It might interest you.   (BIGGER'S *mouth flies open and a horrified gasp breaks from him.* BRITTEN *takes the earring and looks at it inquiringly.*)

BRITTEN   Where'd you get it?

NEWSPAPERMAN JED   Just picked it up. Tell him where I got it, Bigger.

BIGGER   (*Screaming.*)   Let me out of here! Let me out! (*He staggers as if about to fall, then stumbles drunkenly across the room and flies through the door, yelling as he goes.*)   Help me! Help me!

BRITTEN   (*Pushing back his hat.*)   Holy smoke! What's the matter with him—having a fit or something.

NEWSPAPERMAN JED   You'd better catch him. He killed Mary Dalton and burned her body in that furnace.   (BRITTEN *stares at him, dumbfounded, then pulling a whistle from his pocket begins blowing it wildly as he rushes toward the door at the right. In the distance other whistles immediately take up the sound. They continue as the scene fades out. Suddenly they stop, and the lights from overhead at the right wash in on* BUCKLEY *again as he reappears on the upper stage.*)

BUCKLEY   I have tried and shall continue to try to keep my remarks within the limits of immediate fact. Justice is all that I ask. As a prosecuting officer of this sovereign commonwealth I say that the law is sacred because it makes us human. And woe to the men and the civilization of those men who in misguided sympathy or fear weaken the stout structure of that law. Justice must be dispensed fairly and equally in accordance with the facts. And the facts are that this criminal is guilty and in his soul he knows it. The intellectual and moral faculties of mankind may as well be declared impotent and of no avail and our very civilization itself a mockery and a sham if the evidence and testimony submitted by the State are not enough to compel the sentence of death upon this despoiler of innocent and helpless women—this murderer and rapist, Bigger Thomas! (*The lights black out, and* BUCKLEY *disappears. The whooming of a bitter wind blowing across the scene is heard in the distance, interspersed with the repeated and scattered sounds of a far-off tinny banging.*)

Scene 8

The next night—an empty room on the top floor of a snowy abandoned house. The rear wall of the room has collapsed and gives a view of a ruined balcony at the back, with frozen roof-tops, chimneys, and a stretch of night sky beyond. In the distance at the rear an advertising sign flashes on and off. In the extreme left rear a jagged section of wall remains, on which is hanging a once ornate and gilded picture frame, now cankered and dark from the beatings of the weather. The frame contains a semblance of a family portrait—a bearded gentleman with tattered face and faded blue uniform wiggling in the wind. Part of the wall at the right rear leans forward and in to form a sort of shelter. In the shadow at the right front is the distorted shape of a doorframe. The piece of wall at the left stands pretty much upright, in the center of which is the empty criss-cross of a paneless window. The walls, the window sill, and balcony at the rear are caked with ice, and long sharp icicles hang freezingly down from the ruins of the room. The color of the scene runs from thick black shadow at the right to a diffused yellowish glare in the center and back. The ice and snow have an unreal glassy sheen, contrasting sharply with the pure and luminous winter sky which hangs like a cyclorama of dark silk around the stenciled and faint outlines of distant skyscrapers. Drifts of wind-flattened snow show here and there on the floor amid the debris of bricks, sticks, and old papers. The wind moans intermittently about, rising from the caverns of the surrounding buildings like the low breathing of some giant and expiring creature. Now and then a piece of loose tin is heard banging and flopping in the distance, and ever and anon the old building yields to the surging of the wind with creaks and low groanings of its failing timbers. From the deep canyon below comes the muffled drone of the great city, punctuated by an auto horn, a snatch of radio music, and vague wandering noises— all hushed and muted down by the thick snow enveloping the world.

When the curtain rises Bigger is seen standing half-crouched in the shadow of the wall at the right rear. An old piece of rotted blanket is pulled protectingly around his shoulders, and his feet are tied up in pieces of wrapped tow-sacking. He is peering out toward the rear and listening, as if some sound had just disturbed him and he is trying to discover what it is. The glint of his pistol barrel shows from beneath the blanket where he holds it in his hand. Presently he turns and begins to pace up and down, beating himself with his arms to keep from freezing. A mumble of words rises from his lips.

BIGGER   Pshaw, nothing but that old piece of tin banging. They ain't found me yet! From the first jump I out-figure 'em. (*Stopping.*)   Uhm—everything sleepy and 'way off— (*With sudden loudness.*)   I ain't scared, naw. Yeh, all this time back I been afraid, feeling something bad was gonna happen. Well, it's happened. It's come on me at last—and took away my fear. And they all scared now, feeling me in the night, feel me walking behind 'em— And everywhere, the bulls is searching them old ratty Negro houses—Indiana Avenue, Calumet, Prairie, Wabash! Ha! But I ain't 'mong the black trash in the ghetto. (*Calling softly.*)   Clara!   (*He listens at the door at the right.*)   Why don't she come on here?   (*He sinks down on an old box and pulls his blanket shiveringly about him. The flopping tin bangs off at the left. He springs instinctively and nervously up, then sits down again.*)   Ain't nothing— that old tin banging, hanging loose and ready to fall. Fall on down, old tin, but I ain't gonna fall. They ain't gonna get me. (*Gazing back over his shoulder at the night sky and chuckling with low and bitter irony.*)   They smart, them white folks! Yeh, they get the niggers. But, maybe not too smart— (*He spits in the air. He beats his arms about him and stares out into the night.*)   That's right! Flash away, old sign! "Sun-kissed California oranges." Ha! I'll be in them orange-groves soon. . . with the sun on my back! (*He raises his head once more and sees far away, above him, the revolving beam of the beacon in the sky.*) Uhmm —an' look at that old Lindbergh beacon, shining there 'way out through the darkness— (*Musingly.*) Old Lindbergh—he knowed the way. Boiling icy water below him, the thunder and the lightning, the freezing and the hail around him. Keep on driving—riding through. (*Imitating the sound of an airplane propeller with his numbed lips.*) V-r-r-r—rh-h-h-h! V-r-r-r—ruh-uh-uh! Yeh, he made it, got there. And all the people running and shouting, and the headlights switching and sweeping the sky! And the big hats and clawhammer coats, and the furry babbling dolls, and the flowers—and all the spangled glory wrapped like a rainbow round him. (*Singing.*) "Rainbow —I got a rainbow round my shoulder." (*Murmuring.*) Old Lindbergh—he made it—got home, safe home. He not scared! (*Snapping his head up, his hollow eyes burning through the shadows before him.*) Aw, I ain't scared neither! (*He laughs.*) And when I light, ain't going to be no lot of people running to *me* with flowers! Hell, no! When I come, they run! Run like hell the other way!

> (*And now from the depths of the great city below comes the sound of a siren. He springs around, the piece of rotted blanket falling from his shoulders. He grips his gun tightly in his hand and crouching down, moves swiftly to the window at the left. Inching his head up above the sill, he peers over. The sound dies away. He turns from the window.*)

Sure, nothing but a' ambulance! Another fool white boy done broke his neck somewhere driving too fast. (*He moves back toward the box; flapping his arms like a bird to restore the circulation of his blood. A soft sound of fum-*

bling footsteps is heard at the right. Holding his pistol, he backs away, keeping his eyes fastened on the door. The footsteps come nearer, then stop. He calls out softly.)

That you, Clara?

CLARA'S VOICE   (*Outside.*)   Open the door.   (*He springs over, unbars the door, and lets* CLARA *in. Ramming the bar of plank back in place, he grabs a package from her.*)

BIGGER   Okay?

CLARA   (*In a low dull voice.*)   Some grub.   (*With shaking, eager hands, he opens the bag of food and begins devouring the sandwiches she has brought.*)

BIGGER   Thought you was never coming back. And me sitting here freezing to death. Things going 'round in my head! How everything look?

CLARA   Go ahead and eat—

BIGGER   (*His mouth full of food.*)   Anybody notice you?

CLARA   Went to a new delicatessen—Thirty-ninth and Indiana.

BIGGER   And you come back under the El like I told you?

CLARA   I come back that way.

BIGGER   Get the newspapers?

CLARA   Here's some liquor—you 'bout froze.   (*She pulls a bottle from her pocket. He grabs it, unstops it and drinks half of it swiftly down, then lays the bottle on the floor. She stands with her hands shoved by each other into her coat sleeves, looking at him.*)

BIGGER   Where the papers? I ask you.

CLARA   Didn't get 'em, Bigger.

BIGGER   Damn it, told you to—See what they say?

CLARA   They got your picture.

BIGGER   On the front page?

CLARA   On the front page.

BIGGER   Reckon they have. And big headlines—huh?

CLARA   Big headlines, black— (*Her mouth twists with pain.*)

BIGGER   Humm. Where they think I hid?

CLARA   Section down by Ernie's Shack is all surrounded.

BIGGER   Hah—knowed it. Dumb nuts. If them cops' brains was dynamite, wouldn't have enough to make 'em sneeze! (*Angrily.*) Why'n hell didn't you bring me that newspaper? (*She stares at him with dull, dead eyes, saying nothing.*) What's the matter? What time is it?

CLARA   Forgot to wind my watch.

BIGGER   What the big clock down there say?

CLARA   Ten till one, it say.

BIGGER   Ten more minutes and I'm gone from here. Ten more minutes and that big old sign out there goes off for the night, and I make it 'cross that old stairway over there in the dark to the next building and down that long alley.

CLARA   (*Piteously.*) Then what, Bigger?

BIGGER   I find somebody with a car— (*With the gun, he indicates a jab in the side.*) He drive me till I say stop. Then I catch a train to the west—Still got that money?

CLARA   I got it.

BIGGER   How much?

CLARA   'Bout eighty dollars left.

BIGGER   Gimme. (*She pulls the money out of her pocket and hands it to him.*)

CLARA   Bigger, you can't make it that way—You can't.

BIGGER   Goddammit, what do you think? Set here and freeze stiff as a pool stick and wait for 'em to come and pick me up? I got everything figured to the minute. (*Now from the city below comes the sound of the siren again. It continues longer than before. He jerks his head around.*) Don't like the sound of that. Jesus, won't that sign hurry and go off?

CLARA Bigger, you can't do it.

BIGGER (*With a shout.*) Cut that out!

CLARA They offer twenty-five thousand dollars reward—the paper say.

BIGGER (*After an instant of silence.*) Uhm—they want me bad. Well, they ain't gonna get me. (*Thoughtfully.*) Twenty-five thousand—same we put in that kidnap note—

CLARA It say you killed her, Bigger.

BIGGER All right, then, I killed her. I didn't mean to. (*Angrily.*) But hell, we got no time to talk about that. Got to keep my mind clear, my feet free. (*He bends down and begins unwrapping the sacking from around his feet.*)

CLARA You told me you wasn't never gonna kill nobody, Bigger. (*She chokes down the sob that keeps rising up in her throat.*)

BIGGER I tell you, I wasn't trying to kill her. It was an accident—

CLARA Accident—

BIGGER She was drunk—passed out cold—She was so drunk she didn't even know where she was—And her ma might hear her bumbling about.

CLARA And what she do?

BIGGER Nothing—I just put her on the bed and her blind ma come in— (*Shuddering.*) Blind. She come in and I got scared. Scared, I tell you. She was like all the white folks in the world had been rolled into one. (*His voice quickening.*) Yeh, her ma come into the room—had her hands stretched out like. So I just pushed the pillow hard over the gal's mouth to keep her from talking. (*There is *a pause. His voice drops to a low note of helpless confession.*) Then when she left I looked at that gal and she was dead—that's all—it happened just like that— (*He looks at* CLARA *as though imploring her belief.*) She was dead!

CLARA   You—you smothered her.

BIGGER   Yeh, I reckon I did—I reckon I did—but I didn't mean to—I swear to God I didn't. (*In a hopeless tone.*) But what difference do it make? Nobody'll believe me. I'm black and they'll say— (*Flinging a rag savagely away.*)

CLARA   The paper say—

BIGGER   Yeah, I know what they say. They say rape. But I didn't. . . I never touched that girl that way. (*Pause.*) And then when I see she dead, I, oh. . . Clara, I didn't know what to do— I took her to the basement and put her—burnt her up in that furnace. (CLARA *stares at him, her fist stuffed against her mouth as if to keep herself from screaming.*) Jesus, I couldn't help it! (*He stands up suddenly.*) It don't seem like I really done it now—really it don't seem like I done it. (*He looks off, his face hard and tense.*) Maybe I didn't do it. Maybe I just think I did. Maybe somebody else did all that— (*His body relaxes and his shoulders slump.*) But I did. Yeh—this freezing cold makes me know it. Your face say so— (*He goes on unwinding the rags. She gazes at him, her eyes filled with their dull nameless look of horror and despair. He looks anxiously off at the rear.*) Damn snow quit falling hours ago—Roads be cleared up now. Jesus, that blizzard—like it stopped all the traffic to keep me shut up here. (*He picks up the bottle and takes another drink.*)

CLARA   (*Monotonously.*) You can't get away. You got to walk down—meet 'em—tell 'em how it happened—

BIGGER   (*With a wild laugh.*) And they believe me, huh? Goddammit, I stick my head out that door, my life ain't worth a snowflake in hell. They shoot me down like a dog. Jesus, that tin keeps banging. (*And now a strange light flares into the scene an instant and then is gone.* BIGGER *leaps to his feet with a cry.*) What the hell was that? (*Across the dark blue sky at the rear, a tall, slender cone of penciled light begins weaving back and forth. It continues its slow and monotonous sweep a moment like a gigantic metronome finger silently ticking out the minutes of* BIGGER'S *life, and then is gone. He turns and stares at it.*) Look at that light moving. (*He tilts the bottle again, finishes it, then throws it away into the darkness.*) But I ain't scared now. (*His voice beginning to grow vacant and dreamy.*) I'd begun to see something. Aw, Christ, it's gone again. I'm all mixed up, but I ain't scared now, I say.

CLARA   Maybe you ought to be scared—Scared maybe 'cause you ain't scared.

BIGGER   Huh? Aw, to hell with it.

CLARA   What you gonna do?

BIGGER   (*With sudden rage.*) Gonna scram, I tell you. (*With rough brutality.*) And I don't need you now.

CLARA   I know—all last night and today, I know. Don't do no good now—nothing do any good. Your eyes so cold, your face so hard—like you want to kill me. And my heart's all heavy like a lump of lead—and dead.

BIGGER   Yeh. Anything get in my way now, I kill it.

          (*Another siren sounds in the streets below, and now, faintly comes the sound of mumbling voices.* BIGGER *darts back into the shadow and stops.*)

Listen there! (*Again as if from an unseen brilliant eye, the ruined room is illuminated in a white light reflected in a million diamond facets from the icicles, frost and snow.* BIGGER *draws his gun.*) Goddamn, they got a spotlight somewhere. They found me. (*Whirling on* CLARA *and seizing her by the throat.*) They seen you coming back. (*Hissing.*) I ought to kill you. You tell 'em.

CLARA No! No! Bigger! Bigger!

BIGGER (*His lips snarled back, his eyes cold as a snake's.*) Yeh, weak, blind—couldn't do without you. You tell 'em where I am. (*He shakes her like a rag-doll. He hurls her from him against the ruined wall at the right. She lies there in the darkness, shivering and gasping. A low, dog-like whimper rises from her. He rushes over and kicks her.*) Goddammit, stop that whining. (*She crawls toward him.*) Don't you come toward me. I'll kill you. (*The noise in the streets below has increased in volume.*)

CLARA (*Now clinging to his feet.*) Go ahead. Shoot me. Kill us both—and then, no more worry. . . no more pain— Do it, Bigger. (*He jerks his foot loose from her. She falls forward on her face and lies still. The brilliant light floods into the scene again from the faraway hidden spot, and* BIGGER *stands, naked and alone, outlined in it. He whirls around him as if trying to beat it from him. He runs to the window and looks out. Suddenly the electric-sign falters in its cycle of going on and off—then goes out entirely. A clock is heard striking one. In a convulsive gesture, his hand rises to his lips, then drops to his side.*)

BIGGER Yeh, you done it. They coming along that roof over there with their saw-off guns. I see 'em! (*He rushes to the right, starts to unbar the door when a heavy pounding sets up below. He springs back.*) They coming up there, too. (*He runs over and jerks* CLARA *violently from the floor. An ooze of blood is seeping from her mouth.*) You set 'em on me, you bitch! (*Her head sways weakly from side to side, saying "no." He throws her from him again. She stands tottering and about to fall. He runs out on the balcony at the rear. The powerful light remains on him. He starts back with an oath, then runs wildly along the balcony toward the left. The sound of the distant voices rises more loudly.*)

CLARA   They kill you! Kill you! (*She moves blindly toward the rear. A shot rings out.* BIGGER *ducks back into the room behind the piece of ruined wall. Another shot barks, and the sound of breaking glass is heard.*)

BIGGER   (*Yelling.*)   Shoot! Shoot! (*The pounding at the right increases and shouts are heard near at hand off at the left. He grabs* CLARA *and holds her in front of him, moving swiftly over to the right rear.*)

VOICES   (*At the left.*)   There he is! Let him have it! We've got him! (BIGGER *whirls now, holding* CLARA *protectingly in front of him with one hand. Her arms go up and about him in an impulsive gesture of love. Another shot rings out and she sags down in his arms. He looks at her, then lets her slide out of his arms onto the floor.*)

BIGGER   Yeh. In front of me, and they shot you—All right, goddammit, I killed you. (*Wagging his head.*)   Yeh. I said I would. I said so.

A VOICE   (*Beyond the door at the right.*)   Come on out of there, Bigger Thomas! (BIGGER *fires at the door. And now the air is permeated with a multitude of voices, as if an invisible ring of people were squeezing the scene in a tightening circle. A voice at the left calls out.*)

VOICE   Come on out, you black bastard!

SECOND VOICE   You're going to wish you were dead!

VOICE   Drop that gun.

        (*The sound of horns, sirens, and voices from the distance have grown to a roaring volume now. Above the tumult,* BIGGER'S *voice lashes out, high and clear.*)

BIGGER   Yeh, white boys! Come on and get me! You ain't scared of me, is you? Ain't nobody but Bigger in here— (*He shoots at the door.*)   Bigger! Bigger! Bigger standing against the lot of you! Against your thousand . . . two thousand . . . three thousand . . . (*He fires again, and a volley of shots answers him. He is hit, tumbled completely over by the impact of a bullet. His gun flies from his hand and he falls back against the wall. Mouthing and snarling, he crawls toward the pistol, then collapses over* CLARA'S *body. The door at the right is kicked in, and a policeman steps swiftly out of the shadow, his gun drawn.*)

POLICEMAN   One move, boy, and I'll blow your brains out.

(*A second policeman runs in along the balcony from the left rear, his gun also drawn. Through the open door, two plainclothesmen enter behind the policemen.*)

FIRST MAN   (*Bending over* CLARA'S *dead body.*)   Uhm, bullet drilled her in the heart—from the looks.

FIRST POLICEMAN   The sonofabitch—killed her too. Just let that mob get at him!

SECOND POLICEMAN   Come on, get him downstairs. They'll fix 'im! (*He seizes* BIGGER'S *heels and lifts them up. Walking into the scene at the right comes a heavy elderly man in an enveloping overcoat. An old plug hat is pulled low over his forehead. He stops and stares down at* BIGGER.)

FIRST POLICEMAN   (*Looking around.*)   Hum—better be law and order, boys—Here's old Edward Max.

SECOND POLICEMAN   (*Hurriedly.*)   Yeh, law and order and the electric chair later—if he lives.

FIRST POLICEMAN   He'll live all right. He's too mean to die now. (*The sound of the sirens rises and continues as the scene fades out.*)

Scene 9

The shriek of the siren dies as the lights come up, illuminating both the pit and the main stage. Judge Alvin C. Hanley is seated behind his desk on the upper level, center, and Buckley is standing in the courtroom down below. The judge is about

*fifty years old with a massive, clean-shaven, somewhat bulldog
face and iron-gray hair. He is wearing a dark robe. Black
curtains shroud around behind the desk, and up above to the
right and left are two flags—the Stars and Stripes and the State
flag. On the simulated wall behind the judge is the huge
portrait of an eighteenth century statesman resembling
Thomas Jefferson. Somewhat framing the scene on the upper
level are two militiamen at stiff attention, their bayoneted
rifles held straight by their side. Throughout the scene they
remain motionless. In the courtroom pit Mr. and Mrs. Dalton
sit at the table to the left, facing the theatre audience, and
Peggy is near them. The women wear dark veils. Bigger and
his attorney, Edward Max, are seated at the table to the right.
Bigger is handcuffed and his right shoulder is bandaged. Max,
now that we see him better, is a big, flabby, kindly-faced man,
with something sad and tragic in the pallid whiteness of his
skin and the melancholy depths of his deep brown eyes. His
hair is silvery white and bunched in ringlets above and behind his ears. His clothes are shabby and there is a general air
of poverty and yet of peace about him. The smile which
sometimes breaks over his thin almost feminine lips is sweet
and graceful. Just behind Bigger and Max sit Hannah, Vera
and Buddy. Between the two tables at the back sit the sheriff,
the clerk and the court stenographer with a stenotype machine. As the lights come on, we hear a volume of indistinguishable vocables rising from the invisible courtroom audience. The judge is banging loudly with his gavel.*

JUDGE HANLEY   If there is another disturbance I shall clear
the court! (*The noise subsides, and* BUCKLEY *continues
his argument for the prosecution.*)   Proceed, Mr. Buckley.

BUCKLEY   I could call the long roll of the defendant's mis-
demeanors and crimes, describe him as a thug, as a degenerate who abused and cursed his Christian mother, describe him as a deep-dyed criminal, a murderer at heart,
who preyed upon innocent people, who stalked about in
the darkness, thieving, robbing and lying in wait. I could
describe him as a black ape who climbed his way into a
beautiful home and deflowered, mutilated, and destroyed
the light of that home, the joy of those parents—a beauti-

ful girl. But I will not. For I shrink from the mere recital
of the facts connected with this most horrible crime—a
crime that has marked him in every newspaper in the land
as a sub-human killer who in his idle and leisure moments
loafed about the streets, pilfered from news-stands, robbed
the stores, molested women, frequented dives, attended
cheap movies and chased prostitutes.

A few more words, your honor, and I am done. The defendant, Bigger Thomas, pleads guilty to the charges of
the indictment. The rest is simple and brief. Punishment
must follow—punishment laid down by the sacred laws of
this commonwealth, laws created to protect that society
and that social system of which we are a part. (*With
heavy juridical gravity.*)   A criminal is one who goes
against those laws. He attacks the laws. Therefore the law
must destroy him. If thine eye offend thee, pluck it out!
And if a branch of the tree withers and dies, it must be
cut off lest it contaminate the rest of the tree. Such a tree
is the State through whose flourishing and good health we
ourselves exist and carry on our lives on this earth. I pity
this diseased and ruined defendant, but as a true surgeon
looking to the welfare of the organic body of our people,
I repeat that it is necessary this diseased member be cut
off—be cut off and obliterated lest it infect us all unto
death. (*Fervently.*)   Your honor, in the name of the people of this city, in the name of truth and in the name of
Almighty God, I demand that Bigger Thomas justly die
in the electric chair for the brutal murder of beautiful
and innocent Mary Dalton!

> (*He looks at* BIGGER, *then crosses to his chair at the
> end of the table at the left and sits down, with his back
> to the audience.* JUDGE HANLEY *recognizes* MAX *who
> already is on his feet.*)

MAX   Your honor, I want the mind of the Court to be free
and clear, and then if the court says death, let it mean

death, and if the Court says life, let it mean that too. But whatever the Court says, let it be known upon what grounds its verdict is being rendered. Night after night, I have lain without sleep trying to think of a way to picture to you, and to the world, the causes, the reason, why this boy, Bigger Thomas, sits here today—and why our city is boiling with a fever of excitement and hate. (*He gestures toward the two militiamen.*)   I have pled the cause of other criminal youths in this Court as Your Honor well knows. And when I took this case I thought at first it was the same old story of a boy run afoul of the law. But I am convinced it is more terrible than that—with a meaning far more reaching. Where is the responsibility? Where is the guilt? For there is guilt in the rage that demands that this boy's life be stamped out! There is guilt and responsibility in the hate that inflames the crowds of people gathered in the streets below these windows. (*He turns and gestures through the air.*)   What is the atmosphere that surrounds this trial? Are the citizens intent upon seeing that the majesty of the law is upheld? That retribution be dealt out in measure with the facts? That the guilty and only the guilty be caught and punished? No!   (*He looks around at* BUCKLEY.)   Every conceivable prejudice has been dragged into this case. The press, radio, television, even the authorities of the city and state have inflamed the public mind to the point where martial law is threatened in this city.

BUCKLEY   (*Rising angrily.*)   I object, your honor.

JUDGE   Objection sustained.   (BUCKLEY *sits down. The judge looks sternly at* MAX.)   Counsel will please confine his remarks to the evidence in the case!

MAX   Your honor, for the sake of this boy I wish I could bring to you evidence of a morally worthier nature. I wish I could say that love or ambition or jealousy or the quest for adventure, or any of the more romantic emotions were back of this case. But I have no choice in this matter. Life has cut this cloth, not I. Fear and hate and guilt are the keynotes of this drama. You see, Your Honor, I am not afraid to assign blame, for thus I can the more honestly plead for mercy. I do not claim that this boy is the victim of injustice only, but he is a victim of a way of life that has grown like a cancer into the very blood and bones of our social structure. Bigger Thomas sits here today as a symbol of that way, and the judgment delivered upon him is a judgment delivered upon ourselves.

JUDGE   (*Who has begun to lean forward with signs of attention.*)   But you and I are not on trial in this court, Mr. Max. (*He gestures quietly with his hand for* MAX *to continue.*)

MAX   But in a deeper way, Your Honor, we are on trial. And if you and I, as representative citizens of this city and nation, refuse to see it, if we too are caught in the mire of blind emotion like Bigger Thomas, then this vicious evil will roll on like a bloody river to a bloodier sea. I repeat, let us clear our minds of the contention that the defendant here is the victim of an injustice. I do not claim so. Rather I say he is a symbol of an evil way of life. And his case history proves how widespread and widereaching are the causes that have brought him before this bar of judgment. Let us look back into his boyhood. On a certain day as a little child he stood and saw his own father shot down in a race riot—his father who was an humble worker for the white man and who was trying to protect one of his own kind from violence and hate. And then with his mother and sister and little brother he fled here to our great city hoping to find a better environment, a freer life, a chance for him and those he loved. And what did he find here? The same methods of cruelty and degradation. Poverty, idleness, race discrimination, economic injustice, and all the squeezing oppression of a blind and heartless world.

Our world, Your Honor, yours and mine. Here again he found the same frustrated way of life but intensified by the cruelty of a huge and blind and enslaving industrial mechanism. It is that way of life that stands on trial today, Your Honor, in the person of Bigger Thomas. Like his forefathers, he has been a slave. But unlike his forefathers there was something in him that refused to accept this slavery. And why did he refuse to accept it? Because through the very teachings exemplified by the flag that hangs above that portrait there, and the very portrait itself, he was led to believe with one part of his mind that what we have taught him was true—and with the other part of his mind he saw he was denied the right to accept that belief. On the one hand he was stimulated by every token around him to aspire, to be a free individual. And on the other hand by every method of our social system he was frustrated in that desire and urge. Everywhere he turned, he was met with an enclosing wall—on which wall, as it were, stood the sign and political statement telling him that he was free to walk and live beyond these walls— but no doorway through that wall nor any way told him how to make one. And in this contradiction he wandered until his very soul was distracted into confusion, into the by-paths of subterfuge, cheap sex, and crime. And in this confusion and sensitiveness fear was born. And everything around him became symbolic of this fear. And fear breeds hate and hate breeds guilt and guilt again breeds the urge to destroy the symbols of that fear and guilt. (*The Judge is now listening intently to* MAX.) Your Honor, it has taken me days and nights to think my way through this labyrinth of darkness and evil, but I feel I see the truth now, and I am trying to make you see it, in order that this chain of woeful circumstances may be broken here and that the blot of killing Bigger Thomas in the electric chair will not add another item of murder to this lurid story. Yes, I will go so far as to say that in the very evil which

Bigger Thomas wrought so violently upon our body politic, he for the first time in his twisted and misshapen life was borne into the world as a free and responsible soul. What an awful fact to contemplate!

BUCKLEY   (*Suddenly shouting out.*)   He is pleading the prisoner insane, Your Honor!

JUDGE   (*Rapping with his gavel.*)   Silence!

MAX   I am not making that claim, Your Honor. For the one time, horrible as it seems and as true as it is, Bigger Thomas acted in the full capacity of himself. In the evil of his deed he had for the first time in his life found himself. For the first time he was completely alive, and all the pent-up emotion, the frustrated urges of his life flowered into expression. But we ourselves, not he, are to be judged, because this expression was criminal and evil and not healthy and socially good. Bigger Thomas is an organism which our American system has bred. He represents but a tiny aspect of a problem whose reality sprawls all over this nation—as is shown by the civil disturbances now shaking the land. Kill him, burn the life out of him, and still more this living death continues. In this courtroom today not only Bigger Thomas is on trial but our civilization. In one sense you cannot kill Bigger Thomas. He is already dead. He was born dead. Born dead among the wild forests of our great cities, amid the rank and choking vegetation of the slums, in the dark Jim Crow corners of our buses and trains—in the muffled closets and corridors and rest rooms marked off by the fingers of the law as Black against White. And would the great justice of this court commit a double legal and mutilating death upon a soul we have already killed. (*Turning toward* MR. AND MRS. DALTON.)   I have only sympathy for these kind-hearted and grieving parents. You have their testimony, and you have heard them plead for mercy for this boy. Well may they so plead, for they too share the guilt of this terrible crime.

BUCKLEY   (*Loudly.*) Your Honor!—

MAX   Unconsciously and against their will perhaps. They intended no evil, yet they produced evil.

BUCKLEY   I object! He is impugning the character of my witnesses. (*He stands up.*)

MAX   (*Facing him.*) I am not. I am trying to state the facts— (*Turning toward the judge.*) And these are the facts, Your Honor. (BUCKLEY *reseats himself in fuming silence.*) Mr. Dalton rents his vast real estate holdings to hundreds, to thousands of Negroes, and among these thousands is the family of this Bigger Thomas. The rents in those tenements, those foul ghetto buildings—

BUCKLEY   (*On his feet again.*) I object, Your Honor.

JUDGY HANLEY   Objection sustained. (*Calling down to the stenographer.*) Strike the words "foul ghetto" from the record.

MAX   The conditions in those buildings are among the worst in the city. Yet this man is held in high esteem. Why? Because out of the profits he makes, he turns around and gives back to the Negroes a small part of that charity. For this he is lauded in the press and held up as an example of fine citizenship. But where do the Negroes come in? What have they to say about how they live? Nothing! Around the whole vicious circle they move and act at Dalton's behest and must accept the crumbs of their own bread of charity fed back at them as this man wills or wills not. It is a form of bribery that continues and will continue until we see the truth and stop it. And such living corpses as Bigger Thomas here are warnings to stop it and stop it soon or take the consequences. Yes, corpses cannot be bribed. And to you, Mr. Dalton, and you, Mrs. Dalton, I say your philanthropy was as tragically blind as the means by which you made it.

BUCKLEY   Your Honor! (*The* JUDGE *waves him down, and* MAX *goes on.*)

MAX   One word more, Your Honor, and I am through. (*Pointing toward the rear.*)   There under that mighty American flag is the likeness of one of our forefathers— our forefathers who came to these strange shores hundreds of years ago—men who found a land whose tasks called forth the deepest and best we have. And these men and we who followed them built a nation mighty and powerful, today the most powerful nation—physically—on earth. We poured and are still pouring our living soul into it. But we have denied one of the basic truths of Thomas Jefferson who said "We hope to avail the state of those talents which nature has sown as liberally among the poor as the rich, but which perish without use, if not sought for and cultivated." Yes, perish or turn to crime. We have said to those we enslaved to help us build this nation, this is a white man's country, and we have kept it a white man's country. But night and day millions of turmoiling souls, the souls of our black people, are pleading— "This is our country too. We helped to build it. Give us a part in it, a part free and hopeful and wide as the everlasting horizon." And in this fear-crazed, guilt-ridden body of Bigger Thomas that vast multitude cries out in a mighty voice saying, "Give us our full freedom now, our chance and our hope to be men!" Your Honor, I beg you, not in the name of Almighty God, but in the name of ourselves—spare the life of Bigger Thomas!

> (*He turns and sits down. The scene fades out. Somewhere the tones of a deep chime are heard. They continue.*)

Scene 10

The lights come up on a cell in Death's Row in the State prison. Bigger is standing near his bunk, looking out through the bars which he grasps with his left hand. His right shoulder is still bandaged. Edward Max comes along the corridor lead-

*ing in from the right. He carries an open telegram in his hand.
He goes up to the cell and hands it through to Bigger. The
sound of the chimes stops.*

MAX   I've got some bad news. I'm sorry, Bigger. (BIGGER
*reads the wire, then crumples it up and throws it on the
floor.*)

BIGGER   I know you did all you could. They're going to
change my looks in a few minutes, Mr. Max.

MAX   Mrs. Dalton went to the governor with me, Bigger.
(*He shakes his head.*)

BIGGER   Wish she hadn't. Aw, I'm all right, Mr. Max. You
ain't to blame for what's happening to me. I reckon—uh—
I—uh. I just reckon, I had it coming.

MAX   Is there anything I can do for you, Bigger? Anything
you want to tell anybody?

BIGGER   I . . . I . . . I . . .

MAX   (*Eagerly.*)   Yes, Bigger. What is it?

BIGGER   Naw.

MAX   What's on your mind?

BIGGER   I don't know. You go home, Mr. Max. Ain't nothing
more you can do. Ain't nothing nobody can do now.

MAX   Yes, something—in my heart—a friend to—the—
(*His voice dies out.*)

BIGGER   —to the end. I'm glad I got to know you before I
go, Mr. Max.

MAX   I'm glad I got to know you too. I'm sorry to have to
part this way. But I'm old, son. I'll be going soon myself.

BIGGER   Ain't nobody ever talked to me like you before. How
come you do this—you being a white man? Goddammit.
(*Twisting his shoulder.*)   You oughta let me alone. How
come you want to help me in the first place—and me black
and a murderer.

MAX   Bigger, in the work I'm doing, I look at the world in a way that knows no whites and no blacks. The reason I spoke to you as I did is because you made me feel how badly men need to help one another live in this world—live, not die, Bigger.

BIGGER   Yeh, die! I was all set to die—maybe. I was all right—sorter like being already gone—then you come and start talking, digging into me—opening up my guts.

MAX   I just want to understand you, Bigger.

BIGGER   Understand me—she said that!

MAX   Mary was trying to help you, wasn't she?

BIGGER   Naw—I hated her—and I ain't sorry she's dead.

MAX   Take it easy, son.

BIGGER   I hated her.

MAX   Because she was white, Bigger.

BIGGER   She made me feel like a dog—Yeh—that's the way all of them made me feel—in their big house I was all trembling and afraid.

MAX   (*Suddenly, almost sharply.*)   Didn't you ever love anybody, Bigger?

BIGGER   Maybe I loved my daddy—long time ago. They killed him.

MAX   Didn't you love your mother and sister?

BIGGER   Reckon so. Goddammit there you start again. (*He turns and steps to the rear wall of the cell.*)   You mix me all up— Make me feel something could happen—something good, maybe—you make me think—maybe I can't go this way—can't die like this. (*He turns back.*)   You creep in on me—crowd me to the wall—smother me—and I want to breathe—right up till that lightning hits me. Go away, Mr. Max.

MAX   In a few minutes, Bigger.

BIGGER   All the time I lie here thinking, beating my head
    against a wall, trying to dodge what's coming. And there
    ain't no dodging. Mr. Max, maybe I ain't never wanted to
    hurt anybody—for real I ain't.

MAX   I believe you, Bigger.

BIGGER   That time I was thinking about robbing old man
    Blum, or cutting Gus with a knife—yeh, that time I was
    threatening to carve Ernie's belly-button out, I didn't
    really intend to at first—and then all of a sudden I did
    intend to. And then I got sick inside like wanting to vomit
    —my hands shaking and sweating like an old woman's.
    And when Ernie's eyes looked out at me all scared like
    and begging I felt sorry for him and while I was feeling
    sorry for him that sickness went away, that vomit feeling
    went away. (*Shaking his head.*)   It's queer, Mr. Max,
    all queer and strange.

MAX   (*Staring at him.*)   Go on, Bigger.

BIGGER   In the court room you told 'em how I was ruined
    and how the prejudice and old Jim Crow had bred me in
    the dark black corners of the earth. 'Member?

MAX   Yes, Bigger.

BIGGER   And I was born dead, you said—a corpse. Then
    what about her—about Mary? No Jim Crow for her! Naw.
    No Nigger restroom, naw. She was ruined, lost. I had noth-
    ing and I was ruined. She had everything—money—
    friends—everything—and she was like me, ruined—lost.
    (*With a sort of raging mockery.*)   Goddammit, you're
    wrong, Mr. Max. You're wrong. You take away our lives,
    wipe us out, her and me. And when we say something else
    made us and we didn't count, we was dead. Naw! We
    lived, I tell you, lived!   (*Vehemently.*)   We were us—we.
    And we must be the blame too, somehow—in ourselves.
    We had something to do with all this.   (*Shouting.*)   Me—
    me! Hear me!

MAX   (*Still staring at him.*)   I hear you, Bigger!

BIGGER   (*Shaking his head again.*)   All wrong maybe, but I counted. Reckon I ain't never done nothing right the way it ought to be done. That damn chaplain come in here and read me from the Bible all about when a man would do good evil was present with him. What the hell good does it do to tell me that? I already knowed it. And he got down and he prayed and said, believe on Jesus Christ and him crucified. And I told him my daddy believed on Jesus and they crucified him. Get out. And he kept on praying and I started screaming, and he left.

MAX   A man must believe in something, Bigger.

BIGGER   Maybe, Mr. Max, yeah, maybe.

MAX   (*Staring at him as before.*)   You believe in yourself, don't you?

BIGGER   I got nothing else to believe in now, Mr. Max. But like Jesus it don't do me no good.   (*Tugging at the bars.*) I'm all right, though. You go on now. I'm all right.

MAX   You want me to go, Bigger?

BIGGER   Yeh. You go on. I'm okay. For real I am. Tell Ma and the others I was all right at the last—wasn't crying none—see? Tell 'em, Mr. Max—I wasn't crying none, like that night she come. Standing up straight, see?

MAX   Yes, Bigger.

BIGGER   (*After a pause.*)   Goodbye, Mr. Max.

MAX   (*Hopelessly.*)   Goodbye, Bigger.

(*They shake hands through the bars.* MAX *turns and goes away down the corridor, never looking back.* BIGGER *looks straight out before him. The lights hold on him. Suddenly his face starts breaking up. He begins to cry—helplessly, piteously, childishly. He goes on crying, his hands grasping the bars. The lights fade out.*)

THE END

DAY OF ABSENCE

A Satirical Fantasy

Douglas Turner Ward

DOUGLAS TURNER WARD born on a sugar cane and rice plantation near Burnside, Louisiana, grew up in New Orleans. He attended Wilberforce College and the University of Michigan for a year each. Stopping his formal education for personal reasons, he declared, "Once I was exposed to a library and learned how to use it I felt there was nothing more important to learn in my craft."

In 1948 he settled in New York and became a part-time journalist. In order to improve his skills as a writer, he joined Paul Mann's Actors Workshop and began to train as an actor for over two years. As an actor he made his debut off-Broadway in the Circle In The Square production of *The Iceman Cometh*. Next he was featured in the New York City Center production of *Lost in the Stars* and understudied Sidney Poitier in *A Raisin in the Sun*, eventually playing the leading role during the national tour of the play.

His first two plays, *Happy Ending* and *Day of Absence*, were produced at St. Mark's Playhouse on November 15, 1965, and ran for 504 performances. The plays won a Vernon Rice Drama Desk Award and an Obie Award. It is true, as some critics have noted, that *Happy Ending* and *Day of Absence* are each an extension of a single joke. Although the story lines are that of a joke, each play derives from a dramatic form both popular and traditional within the American theatre. *Day of Absence* recalls the pattern of the first part of a minstrel show, but with the comic inversion of white face used. *Happy Ending* is close in form to the serio-comic sketch inserted towards the close of a vaudeville bill. In utilizing traditional forms, Ward enlarges the plays from a single bright gag into meaningful statements on the identity of Blackness and provides actors with dramatic schemas on which to elaborate comic turns.

Joining with David Hooks in 1968, Douglas Turner Ward founded the Negro Ensemble Company and at present he is Artistic Director of this important producing theatrical company, which won a special Tony Award in 1969. In addition to his administrative duties, he has both acted and directed for the company.

DAY OF
ABSENCE

Characters

CLEM

LUKE

JOHN

MARY

FIRST OPERATOR

SECOND OPERATOR

THIRD OPERATOR

SUPERVISOR

JACKSON

MAYOR

FIRST CITIZEN

SECOND CITIZEN

THIRD CITIZEN

INDUSTRIALIST

BUSINESSMAN

CLUB WOMAN

COURIER

ANNOUNCER

CLAN

AIDE

PIOUS

DOLL WOMAN

BRUSH MAN

MOP MAN

RASTUS

All characters are played by Black Actors in White Face.

CLEM   (*Sitting under a sign suspended by invisible wires and bold-printed with the lettering: "STORE."*) 'Morning, Luke. . . .

LUKE   (*Sitting a few paces away under an identical sign.*) 'Morning, Clem. . . .

CLEM   Go'n' be a hot day.

LUKE   Looks that way. . . .

CLEM   Might rain though. . . .

LUKE   Might.

CLEM   Hope it does. . . .

LUKE   Me, too. . . .

CLEM   Farmers could use a little wet spell for a change. . . . How's the Missis?

LUKE   Same.

CLEM   'N' the kids?

LUKE   Them, too. . . . How's yourns?

CLEM   Fine, thank you. . . . (*They both lapse into drowsy silence, waving lethargically from time to time at imaginary passersby.*) Hi, Joe. . . .

LUKE   Joe. . . .

CLEM   . . . How'd it go yesterday, Luke?

LUKE   Fair.

CLEM   Same wit' me. . . . Business don't seem to git no better or no worse. Guess we in a rut, Luke, don't it 'pear that way to you?—Morning, ma'am.

The text printed here is from the Dramatists Play Service Acting Edition (New York: Dramatists Play Service, 1966).

LUKE   Morning. . . .

CLEM   Tried display, sales, advertisement, stamps—every-
          thing, yet merchandising stumbles 'round in the same old
          groove. . . . But—that's better than plunging downwards,
          I reckon.

LUKE   Guess it is.

CLEM   Morning, Bret. How's the family? . . . That's good.

LUKE   Bret—

CLEM   Morning, Sue.

LUKE   How do, Sue.

CLEM   (*Staring after her.*) . . . Fine hunk of woman.

LUKE   Sure is.

CLEM   Wonder if it's any good?

LUKE   Bet it is.

CLEM   Sure like to find out!

LUKE   So would I.

CLEM   You ever try?

LUKE   Never did. . . .

CLEM   Morning, Gus. . . .

LUKE   Howdy, Gus.

CLEM   Fine, thank you. (*They lapse into silence again.*
          CLEM *rouses himself slowly, begins to look around quiz-
          zically.*) Luke . . . ?

LUKE   Huh?

CLEM   Do you . . . er, er—feel anything—funny . . . ?

LUKE   Like what?

CLEM   Like . . . er—something—strange?

LUKE   I dunno . . . haven't thought about it.

CLEM   I mean . . . like something's wrong—outta place, un-
          usual?

LUKE   I don't know. . . . What you got in mind?

CLEM   Nothing . . . just that—just that—like somp'ums
outta kilter. I got a funny feeling somp'ums not up to snuff.
Can't figger out what it is . . .

LUKE   Maybe it's in your haid?

CLEM   No, not like that. . . . Like somp'ums happened—or
happening—gone haywire, loony.

LUKE   Well, don't worry 'bout it, it'll pass.

CLEM   Guess you right. (*Attempts return to somnolence
but doesn't succeed.*) . . . I'm sorry, Luke, but you sure
you don't feel nothing peculiar . . . ?

LUKE   (*Slightly irked.*) Toss it out your mind, Clem! We
got a long day ahead of us. If something's wrong, you'll
know 'bout it in duc time. No use worrying about it 'till it
comes and if it's coming, it will. Now, relax!

CLEM   All right, you right. . . . Hi, Margie. . . .

LUKE   Marge.

CLEM   (*Unable to control himself.*) Luke, I don't give a
damn what you say. Somp'ums topsy-turvy, I just know it!

LUKE   (*Increasingly irritated.*) Now look here, Clem—it's
a bright day, it looks like it's go'n' git hotter. You say the
wifc and kids are fine and the business is no better or no
worse? Well, what else could be wrong? . . . If somp'ums
go'n' happcn, it's go'n' happen anyway and there ain't a
damn fool thing you kin do to stop it! So you ain't helping
me, yourself or nobody else by thinking 'bout it. It's not
go'n' be no better or no worse when it gits here. It'll come
to you when it gits ready to come and it's go'n' be the same
whether you worry about it or not. So stop letting it upset
you! (LUKE *settles back in his chair.* CLEM *does likewise.*
LUKE *shuts his eyes. After a few moments, they reopen.
He forces them shut again. They reopen in greater curi-
osity. Finally, he rises slowly to an upright position in the
chair, looks around frowningly. Turns slowly to* CLEM.)

. . . Clem? . . . You know something? . . . Somp'um is peculiar . . .

CLEM   (*Vindicated.*)   I knew it, Luke! I just knew it! Ever
since we been sitting here, I been having that feeling!
(*Scene is blacked out abruptly. Lights rise on another section of the stage where a young couple lie in bed under
an invisible-wire-suspension-sign lettered: "HOME." Loud
insistent sounds of baby yells are heard.* JOHN, *the husband,
turns over trying to ignore the cries,* MARY, *the wife, is
undisturbed.* JOHN'S *efforts are futile, the cries continue
until they cannot be denied. He bolts upright, jumps out
of bed and disappears offstage. Returns quickly and tries
to rouse* MARY.)

JOHN   Mary . . .   (*Nudges her, pushes her, yells into her
ear, but she fails to respond.*)   Mary, get up. . . . Get up!

MARY   Ummm . . .   (*Shrugs away, still sleeping.*)

JOHN   GET UP!

MARY   UMMMMMMMMM!

JOHN   Don't you hear the baby bawling! . . . NOW GET
UP!

MARY   (*Mumbling drowsily.*) . . . What baby . . . whose
baby . . . ?

JOHN   Yours!

MARY   Mine? That's ridiculous. . . . what'd you say . . . ?
Somebody's baby bawling? . . . How could that be so?
(*Hearing screams.*)   Who's crying? Somebody's crying!
. . . What's crying? . . . WHERE'S LULA?!

JOHN   I don't know. You better get up.

MARY   That's outrageous! . . . What time is it?

JOHN   Late 'nuff! Now rise up!

MARY   You must be joking. . . . I'm sure I still have four or
five hours sleep in store—even more after that head-

splittin' blow-out last night . . .   (*Tumbles back under covers.*)

JOHN   Nobody told you to gulp those last six bourbons—

MARY   Don't tell me how many bourbons to swallow, not after you guzzled the whole stinking bar! . . . Get up? . . . You must be cracked. . . . Where's Lula? She must be here, she always is . . .

JOHN   Well, she ain't here yet, so get up and muzzle that brat before she does drive me cuckoo!

MARY   (*Springing upright, finally realizing gravity of situation.*)   Whaddaya mean Lula's not here? She's always here, she must be here. . . . Where else kin she be? She supposed to be. . . . She just can't *not* be here—CALL HER! (*Blackout as* JOHN *rushes off-stage. Scene shifts to a trio of Telephone Operators perched on stools before imaginary switchboards. Chaos and bedlam are taking place to the sound of buzzes.* PRODUCTION NOTE: *Effect of following dialogue should simulate rising pandemonium.*)

FIRST OPERATOR   The line is busy—

SECOND OPERATOR   Line is busy—

THIRD OPERATOR   Is busy—

FIRST OPERATOR   Doing best we can—

SECOND OPERATOR   Having difficulty—

THIRD OPERATOR   Soon as possible—

FIRST OPERATOR   Just one moment—

SECOND OPERATOR   Would you hold on—

THIRD OPERATOR   Awful sorry, madam—

FIRST OPERATOR   Would you hold on, please—

SECOND OPERATOR   Just a second, please—

THIRD OPERATOR   Please hold on, please—

FIRST OPERATOR   The line is busy—

SECOND OPERATOR   The line is busy—

THIRD OPERATOR   The line is busy—

FIRST OPERATOR   Doing best we can—

SECOND OPERATOR   Hold on please—

THIRD OPERATOR   Can't make connections—

FIRST OPERATOR   Unable to put it in—

SECOND OPERATOR   Won't plug through—

THIRD OPERATOR   Sorry madam—

FIRST OPERATOR   If you'd wait a moment—

SECOND OPERATOR   Doing best we can—

THIRD OPERATOR   Sorry—

FIRST OPERATOR   One moment—

SECOND OPERATOR   Just a second—

THIRD OPERATOR   Hold on—

FIRST OPERATOR   YES—

SECOND OPERATOR   STOP IT!—

THIRD OPERATOR   HOW DO I KNOW—

FIRST OPERATOR   YOU ANOTHER ONE!

SECOND OPERATOR   HOLD ON DAMMIT!

THIRD OPERATOR   UP YOURS, TOO!

FIRST OPERATOR   THE LINE IS BUSY—

SECOND OPERATOR   THE LINE IS BUSY—

THIRD OPERATOR   THE LINE IS BUSY— (*The switch-board clamors a cacophony of buzzes as Operators plug connections with the frenzy of a Chaplin movie. Their replies degenerate into a babble of gibberish. At the height of frenzy, the* SUPERVISOR *appears.*)

SUPERVISOR   WHAT'S THE SNARL-UP???!!!

FIRST OPERATOR   Everybody calling at the same time, ma'am!

SECOND OPERATOR   Board can't handle it!

THIRD OPERATOR   Like everybody in big New York City is trying to squeeze a call through to li'l' ole us!

SUPERVISOR   God! . . . Somp'un terrible musta happened! . . . Buzz the emergency frequency hookup to the Mayor's office and find out what the hell's going on! (*Scene blacks out quickly to* CLEM *and* LUKE.)

CLEM   (*Something slowly dawning on him.*)   Luke . . . ?

LUKE   Yes, Clem?

CLEM   (*Eyes roving around in puzzlement.*)   Luke . . . ?

LUKE   (*Irked.*)   I said what, Clem!

CLEM   Luke . . . ? Where—where is—the—the?

LUKE   THE WHAT?!

CLEM   Nigras . . . ?

LUKE   ?????What . . . ?

CLEM   Nigras. . . . Where is the Nigras, where is they, Luke . . . ? ALL THE NIGRAS! . . . I don't see no Nigras . . . ?!

LUKE   Whatcha mean . . . ?

CLEM   (*Agitatedly.*)   Luke, there ain't a darky in sight. . . . And if you remember, we ain't spied a nappy hair all morning. . . . The Nigras, Luke! We ain't laid eyes on nary a coon this whole morning!!!

LUKE   You must be crazy or something, Clem!

CLEM   Think about it, Luke, we been sitting here for an hour or more—try and recollect if you remember seeing jist *one* go by?!!!

LUKE   (*Confused.*)   . . . I don't recall. . . . But . . . but there musta been some. . . . The heat musta got you, Clem! How in hell could that be so?!!!

CLEM   (*Triumphantly.*)   Just think, Luke! . . . Look around ya. . . . Now, every morning mosta people walkin' 'long this street is colored. They's strolling by going to work, they's waiting for the buses, they's sweeping sidewalks, cleaning stores, starting to shine shoes and wetting the mops—right?! . . . Well, look around you, Luke—where is they? (LUKE *paces up and down, checking.*) I told you, Luke, they ain't nowheres to be seen.

LUKE   ???? . . . This . . . this . . . some kind of holiday for 'em—or something?

CLEM   I don't know, Luke . . . but . . . but what I do know is they ain't here 'n' we haven't seen a solitary one. . . . It's scaryfying, Luke . . . !

LUKE   Well . . . maybe they's jist standing 'n' walking and shining on other streets.—Let's go look! (*Scene blacks out to* JOHN *and* MARY. *Baby cries are as insistent as ever.*)

MARY   (*At end of patience.*) SMOTHER IT!

JOHN   (*Beyond his.*) That's a hell of a thing to say 'bout your own child! You should know what to do to hush her up!

MARY   Why don't you try?!

JOHN   You had her!

MARY   You shared in borning her?!

JOHN   Possibly not!

MARY   Why, you lousy—!

JOHN   What good is a mother who can't shut up her own daughter?!

MARY   I told you she yells louder every time I try to lay hands on her.—Where's Lula? Didn't you call her?!

JOHN   I told you I can't get the call through!

MARY   Try ag'in—

JOHN   It's no use! I tried numerous times and can't even git through to the switchboard. You've got to quiet her down yourself. (*Firmly.*) Now, go in there and clam her up 'fore I lose my patience! (MARY *exits. Soon, we hear the yells increase. She rushes back in.*)

MARY   She won't let me touch her, just screams louder!

JOHN   Probably wet 'n' soppy!

MARY   Yes! Stinks something awful! Phooooey! I can't stand that filth and odor!

JOHN   That's why she's screaming! Needs her didee changed.—Go change it!

MARY   How you 'spect me to when I don't know how?! Suppose I faint?!

JOHN   Well let her blast away. I'm getting outta here.

MARY   You can't leave me here like this!

JOHN   Just watch me! . . . See this nice split-level cottage, peachy furniture, multi-colored teevee, hi-fi set 'n' the rest? . . . Well, how you think I scraped 'em together while you curled up on your fat li'l' fanny? . . . By gitting outta here—not only *on time* . . . but EARLIER! Beating a frantic crew of nice young executives to the punch—gitting there fustest with the mostest brown-nosing you ever saw! Now if I goof one day—just ONE DAY!—You reckon I'd stay ahead? NO! . . . There'd be a wolf-pack trampling over my prostrate body, racing to replace my smiling face against the boss' left rump! . . . NO, MAM! I'm zooming outta here on time, just as I always have and what's more—you go'n' fix me some breakfast, I'M HUNGRY!

MARY   But—

JOHN   No buts about it! (*Flash blackout as he gags on a mouthful of coffee.*) What you trying to do, STRANGLE ME!!! (*Jumps up and starts pulling on jacket.*)

MARY   (*Sarcastically.*) What did you expect?

JOHN   (*In biting fury.*)   That you could possibly boil a pot
of water, toast a few slices of bread and fry a coupler eggs!
. . . It was a mistaken assumption!

MARY   So they aren't as good as Lula's!

JOHN   That is an overstatement. Your efforts don't result in
anything that could possibly be digested by man, mammal,
or insect! . . . When I married you, I thought I was fairly
acquainted with your faults and weaknesses—I chalked
'em up to human imperfection. . . . But now I know I was
being extremely generous, over-optimistic and phenome-
nally deluded!—You have no idea how useless you really
are!

MARY   Then why'd you marry me?!

JOHN   Decoration!

MARY   You shoulda married Lula!

JOHN   I might've if it wasn't 'gainst the segregation law!
. . . But for the sake of my home, my child and my sanity,
I will even take a chance on sacrificing my slippery grip
on the status pole and drive by her shanty to find out
whether she or someone like her kin come over here and
prevent some ultimate disaster. (*Storms toward door,
stopping abruptly at exit.*)   Are you sure you kin make it
to the bathroom wit'out Lula backing you up?!!!   (*Blackout. Scene shifts to* MAYOR'S *office where a cluttered desk
stands amid papered debris.*)

MAYOR   (*Striding determinedly toward desk, stopping mid-
ways, bellowing.*)   WOODFENCE! . . . WOODFENCE!
. . . WOODFENCE!   (*Receiving no reply, completes
distance to desk.*)   JACKSON! . . . JACKSON!

JACKSON   (*Entering worriedly.*)   Yes, sir . . . ?

MAYOR   Where's Vice-Mayor Woodfence, that no-good
brother-in-law of mine?!

JACKSON   Hasn't come in yet, sir.

MAYOR   HASN'T COME IN?!!! . . . Damn bastard! Knows we have a crucial conference. Soon as he staggers through that door, tell him to shoot in here! (*Angrily focusing on his disorderly desk and littered surroundings.*) And git Mandy here to straighten up this mess—Rufus too! You know he shoulda been waiting to knock dust off my shoes soon as I step in. Get 'em in here! . . . What's the matter wit' them lazy Nigras? . . . Already had to dress myself because of JC, fix my own coffee without MayBelle, drive myself to work 'counta Bubber, feel my old Hag's tits after Sapphi—NEVER MIND!—Git 'em in here— QUICK!

JACKSON   (*Meekly.*) They aren't . . . they aren't here, sir . . .

MAYOR   Whaddaya mean they aren't here? Find out where they at. We got important business, man! You can't run a town wit' laxity like this. Can't allow things to git snafued jist because a bunch of lazy Nigras been out gitting drunk and living it up all night! Discipline, man, discipline!

JACKSON   That's what I'm trying to tell you, sir . . . they didn't come in, can't be found . . . none of 'em.

MAYOR   Ridiculous, boy! Scare 'em up and tell 'em scoot here in a hurry befo' I git mad and fire the whole goddamn lot of 'em!

JACKSON   But we can't find 'em, sir.

MAYOR   Hogwash! Can't nobody in this office do anything right?! Do I hafta handle every piddling little matter myself?! Git me their numbers, I'll have 'em here befo' you kin shout to— (*Three men burst into room in various states of undress.*)

ONE   Henry—they vanished!

TWO   Disappeared into thin air!

THREE   Gone wit'out a trace!

TWO   Not a one on the street!

THREE   In the house!

ONE   On the job!

MAYOR   Wait a minute!! . . . Hold your water! Calm down—!

ONE   But they've gone, Henry—GONE! All of 'em!

MAYOR   What the hell you talking 'bout? Gone? Who's gone—?

ONE   The Nigras, Henry! They gone!

MAYOR   Gone? . . . Gone where?

TWO   That's what we trying to tell ya—they just disappeared! The Nigras have disappeared, swallowed up, vanished! All of 'em! Every last one!

MAYOR   Have everybody 'round here gone batty? . . . That's impossible, how could the Nigras vanish?

THREE   Beats me, but it's happened!

MAYOR   You mean a whole town of Nigras just evaporate like this—poof!—Overnight?

ONE   Right!

MAYOR   Y'all must be drunk! Why, half this town is colored. How could they just sneak out!

TWO   Don't ask me, but there ain't one in sight!

MAYOR   Simmer down 'n' put it to me easy-like.

ONE   Well . . . I first suspected somp'um smelly when Sarah Jo didn't show up this morning and I couldn't reach her—

TWO   Dorothy Jane didn't 'rive at my house—

THREE   Georgia Mae wasn't at mine neither—and SHE sleeps in!

ONE   When I reached the office, I realized I hadn't seen nary one Nigra all morning! Nobody else had either—wait a minute—Henry, have you?!

MAYOR   ???Now that you mention it . . . no, I haven't . . .

ONE   They gone, Henry. . . . Not a one on the street, not a one in our homes, not a single, last living one to be found nowheres in town. What we gon' do?!

MAYOR   (*Thinking.*)   Keep heads on your shoulders 'n' put clothes on your back. . . . They can't be far. . . . Must be 'round somewheres. . . . Probably playing hide 'n' seek, that's it! . . . JACKSON!

JACKSON   Yessir?

MAYOR   Immediately mobilize our Citizens Emergency Distress Committee!—Order a fleet of sound trucks to patrol streets urging the population to remain calm—situation's not as bad as it looks—everything's under control! Then, have another squadron of squawk buggies drive slowly through all Nigra alleys, ordering them to come out wherever they are. If that don't git 'em, organize a vigilante search-squad to flush 'em outta hiding! But most important of all, track down that lazy goldbricker, Woodfence and tell him to git on top of the situation! By God, we'll find 'em even if we hafta dig 'em outta the ground! (*Blackout. Scene shifts back to* JOHN *and* MARY *a few hours later. A funereal solemnity pervades their mood.* JOHN *stands behind* MARY *who sits, in a scene duplicating the famous "American Gothic" painting.*)

JOHN   . . . Walked up to the shack, knocked on door, didn't git no answer. Hollered: "LULA? LULA . . . ?"—Not a thing. Went 'round the side, peeped in window—nobody stirred. Next door—nobody there. Crossed other side of street and banged on five or six other doors—not a colored person could be found! Not a man, neither woman or child—not even a little black dog could be seen, smelt or heard for blocks around. . . . They've gone, Mary.

MARY   What does it all mean, John?

JOHN   I don't know, Mary . . .

MARY   I always had Lula, John. She never missed a day at my side. . . . That's why I couldn't accept your wedding proposal until I was sure you'd welcome me and her together as a package. How am I gonna git through the day? My baby don't know *me*, I ain't acquainted wit' *it*. I've never lifted cover off pot, swung a mop or broom, dunked a dish or even pushed a dustrag. I'm lost wit'out Lula, I need her, John, I need her. (*Begins to weep softly.* JOHN *pats her consolingly.*)

JOHN   Courage, honey. . . . Everybody in town is facing the same dilemma. We mustn't crack up . . . (*Blackout. Scene shifts back to* MAYOR'S *office later in day. Atmosphere and tone resembles a wartime headquarters at the front.* MAYOR *is poring over huge map.*)

INDUSTRIALIST   Half the day is gone already, Henry. On behalf of the factory owners of this town, you've got to bail us out! Seventy-five percent of all production is paralyzed. With the Nigra absent, men are waiting for machines to be cleaned, floors to be swept, crates lifted, equipment delivered and bathrooms to be deodorized. Why, restrooms and toilets are so filthy until they not only cannot be sat in, but it's virtually impossible to get within hailing distance because of the stench!

MAYOR   Keep your shirt on, Jeb—

BUSINESSMAN   Business is even in worse condition, Henry. The volume of goods moving 'cross counters has slowed down to a trickle—almost negligible. Customers are not only not purchasing—but the absence of handymen, porters, sweepers, stock-movers, deliverers and miscellaneous dirty-work doers is disrupting the smooth harmony of marketing!

CLUB WOMAN   Food poisoning, severe indigestitis, chronic diarrhea, advanced diaper chafings and a plethora of un-sanitary household disasters dangerous to life, limb and property! . . . As a representative of the Federation of Ladies' Clubs, I must sadly report that unless the trend is reversed, a complete breakdown in family unity is immi-nent. . . . Just as homosexuality and debauchery signalled the fall of Greece and Rome, the downgrading of South-ern Bellesdom might very well prophesy the collapse of our indigenous institutions. . . . Remember—it has always been pure, delicate, lily-white images of Dixie femininity which provided backbone, inspiration and ideology for our male warriors in their defense against the on-rushing black horde. If our gallant men are drained of this wor-ship and idolatry—God knows! The cause won't be worth a Confederate nickel!

MAYOR   Stop this panicky defeatism, y'all hear me! All ma-chinery at my disposal is being utilized. I assure you wit' great confidence the damage will soon repair itself.—Cheerful progress reports are expected any moment now.—Wait! See, here's Jackson. . . . Well, Jackson?

JACKSON   (*Entering.*)   As of now, sir, all efforts are fruit-less. Neither hide nor hair of them has been located. We have not unearthed a single one in our shack-to-shack search. Not a single one has heeded our appeal. Scoured every crick and cranny inside their hovels, turning furni-ture upside down and inside out, breaking down walls and tearing through ceilings. We made determined efforts to discover where 'bouts of our faithful uncle Toms and in-formers—but even they have vanished without a trace. . . . Searching squads are on the verge of panic and hysteria, sir, wit' hotheads among 'em campaigning for scorched earth policies. Nigras on a whole lack cellars, but there's rising sentiment favoring burning to find out whether they're underground—DUG IN!

MAYOR   Absolutely counter such foolhardy suggestions! Suppose they are tombed in? We'd only accelerate the gravity of the situation using incendiary tactics! Besides, when they're rounded up where will we put 'em if we've already burned up their shacks—IN OUR OWN BED-ROOMS?!!!

JACKSON   I agree, sir, but the mood of the crowd is becoming irrational. In anger and frustration, they's forgetting their original purpose was to FIND the Nigras!

MAYOR   At all costs! Stamp out all burning proposals! Must prevent extremist notions from gaining ascendancy. Git wit' it. . . . Wait—'n' for Jehovah's sake, find out where the hell is that trifling slacker, WOODFENCE!

COURIER   (*Rushing in.*)   Mr. Mayor! Mr. Mayor! . . . We've found some! We've found some!

MAYOR   (*Excitedly.*)   Where?!

COURIER   In the—in the—   (*Can't catch breath.*)

MAYOR   (*Impatiently.*)   Where, man? Where?!!!

COURIER   In the colored wing of the city hospital!

MAYOR   The hos—? The hospital! I shoulda known! How could those helpless, crippled, cut and shot Nigras disappear from a hospital! Shoulda thought of that! . . . Tell me more, man!

COURIER   I—I didn't wait, sir. . . . I—I ran in to report soon as I heard—

MAYOR   WELL GIT BACK ON THE PHONE, YOU IDIOT, DON'T YOU KNOW WHAT THIS MEANS!

COURIER   Yes, sir. (*Races out.*)

MAYOR   Now we are gitting somewhere! . . . Gentlemen, if one sole Nigra is among us, we're well on the road to rehabilitation! Those Nigras in the hospital must know somp'um 'bout the others where'bouts. . . . Scat back to your colleagues, boost up their morale and inform 'em that things will zip back to normal in a jiffy! (*They start to file out, then pause to observe the* COURIER *reentering dazedly.*) Well . . . ? Well, man . . . ? WHAT'S THE MATTER WIT' YOU, NINNY, TELL ME WHAT ELSE WAS SAID?!

COURIER   They all . . . they all . . . they all in a—in a—a coma, sir . . .

MAYOR   They all in a what . . . ?

COURIER   In a coma, sir . . .

MAYOR   Talk sense, man! . . . Whaddaya mean, they all in a coma?

COURIER   Doctor says every last one of the Nigras are jist laying in bed . . . STILL . . . not moving . . . neither live or dead . . . laying up there in a coma . . . every last one of 'em . . .

MAYOR   (*Sputters, then grabs phone.*) Get me Confederate Memorial. . . . Put me through to the Staff Chief. . . . YES, this is the Mayor. . . . Sam? . . . What's this I hear? . . . But how could they be in a coma, Sam? . . . You don't know! Well, what the hell you think the city's paying you for! . . . You've got 'nuff damn hacks and quacks there to find out! . . . How could it be somp'um unknown? You mean Nigras know somp'um 'bout drugs your damn butchers don't?! . . . Well, what the crap good are they! . . . All right, all right, I'll be calm. . . . Now, tell me. . . . Uh huh, uh huh. . . . Well, can't you give 'em some injections or somp'um . . . ?—You did . . . uh huh . . . DID YOU TRY A LI'L' ROUGH TREATMENT?—that too, huh. . . .

All right, Sam, keep trying. . . . (*Puts phone down deli-cately, continuing absently.*) Can't wake 'em up. Just lay there. Them that's sick won't git no sicker, them that's half-well won't git no better, babies that's due won't be born and them that's come won't show no life. Nigras wit' cuts won't bleed and them which need blood won't be transfused. . . . He say dying Nigras is even refusing to pass away! (*Is silently perplexed for a moment, then suddenly breaks into action.*) JACKSON?! . . . Call up the police—THE JAIL! Find out what's going on there! Them Nigras are captives! If there's one place we got darkies under control, it's there! Them sonsabitches too onery to act right either for colored or white! (JACKSON *exits. The* COURIER *follows.*) Keep your fingers crossed, citizens, them Nigras in jail are the most important Nigras we got! (*All hands are raised conspicuously aloft, fingers prominently ex-ed. Seconds tick by. Soon* JACKSON *returns crestfallen.*)

JACKSON   Sheriff Bull says they don't know whether they still on premises or not. When they went to rouse Nigra jailbirds this morning, cell-block doors refused to swing open. Tried everything—even exploded dynamite charges —but it just wouldn't budge. . . . Then they hoisted guards up to peep through barred windows, but couldn't see good 'nuff to tell whether Nigras was inside or not. Finally, gitting desperate, they power-hosed the cells wit' water but had to cease 'cause Sheriff Bull said he didn't wanta jeopardize drowning the Nigras since it might spoil his chance of shipping a record load of cotton pickers to the State Penitentiary for cotton-snatching jubilee. . . . Anyway—they ain't heard a Nigra-squeak all day.

MAYOR   ???That so . . . ? WHAT 'BOUT TRAINS 'N' BUSSES PASSING THROUGH? There must be some dinges riding through?

JACKSON   We checked . . . not a one on board.

MAYOR   Did you hear whether any other towns lost their Nigras?

JACKSON   Things are status-quo everywhere else.

MAYOR   (*Angrily.*)   Then what the hell they picking on us for!

COURIER   (*Rushing in.*)   MR. MAYOR! Your sister jist called—HYSTERICAL! She says Vice-Mayor Wood-fence went to bed wit' her last night, but when she woke up this morning he was gone! Been missing all day!

MAYOR   ???Could Nigras be holding brother-in-law Wood-fence hostage?!

COURIER   No, sir. Besides him—investigations reveal that dozens or more prominent citizens—two City Council members, the chairman of the Junior Chamber of Commerce, our City College All-Southern half-back, the chair-lady of the Daughters of the Confederate Rebellion, Miss Cotton-Sack Festival of the Year and numerous other miscellaneous nobodies—are all absent wit'out leave. Dangerous evidence points to the conclusion that they have been infiltrating!

MAYOR   Infiltrating???

COURIER   Passing all along!

MAYOR   ???PASSING ALL ALONG???

COURIER   Secret Nigras all the while!

MAYOR   NAW!   (CLUB WOMAN *keels over in faint.* JACKSON, BUSINESSMAN *and* INDUSTRIALIST *begin to eye each other suspiciously.*)

COURIER   Yessir!

MAYOR   PASSING???

COURIER   Yessir!

MAYOR   SECRET NIG—!???

COURIER   Yessir!

MAYOR   (*Momentarily stunned to silence.*)   The dirty mongrelizers! . . . Gentlemen, this is a grave predicament indeed. . . . It pains me to surrender priority of our states' right credo, but it is my solemn task and frightening duty to inform you that we have no other recourse but to seek outside help for deliverance. (*Blackout. Lights rerise on Huntley-Brinkley-Murrow-Severeid-Cronkite-Reasoner-type* ANNOUNCER *grasping a hand-held microphone* [*imaginary*] *a few hours later. He is vigorously, excitedly mouthing his commentary, but no sound escapes his lips. . . . During this dumb, wordless section of his broadcast, a bedraggled assortment of figures marching with picket signs occupy his attention. On their picket signs are inscribed various appeals and slogans. "CINDY LOU UNFAIR TO BABY JOE"* . . . *"CAP'N SAM MISS BIG BOY"* . . . *"RETURN LI'L' BLUE TO MARSE JIM"* . . . *"INFORMATION REQUESTED 'BOUT MAMMY GAIL"* . . . *"BOSS NATHAN PROTEST TO FAST LEROY." Trailing behind the marchers, forcibly isolated, is a woman dressed in widow-black holding a placard which reads: "WHY DIDN'T YOU TELL US—YOUR DEFILED WIFE AND TWO ABSENT MONGRELS."*)

ANNOUNCER   (*Who has been silently mouthing his delivery during the picketing procession, is suddenly heard as if caught in the midst of commentary.*)   . . . Factories standing idle from the loss of non-essential workers. Stores shuttered from the absconding of uncrucial personnel. Uncollected garbage threatening pestilence and pollution. . . . Also, each second somewheres in this former utopia below the Mason and Dixon, dozens of decrepit old men and women usually tended by faithful nurses and servants are popping off like flies—abandoned by sons, daughters and grandchildren whose refusal to provide their doddering relatives with bedpans and other soothing necessities result in their hasty, nasty, messy corpus delicties. . . . But most critically affected of all by this complete drought of Afro-American resources are policemen and other public safety guardians denied their daily quota of Negro arrests. One officer known affectionately as "TWO-A-DAY-PETE" because of his unblemished record of TWO Negro headwhippings per day has already been carted off to the County Insane Asylum—straight-jacketed, screaming and biting, unable to withstand the shock of having his spotless slate sullied by interruption. . . . It is feared that similar attacks are soon expected among municipal judges prevented for the first time in years of distinguished bench-sitting from sentencing one single Negro to a hoosegow or pokey. . . . Ladies and gentlemen, as you trudge in from the joys and headaches of workday chores and dusk begins to descend on this sleepy Southern hamlet, we RE-PEAT—today—before early morning dew had dried upon magnolia blossoms, your comrade citizens of this lovely Dixie village awoke to the realization that some—pardon me! Not some—but ALL OF THEIR NEGROES were missing. . . . Absent, vamoosed, departed, at bay, fugitive, away, gone and so-far unretrieved. . . . In order to dispel your incredulity, gauge the temper of your suffering compatriots and just possibly prepare you for the likelihood of an equally nightmarish eventuality, we have gathered a cross-section of this city's most distinguished leaders for exclusive interviews. . . . First, Mr. Council Clan, grand-dragoon of this area's most active civic organizations and staunch bell-wether of the political opposition. . . . Mr. Clan, how do you ACCOUNT for this incredible disappearance?

CLAN   A PLOT, plain and simple, that's what it is, as plain as the corns on your feet!

ANNOUNCER   Whom would you consider responsible?

CLAN   I could go on all night.

ANNOUNCER   Cite a few?

CLAN   Too numerous.

ANNOUNCER   Just one?

CLAN   Name names when time comes.

ANNOUNCER   Could you be referring to native Negroes?

CLAN   Ever try quaranteening lepers from their spots?

ANNOUNCER   Their organizations?

CLAN   Could you slice a nose off a mouth and still keep a face?

ANNOUNCER   Commies?

CLAN   Would you lop off a titty from a chest and still have a breast?

ANNOUNCER   Your city government?

CLAN   Now you talkin'!

ANNOUNCER   State administration?

CLAN   Warming up!

ANNOUNCER   Federal?

CLAN   Kin a blind man see?!

ANNOUNCER   The Court?

CLAN   Is a pig clean?!

ANNOUNCER   Clergy?

CLAN   Do a polecat stink?!

ANNOUNCER   Well, Mr. Clan, with this massive complicity, how do you think the plot could've been prevented from succeeding?

CLAN   If I'da been in office, it never woulda happened.

ANNOUNCER   Then you're laying major blame at the doorstep of the present administration?

CLAN   Damn tooting!

ANNOUNCER   But from your oft-expressed views, Mr. Clan, shouldn't you and your followers be delighted at the turn of events? After all—isn't it one of the main policies of your society to *drive* the Negroes away? *Drive* 'em back where they came from?

CLAN   DRIVVVE, BOY! DRIIIIVVVE! That's right!... When we say so and not befo'. Ain't supposed to do nothing 'til we tell 'em. Got to stay put until we exercise our God-given right to tell 'em when to git!

ANNOUNCER   But why argue if they've merely jumped the gun? Why not rejoice at this premature purging of undesirables?

CLAN   The time ain't ripe yet, boy.... The time ain't ripe yet.

ANNOUNCER   Thank you for being so informative, Mr. Clan —Mrs. Aide? Mrs. Aide? Over here, Mrs. Aide.... Ladies and gentlemen, this city's Social Welfare Commissioner, Mrs. Handy Anna Aide.... Mrs. Aide, with all your Negroes *AWOL*, haven't developments alleviated the staggering demands made upon your Welfare Department? Reduction of relief requests, elimination of case loads, removal of chronic welfare dependents, et cetera?

AIDE   Quite the contrary. Disruption of our pilot projects among Nigras saddles our white community with extreme hardship.... You see, historically, our agencies have always been foremost contributors to the Nigra Git-A-Job movement. We pioneered in enforcing social welfare theories which oppose coddling the fakers. We strenuously believe in helping Nigras help themselves by participating in meaningful labor. "Relief is Out, Work is In," is our motto. We place them as maids, cooks, butlers, and breast-feeders, cesspool-diggers, wash-basin maintainers, shoe-shine boys, and so on—mostly on a volunteer self-work basis.

ANNOUNCER   Hired at prevailing salaried rates, of course?

AIDE   God forbid! Money is unimportant. Would only make 'em worse. Our main goal is to improve their ethical behavior. "Rehabilitation Through Positive Participation" is another motto of ours. All unwed mothers, loose-living malingering fathers, bastard children and shiftless grand-parents are kept occupied through constructive muscle-therapy. This provides the Nigra with less opportunity to indulge his pleasure-loving amoral inclinations.

ANNOUNCER   They volunteer to participate in these pilot projects?

AIDE   Heavens no! They're notorious shirkers. When I said the program is voluntary, I meant white citizens in over-whelming majorities do the volunteering. Placing their homes, offices, appliances and persons at our disposal for use in "Operation Uplift." . . . We would never dare place such a decision in the hands of the Nigra. It would never get off the ground! . . . No, they have no choice in the mat-ter. "Work or Starve" is the slogan we use to stimulate Nigra awareness of what's good for survival.

ANNOUNCER   Thank you, Mrs. Aide, and good luck. . . . Rev? . . . Rev? . . . Ladies and gentlemen, this city's fore-most spiritual guidance counselor, Reverend Reb Pious. . . . How does it look to you, Reb Pious?

PIOUS   (*Continuing to gaze skyward.*)   It's in *His* hands, son, it's in *His* hand.

ANNOUNCER   How would you assess the disappearance, from a moral standpoint?

PIOUS   An immoral act, son, morally wrong and ethically indefensible. A perversion of Christian principles to be condemned from every pulpit of this nation.

ANNOUNCER   Can you account for its occurrence after the many decades of the Church's missionary activity among them?

PIOUS   It's basically a reversion of the Nigra to his deep-rooted primitivism. . . . Now, at last, you can understand the difficulties of the Church in attempting to anchor

God's kingdom among ungratefuls. It's a constant, unrelenting, no-holds-barred struggle against Satan to wrestle away souls locked in his possession for countless centuries! Despite all our aid, guidance, solace and protection, Old BeezleBub still retains tenacious grips upon the Nigras' childish loyalty—comparable to the lure of bright flames to an infant.

ANNOUNCER   But actual physical departure, Reb Pious? How do you explain that?

PIOUS   Voodoo, my son, voodoo. . . . With Satan's assist, they have probably employed some heathen magic which we cultivated, sophisticated Christians know absolutely nothing about. However, before long we are confident about counteracting this evil witch doctory and triumphing in our Holy Savior's name. At this perilous juncture, true believers of all denominations are participating in joint, 'round-the-clock observances, offering prayers for our Master's swiftest intercession. I'm optimistic about the outcome of his intervention. . . . Which prompts me—if I may, sir—to offer these words of counsel to our delinquent Nigras. . . . I say to you without rancor or vengeance, quoting a phrase of one of your greatest prophets, Booker T. Washington: "Return your buckets to where they lay and all will be forgiven."

ANNOUNCER   A very inspirational appeal, Reb Pious. I'm certain they will find the tug of its magnetic sincerity irresistible. Thank you, Reb Pious. . . . All in all—as you have witnessed, ladies and gentlemen—this town symbolizes the face of disaster. Suffering as severe a prostration as any city wrecker, ravaged and devastated by the holocaust of war. A vital, lively, throbbing organism brought to a screeching halt by the strange enigma of the missing Negroes. . . . We take you now to offices of the one man into whose hands has been thrust the final responsibility of rescuing this shuddering metropolis from the precipice of destruction. . . . We give you the honorable Mayor, Henry R. E. Lee. . . . Hello, Mayor Lee.

MAYOR   (*Jovially.*) Hello, Jack.

ANNOUNCER   Mayor Lee, we have just concluded interviews with some of your city's leading spokesmen. If I may say so, sir, they don't sound too encouraging about the situation.

MAYOR   Nonsense, Jack! The situation's well-in-hand as it could be under the circumstances. Couldn't be better in hand. Underneath every dark cloud, Jack, there's always a ray of sunlight, ha, ha, ha.

ANNOUNCER   Have you discovered one, sir?

MAYOR   Well, Jack, I'll tell you. . . . Of course we've been faced wit' a little crisis, but look at it like this—we've faced 'em befo': Sherman marched through Georgia— ONCE! Lincoln freed the slaves—MOMENTARILY! Carpetbaggers even put Nigras in the Governor's mansion, state legislature, Congress and the Senate of the United States. But what happened?—Ole Dixie bounced right on back up. . . . At this moment the Supreme Court's trying to put Nigras in our schools and the Nigra has got it in his haid to put hisself everywhere. . . . But what you 'spect go'n' happen?—Ole Dixie will kangaroo back even higher. Southern courage, fortitude, chivalry and superiority always wins out. . . . SHUCKS! We'll have us some Nigras befo' daylight is gone!

ANNOUNCER   Mr. Mayor, I hate to introduce this note, but in an earlier interview, one of your chief opponents, Mr. Clan, hinted at your own complicity in the affair—

MAYOR   A LOT OF POPPYCOCK! Clan is politicking! I've beaten him four times outta four and I'll beat him four more times outta four! This is no time for partisan politics! What we need now is level-headedness and across-the-board unity. This typical, rash, mealy-mouth, shooting-off-at-the-lip of Clan and his ilk proves their insincerity and voters will remember that in the next election! Won't you, voters?! (*Has risen to the height of campaign oratory.*)

ANNOUNCER   Mr. Mayor! . . . Mr. Mayor! . . . Please—

MAYOR   . . . I tell you, I promise you—

ANNOUNCER   PLEASE! MR. MAYOR!

MAYOR   Huh? . . . Oh—yes, carry on.

ANNOUNCER   Mr. Mayor, your cheerfulness and infectious good spirits lead me to conclude that startling new developments warrant fresh-found optimism. What concrete, declassified information do you have to support your claim that Negroes will reappear before nightfall?

MAYOR   Because we are presently awaiting the pay-off of a masterful five-point supra-recovery program which can't help but reap us a bonanza of Nigras 'fore sundown! . . . First: Exhaustive efforts to pinpoint the where'bouts of our own missing darkies continue to zero in on the bullseye. . . . Second: The President of the United States, following an emergency cabinet meeting, has designated us the prime disaster area of the century—National Guard is already on the way. . . . Third: In an unusual, but bold maneuver, we have appealed to the NAACP 'n' all other Nigra conspirators to help us git to the bottom of the vanishing act. . . . Fourth: We have exercised our non-reciprocal option and requested that all fraternal southern states express their solidarity by lending us some of their Nigras temporarily on credit. . . . Fifth and foremost: We have already gotten consent of the Governor to round up all stray, excess and incorrigible Nigras to be shipped to us under escort of the State Militia. . . . That's why we've stifled pessimism and are brimming wit' confidence that this full-scale concerted mobilization will ring down a jackpot of jigaboos 'fore light vanishes from sky!—

ANNOUNCER   Congratulations! What happens if it fails?

MAYOR   Don't even think THAT! Absolutely no reason to suspect it will. . . . (*Peers over shoulder, then whispers confidentially while placing hand over mouth by* AN-NOUNCER'S *imaginary mike.*) . . . But speculating on the dark side of your question—if we don't turn up some by nightfall, it may be all over. The harm has already been done. You see the South has always been glued together by the uninterrupted presence of its darkies. No telling how unstuck we might git if things keep on like they have. —Wait a minute, it musta paid off already! Mission accomplished 'cause here's Jackson head a time wit' the word. . . . Well, Jackson, what's new?

JACKSON   Situation on the home front remains static, sir—can't uncover scent or shadow. The NAACP and all other Nigra front groups 'n' plotters deny any knowledge or connection wit' the missing Nigras. Maintained this even after appearing befo' a Senate Emergency Investigating Committee which subpoenaed 'em to Washington post haste and threw 'em in jail for contempt. A handful of Nigras who agreed to make spectacular appeals for ours to come back to us, have themselves mysteriously disappeared. But, worst news of all, sir, is our sister cities and counties, inside and outside the state, have changed their minds, fallen back on their promises and refused to lend us any Nigras, claiming they don't have 'nuff for themselves.

MAYOR   What 'bout Nigras promised by the Governor?!

JACKSON   Jailbirds and vagrants escorted here from chain-gangs and other reservations either revolted and escaped enroute or else vanished mysteriously on approaching our city limits. . . . Deterioration rapidly escalates, sir. Estimates predict we kin hold out only one more hour before overtaken by anarchistic turmoil. . . . Some citizens seeking haven elsewheres have already fled, but on last report were being forcibly turned back by armed sentinels in other cities who wanted no parts of 'em—claiming they carried a jinx.

MAYOR   That bad, huh?

JACKSON   Worse, sir . . . we've received at least five reports of plots on your life.

MAYOR   What?!—We've gotta act quickly then!

JACKSON   Run out of ideas, sir.

MAYOR   Think harder, boy!

JACKSON   Don't have much time, sir. One measly hour, then all hell go'n' break loose.

MAYOR   Gotta think of something drastic, Jackson!

JACKSON   I'm dry, sir.

MAYOR   Jackson! Is there any planes outta here in the next hour?

JACKSON   All transportation's been knocked out, sir.

MAYOR   I thought so!

JACKSON   What were you contemplating, sir?

MAYOR   Don't ask me what I was contemplating! I'm still boss 'round here! Don't forgit it!

JACKSON   Sorry, sir.

MAYOR   . . . Hold the wire! . . . Wait a minute . . . ! Waaaaait a minute—GODAMMIT! All this time crapping 'round, diddling and fotsing wit' puny li'l' solutions—all the while neglecting our ace in the hole, our trump card! Most potent weapon for digging Nigras outta the woodpile!!! All the while right befo' our eyes! . . . Ass! Why didn't you remind me?!!!

JACKSON   What is it, sir?

MAYOR   . . . ME—THAT'S WHAT! ME! A personal appeal from ME! *Directly to them!* . . . Although we wouldn't let 'em march to the polls and express their affection for me through the ballot box, we've always known I'm held highest in their esteem. A direct address from their beloved Mayor! . . . If they's anywheres close within the sound of my voice, they'll shape up! Or let us know by a sign they's ready to!

JACKSON   You sure *that'll* turn the trick, sir?

MAYOR   As sure as my ancestors befo' me who knew that when they puckered their lips to whistle, ole Sambo was gonna come a-lickety-splitting to answer the call! . . . That same chips-down blood courses through these Confederate gray veins of Henry R. E. Lee!!!

ANNOUNCER   I'm delighted to offer our network's facilities for such a crucial public interest address, sir. We'll arrange immediately for your appearance on an international hookup, placing you in the widest proximity to contact them wherever they may be.

MAYOR   Thank you, I'm very grateful. . . . Jackson, re-grease the machinery and set wheels in motion. Inform townspeople what's being done. Tell 'em we're all in this together. The next hour is countdown. I demand absolute cooperation, city-wide silence and inactivity. I don't want the Nigras frightened if they's nearby. This is the most important hour in town's history. Tell 'em if one single Nigra shows up during hour of decision, victory is within sight. I'm gonna git 'em that one—maybe all! Hurry and crack to it! (ANNOUNCER *rushes out, followed by* JACKSON. *Blackout. Scene re-opens, with* MAYOR *seated, eyes front, spotlight illuminating him in semi-darkness. Shadowy figures stand in the background, prepared to answer phones or aid in any other manner.* MAYOR *waits patiently until "GO!" signal is given. Then begins, his voice combining elements of confidence, tremolo and gravity.*) Good evening. . . . Despite the fact that millions of you wonderful people throughout the nation are viewing and listening to this momentous broadcast—and I thank you

for your concern and sympathy in this hour of our peril—
I primarily want to concentrate my attention and address
these remarks solely for the benefit of our departed Nigra
friends who may be listening somewheres in our far-flung
land to the sound of my voice. . . . If you are—it is with
heart-felt emotion and fond memories of our happy association that I ask—"Where are you . . . ?" Your absence
has left a void in the bosom of every single man, woman
and child of our great city. I tell you—you don't know
what it means for us to wake up in the morning and discover that your cheerful, grinning, happy-go-lucky faces
are missing! . . . From the depths of my heart, I can only
meekly, humbly suggest what it means to me personally.
. . . You see—the one face I will never be able to erase
from my memory is the face—not of my Ma, not of Pa,
neither wife or child—but the image of the first woman I
came to love so well when just a wee lad—the vision of
the first human I laid clear sight on at childbirth—the
profile—better yet, the full face of my dear old . . . Jemi-
mah—God rest her soul. . . . Yes! My dear ole mammy,
wit' her round ebony moonbeam gleaming down upon me
in the crib, teeth shining, blood-red bandana standing
starched, peaked and proud, gazing down upon me affectionately as she crooned me a Southern lullaby. . . . OH!
It's a memorable picture I will eternally cherish in perma-
nent treasure chambers of my heart, now and forever
always. . . . Well, if this radiant image can remain so infi-
nitely vivid to me all these many years after her unfortunate demise in the Po' folks home—THINK of the misery
the rest of us must be suffering after being *freshly* denied
your soothing presence?! We need ya. If you kin hear me,
just contact this station 'n' I will welcome you back personally. Let me just tell you that since you eloped, nothing
has been the same. How could it? You're part of us, you
belong to us. Just give us a sign and we'll be contented
that all is well. . . . Now if you've skipped away on a little

fun-fest, we understand, ha, ha. We know you like a good time and we don't begrudge it to ya. Hell—er, er, we like a good time ourselves—who doesn't? . . . In fact, think of all the good times we've had together, huh? We've had some real fun, you and us, yesiree! . . . Nobody knows better than you and I what fun we've had together. You singing us those old Southern coon songs and dancing those Nigra jigs and us clapping, prodding 'n' spurring you on! Lots of fun, huh?! . . . OH BOY! The times we've had together. . . . If you've snucked away for a bit of fun by yourself, we'll go 'long wit' ya—long as you let us know where you at so we won't be worried about you. . . . We'll go 'long wit' you long as you don't take the joke too far. I'll admit a joke is a joke and you've played a LULU! . . . I'm warning you, we can't stand much more horsing 'round from you! Business is business 'n' fun is fun! You've had your fun so now let's get down to business! Come on back, YOU HEAR ME!!! . . . . If you been hoodwinked by agents of some foreign government, I've been authorized by the President of these United States to inform you that this liberty-loving Republic is prepared to rescue you from their clutches. Don't pay no 'tention to their sireeen songs and atheistic promises! You better off under our control and you know it! . . . If you been bamboozled by rabble-rousing nonsense of your own so-called leaders, we prepared to offer same protection. Just call us up! Just give us a sign! . . . Come on, give us a sign . . . give us a sign— even a teeny-weeny one . . . ??!! (*Glances around checking on possible communications. A bevy of headshakes indicate no success.* MAYOR *returns to address with desperate fervor.*) Now look—you don't know what you doing! If you persist in this disobedience, you know all too well the consequences! We'll track you to the end of the earth, beyond the galaxy, across the stars! We'll capture you and chastise you with all the vengeance we command! 'N' you know only too well how stern we kin be when double-

crossed! The city, the state and the entire nation will cru-
cify you for this unpardonable defiance! (*Checks again.*)
No call . . . ? No sign . . . ? Time is running out! Deadline
slipping past! They gotta respond! They gotta! (*Resum-
ing.*) Listen to me! I'm begging y'all, you've gotta come
back . . . ! LOOK, GEORGE! (*Waves dirty rag aloft.*)
I brought the rag you wax the car wit'. . . . Don't this
bring back memories, George, of all the days you spent
shining that automobile to shimmering perfection . . . ?
And you, Rufus?! . . . Here's the shoe polisher and the
brush! . . . 'Member, Rufus? . . . Remember the happy
mornings you spent popping this rag and whisking this
brush so furiously 'till it created music that was sympho-
nee to the ear . . . ? And you—MANDY? . . . Here's the
waste-basket you didn't dump this morning. I saved it just
for you! . . . LOOK, all y'all out there   ? (*Signals and
a three-person procession parades one after the other before the imaginary camera.*)

DOLL WOMAN   (*Brandishing a crying baby* [*doll*] *as she
strolls past and exits.*)   She 's been crying ever since you
left, Caldonia . . .

MOP MAN   (*Flashing mop.*)   It's been waiting in the same
corner, Buster . . .

BRUSH MAN   (*Flagging toilet brush in one hand and toilet
plunger in other.*)   It's been dry ever since you left, Washington . . .

MAYOR   (*Jumping in on the heels of the last exit.*)   Don't
these things mean anything to y'all? By God! Are your
memories so short?! Is there nothing sacred to ya? . . .
Please come back, for my sake, please! All of you—even
you questionable ones! I promise no harm will be done to
you! Revenge is disallowed! We'll forgive everything! Just
come on back and I'll git down on my knees— (*Immediately drops to knees.*)   I'll be kneeling in the middle of
Dixie Avenue to kiss the first shoe of the first one 'a you

to show up. . . . *I'll smooch any other spot you request.* . . .
Erase this nightmare 'n' we'll concede any demand
you make, just come on back—please???!! . . .
PLEEEEEEEZE?!!!

VOICE   (*Shouting.*) TIME!!!

MAYOR   (*Remaining on knees, frozen in a pose of supplication. After a brief, deadly silence, he whispers almost in-
audibly.*) They wouldn't answer . . . they wouldn't answer . . . (*Blackout as bedlam erupts offstage. Total
blackness holds during a sufficient interval where offstage
sound-effects create the illusion of complete pandemonium, followed by a diminution which trails off into an
expressionistic simulation of a city coming to a strickened
standstill: industrial machinery clanks to halt, traffic
blares to silence, etc. . . . The stage remains dark and silent for a long moment, then lights re-arise on the AN-
NOUNCER.*)

ANNOUNCER   A pitiful sight, ladies and gentlemen. Soon
after his unsuccessful appeal, Mayor Lee suffered a vicious
pummeling from the mob and barely escaped with his life.
National Guardsmen and State Militia were impotent in
quelling the fury of a town venting its frustration in an
orgy of destruction—a frenzy of rioting, looting and all
other aberrations of a town gone berserk. . . . Then—suddenly—as if a magic wand had been waved, madness
evaporated and something more frightening replaced it:
Submission. . . . Even whimperings ceased. The city: ex-
hausted, benumbed.—Slowly its occupants slinked off into
shadows, and by midnight, the town was occupied exclu-
sively by zombies. The fight and life had been drained out.
. . . Pooped. . . . Hope ebbed away as completely as the
beloved, absent Negroes. . . . As our crew packed gear and
crept away silently, we treaded softly—as if we were stealing away from a mausoleum. . . . The Face Of A Defeated
City. (*Blackout. Lights rise slowly at the sound of rooster-*

crowing, signalling the approach of a new day, the next morning. Scene is same as opening of play. CLEM *and* LUKE *are huddled over dazedly, trancelike. They remain so for a long count. Finally, a figure drifts on stage, shuffling slowly.*)

LUKE   (*Gazing in silent fascination at the approaching figure.*) . . . Clem . . . ? Do you see what I see or am I dreaming . . . ?

CLEM   It's a . . . a Nigra, ain't it, Luke . . . ?

LUKE   Sure looks like one, Clem—but we better make sure —eyes could be playing tricks on us. . . . Does he still look like one to you, Clem?

CLEM   He still does, Luke—but I'm scared to believe—

LUKE   . . . Why . . . ? It looks like Rastus, Clem!

CLEM   Sure does, Luke . . . but we better not jump to no hasty conclusion . . .

LUKE   (*In timid softness.*)   That you, Rastus . . . ?

RASTUS   (*Stepin Fetchit, Willie Best, Nicodemus, B. McQueen and all the rest rolled into one.*)   Why . . . howdy . . . Mr. Luke . . . Mr. Clem . . .

CLEM   It is him, Luke! It is him!

LUKE   Rastus?

RASTUS   Yas . . . sah?

LUKE   Where was you yesterday?

RASTUS   (*Very, very puzzled.*)   Yes . . . ter . . . day? . . . Yester . . . day . . . ? Why . . . right . . . here . . . Mr. Luke . . .

LUKE   No you warn't, Rastus, don't lie to me! Where was you yestiddy?

RASTUS   Why . . . I'm sure I was . . . Mr. Luke . . . Remember . . . I made . . . that . . . delivery for you . . .

LUKE   That was MONDAY, Rastus, yestiddy was TUES-
DAY.

RASTUS   Tues . . . day . . . ? You don't say. . . . Well . . .
well . . . well . . .

LUKE   Where was you 'n' all the other Nigras yesterday,
Rastus?

RASTUS   I . . . thought . . . yestiddy . . . was . . . Monday,
Mr. Luke—I coulda swore it . . . ! . . . See how . . . things
. . . kin git all mixed up? . . . I coulda swore it . . .

LUKE   TODAY is WEDNESDAY, Rastus. Where was you
TUESDAY?

RASTUS   Tuesday . . . huh? That's somp'um . . . I . . . don't
. . . remember . . . missing . . . a day . . . Mr. Luke . . . but I
guess you right . . .

LUKE   Then where was you!!!???

RASTUS   Don't rightly know, Mr. Luke. I didn't know I had
skipped a day.—But that jist goes to show you how time
kin fly, don't it, Mr. Luke. . . . Uuh, uuh, uuh . . .   (*He
starts shuffling off, scratching head, a flicker of a smile
playing across his lips.* CLEM *and* LUKE *gaze dumbfound-
edly as he disappears.*)

LUKE   (*Eyes sweeping around in all directions.*)   Well. . . .
There's the others, Clem. . . . Back jist like they useta be.
. . . Everything's same as always . . .

CLEM   ??? . . . . Is it . . . Luke . . . !
(*Slow fade.*)

CURTAIN

HAPPY ENDING

Douglas Turner Ward

HAPPY ENDING

Characters

ELLIE

VI

JUNIE

ARTHUR   *Ellie's Husband*

TIME   *The present, an early weekday evening around five or six* P.M.

PLACE   *The spotless kitchen of a Harlem tenement apartment. At stage-left is a closed door providing entry to the outside hallway. On the opposite side of the stage is another door leading into the interior of the railroad flat. Sandwiched between this door and a window facing the brick walls of the apartment's inner shaft is a giant, dazzling white refrigerator. Positioned center-stage is a gleaming, porcelain-topped oval table. Directly behind is a modern stove-range. To the left of the stove, another window looks out upon a backyard court. The window is flanked on its left by a kitchen sink. Adjacent to the refrigerator, upstage-right, a bathroom door completes the setting.*

As curtain rises, waning rays of daylight can be seen streaming through the courtyard window. Two handsome women, both in their late thirties or early forties, are sitting at opposite ends of the kitchen table. They are dressed as if recently entered from work. Hats and coats are still worn, handbags lie on floor propped against legs of respective chairs. They remain in dejected poses, weeping noiselessly.

ELLIE   Let me have your handkerchief, Vi. . . .   (VI *hands it to her absently.* ELLIE *daubs eyes, then rests hankie on table. It lies there until* VI *motions for it to be handed back.*)

VI   What we go'n' do, Ellie?

ELLIE   Don' know. . . . Don't seem like there's much more we kin do. . . .

VI   This time it really might happen. . . .

ELLIE   I know. . . .

VI   Persons kin go but just so far. . . .

ELLIE   Lord, this may be the limit. . . .

VI   End of the line. . . .

ELLIE   Hear us, Savior!

The text printed here is from the Dramatists Play Service Acting Edition (New York: Dramatists Play Service, 1966).

VI   . . . Think it might help if I prayed a novena to him first
          thing tomorrow morning?

ELLIE   . . . Certainly couldn't do no harm. . . . (*They lapse
          into silence once again, passing hankie back and forth on
          request. Suddenly,* JUNIE, *a tall, slender, sharply hand-
          some, tastefully dressed youth in his early twenties, bursts
          upon the scene, rushing through hallway door.*)

JUNIE   (*Rapidly crossing, shedding coat in transit.*)   Hey,
          Vi, Ellie . . .   (*Exits through interior door, talking off-
          stage.*)   Ellie, do I have any more pleated shirts clean . . . ?
          Gotta make fast impression on new chick tonight. . . .
          (*Thrusting head back into view.*)   One of them foxy,
          black "Four-Hundred" debutantes, you dig! All class and
          manners, but nothing underneath but a luscious, V-8
          chassis!—Which is A-O-reeet wit' me since that's all I'm
          after. You hear me talking to ya! Now, tell me what I say!
          Hah, hah, hah!   (*Withdraws head back offstage.*)
          . . . Sure got them petty tyrants straight at the unemploy-
          ment office today.   (*Dripping contempt.*)   Wanted me to
          snatchup one of them jive jobs they try to palm off on ya.
          I told 'em no, thanks!—SHOVE IT!   (*Reentering, busily
          buttoning elegantly pleated shirt.*)   If they can't find me
          something in my field, up to my standards, forgit it! . . .
          Damn, act like they paying you money out their own
          pockets. . . . Whatcha got to eat, Ellie? . . . I'm scarfy as
          a bear. In fact—with little salt 'n' pepper, I could devour
          one of you—or both between a double-decker!   (*Descends
          upon them to illustrate playfully. Pulls up short on noticing
          their tears for the first time.*)   Hey? . . . What'sa mat-
          ter . . . ? What's up?   (*They fail to respond.*)   Is it the kids?
          (*They shake heads negatively.*)   Somebody sick down
          home?   (*Fearfully.*)   Nothing's wrong wit' mother?!!!
          (*They shake heads again.*)   Roy or Jim in jail? . . . Arthur
          or Ben lose their jobs?   (*Another double headshake.*)
          Tell me, I wanta know! Everything was fine this morning.
          Som'um musta happened since. Come on, what is it?!

ELLIE   Should we tell him, Vi?

VI   I don't know. . . . No use gitting him worried and up-set. . . .

ELLIE   (*Sighing heavily.*) Maybe we better. He's got to find out sooner or later.

JUNIE   What are you crying for?

ELLIE   . . . Our bosses—Mr. and Mrs. Harrison, Junie. . . .

JUNIE   ???Mr. and Mrs. Harrison . . . ? (*Suddenly re-lieved, amused and sardonic.*) What happened? They escaped from a car wreck—UNHURT?

ELLIE   (*Failing to grasp sarcasm.*) No.

JUNIE   (*Returning to shirt-buttoning.*) Did you just git disappointing news flashes they go'n' live forever?

VI   (*Also misreading him.*) No, Junie.

JUNIE   Well, what then? . . . I don't get it.

ELLIE   They's getting a divorce. . . .

JUNIE   ???A what—?

VI   A divorce.

JUNIE   ???Why?

ELLIE   'Cause Mr. Harrison caught her wit' a man.

JUNIE   Well, it's not the first time 'cording to you.

ELLIE   The other times wasn't wit' his best friend.

JUNIE   His best friend?! WHEEE! Boy, she really did it up this time. . . . Her previous excursions were restricted to his casual acquaintances! . . . But why the hell should he be so upset? He's put up wit' all the rest. This only means she's gitting closer to home. Maybe next time it'll be him, ha, ha, ha. . . .

ELLIE   (*Reprimandingly.*) It's no joke, Junie.

JUNIE   (*Exiting into bathroom.*) How'd it happen?

ELLIE   (*Flaring at the memory.*)   Just walked in and caught 'em in his own bedroom!

VI   (*Even more outraged.*)   Was that dirty dog, Mr. Heller, lives on the 19th floor of the same building!

ELLIE   (*Anger mounting.*)   I warned her to be careful when she first started messing with him. I told her Mr. Harrison was really gon' kick her out if he found out, but she'd have the snake sneak in sometimes soon as Mr. Harrison left! Even had nerve to invite him to chaperone his wife back later in the evening for a li'l' after-dinner snack!

JUNIE   (*Reentering, merrily.*)   What's a little exchange of pleasantries among rich friends, bosom buddies? Now, all Harrison has to do is return the favor and even things up.

VI   She really cooked her goose this time.

JUNIE   Good for her.

ELLIE   Good . . . ?

JUNIE   Sure—what'd she 'spect? To wait 'till she hauled some cat into bed right next to her old man befo' he got the message?

VI   They is gitting a *divorce*, Junie!

JUNIE   (*Sauntering over to fruit bowl atop refrigerator.*) That's all? . . . I'm surprised I didn't read headlines 'bout a double murder and one suicide. . . . But I forgot!—that's our colored folk's method of clearing up little gummy problems like that—that is, MINUS the suicide bit.

ELLIE   *They's breaking up their home, Junie!*

JUNIE   (*Biting into apple selected from bowl.*)   They'll learn to live wit' it. . . . Might even git to like the idea.

VI   And the chillun?

JUNIE   Delicate li'l' boobies will receive nice fat allowances to ease the pain until they grow up to take over the world.

ELLIE   ???Is that all you feel at a time like this, boy?

VI   Disastrous, that's what it is!

ELLIE   Tragicull 'n' unfair!

JUNIE   Is this what you boohooing 'bout?!!!

ELLIE   Could you think of anything worser?

JUNIE   But, why?!   (*Exits into interior.*)

ELLIE   'Cause this time we KNOW HE MEANS BUSI-
NESS, JUNIE! Ain't no false alarm like them other times.
We were there, right there! . . . Had a feeling somp'um
was go'n' happen soon as I answered the door and let
Mr. Heller in! Like chilly pneumonia on top a breeze. . . .
Miss Harrison tole me she didn't wanta be disturbed for
the rest of the afternoon. Well, she was disturbed all
right! They musta fell asleep 'cause Mr. Harrison even
got home late and still caught 'em. . . .

JUNIE   (*Returns with tie, etc., to continue dressing.*)
Couldn't you have interrupted their togetherness and
sounded a timely danger warning?

ELLIE   We didn't hear him. I was in the kitchen, Vi down
in basement ironing. I didn't know Mr. Harrison had
come in 'till I heard screaming from the bedroom. But
soon as I did, I called Vi and me and her tipped down the
hall and heard Mr. Harrison order Mr. Heller to put his
clothes back on and stop considering hisself a friend for
the rest of his life! " 'N' you—slut! Pack up and git out
soon as you find a suitable apartment." . . . Then he invited
me and Vi into the room and told us he was divorcing
her. . . . That man was hurt, Junie, hurt deep! Could see
it in his eyes. . . . Like a little boy, so sad he made you
wanta grab hold his head and rock him in your arms like
a baby.

VI   Miss Harrison looked a sight herself, po' thing! Like a
li'l' girl caught stealing crackers out the cookie jar.

ELLIE   I almost crowned ole back-stabber Heller! Come
brushing up 'gainst *me* on his way out!

JUNIE   (*Almost cracking up with laughter.*)   Shoulda
pinned medal on him as he flew by. Escaping wit' head
still on shoulder and no bullet-holes dotting through his
chest.

ELLIE   (*Once again taking him literally.*) The skunk really
left us all too high and dry for that, Junie. . . . Oh, don't
think it wouldn't broke your heart, too, nephew. . . .
Sneaky rascal gone, rest of us in sorrow, tears pouring
down our faces 'n' me and Vi jist begging and begging. . . .
(*As if to Harrisons.*)   "Y'all please think twice befo' you
do anything you'll be sorry for. You love each other—and
who's in better position than Vi and me to know how much
you love each other—" (JUNIE *ceases dressing to listen
closely.*)

VI   'Course she love him, just can't help herself.

ELLIE   "—When two hearts love each other as much as we
know y'all do, they better take whole lots of time befo'
doing something so awful as breaking up a marriage—
even if it ain't hunert-percent perfect. Think about your
reputation and the scandal this will cause Mr. Harrison.
Jist 'bout kill your po' mother—her wit' her blood pressure,
artritis, gout, heart tickle 'n' everything. But most of all,
don't orphan the kids! Kids come first. Dear li'l angels!
Just innocents looking on gitting hurt in ways they can't
understand."

JUNIE   (*Incredulous.*)   You told 'em this, Ellie?

ELLIE   Love conquers all, Junie!

JUNIE   Wit' your assistance, Vi?

VI   As much as I could deliver, Junie.

JUNIE   And what impression did your tender concern have
on the bereaved couple?

ELLIE   Mr. Harrison said he understood 'n' appreciated our
feelings and was very grateful for our kindly advice—but

he was sorry, his mind was made up. She'd gone too far and he couldn't forgive her—not EVER! . . . We might judge him a harsh, vindicty man, he said, but he couldn't bring hisself to do it. Even apologized to us for being so cruel.

JUNIE   (*Continuing his slow boil.*)   You accepted his apology, Vi?

VI   I should say not. I pleaded wit' him agin to think it over for sake of home, family and good name!

JUNIE   Well of all the goddamn things I ever heard!

ELLIE   (*Heartened by his misread support.*)   I'm telling ya!

VI   I knew it was go'n' happen if she kept on like she did!

ELLIE   Just wouldn't listen!

JUNIE   It's a disgrace!

ELLIE   Ain't the word!

VI   Lot worse than that!

JUNIE   Did you both plop down on your knees begging him to give her another chance?

VI   NO!—But we woulda if we'd thought about it! Why didn't we, Ellie?!

ELLIE   Things happened so fast—

JUNIE   Never have I been so humiliated in all my life !

VI   (*Self-disgusted by their glaring omission.*)   No excuse not thinking 'bout it, Ellie!

ELLIE   Certainly ain't.

JUNIE   What about your pride—!?

VI   You right! Musta been false pride kept us from dropping to our knees!

JUNIE   Acting like imbeciles! Crying your heart out 'cause Massa and Mistress are go'n' break up housekeeping!!! Maybe I oughta go beat up the adulterous rat crawling in between the sheets!!! (*Pacing up and down in angry indignation as they sit stunned.*) Here we are—Africa rising to its place in the sun wit' prime ministers and other dignitaries taking seats around the international conference table—us here fighting for our rights like never before, changing the whole image, dumping stereotypes behind us and replacing 'em wit' new images of dignity and dimension—and I come home and find my own aunts, sisters of my mother, daughters of my grandpa who never took crap off no cracker even though he did live on a plantation—DROWNING themselves in tears jist 'cause boss man is gonna kick bosslady out on her nose . . . !!! Maybe *Gone With The Wind* was accurate! Maybe we jist can't help "Miss Scarrrrrrlet-ing" and "Oh Lawdying" every time mistress white gets a splinter in her pinky. That's what *I'm* talking about.

VI   Ain't you got no feelings, boy?

JUNIE   Feelings?!!! . . . So you work every day in their kitchen, Ellie, and every Thursday you wash their stinky clothes, Vi. But that don't mean they're paying you to bleed from their scratches! . . . Look—don't get me wrong—I'm not blaming you for being domestics. It's an honorable job. It's the only kind available sometimes, and it carries no stigma in itself—but that's all it is, A JOB! An exchange of work for pay! BAD PAY AT THAT! Which is all the more reason why you shouldn't give a damn whether the Harrisons kick, kill or mangle each other!

ELLIE   You gotta care, Junie—

JUNIE   "Breaking up home and family!"—Why, I've seen both of you ditch two husbands apiece and itching to send third ones packing if they don't toe the line. You don't even cry over that!

ELLIE   Don't have time to—

JUNIE   Boy, if some gray cat was peeping in on you, he'da sprinted back home and wrote five Uncle Tom Cabins and ten Old Black Joes!

ELLIE   Wait a minute, now—

JUNIE   I never heard you shedding such tragic tears when your own li'l' crumbcrushers suffered through fatherless periods! All you grumbled was "good riddance, they better off wit'out the sonsabitches!" . . . Maybe Harrison tots will make out just as well. They got puny li'l' advantages of millions of dollars and slightly less parched skins!

VI   Show some tenderness, boy. Ain't human not to trouble over our bosses' sorrows—

JUNIE   That's what shames me. I gave you credit for more integrity. Didn't figger you had chalk streaks in ya. You oughta be shamed for *yourselves!*

ELLIE   And done what?

JUNIE   NOTHING!—Shoulda told 'em their sticky mess is their own mud puddle. You neutrals. Just work there. Aren't interested in what they do!

ELLIE   That wouldn't be expressing our deepest sentiments—

JUNIE   I'm ashamed you even had any "sentiments!" . . . Look, it's hopeless, I'm not getting anywhere trying to make you understand. . . . I'm going out for a whiff of fresh air! (*Rushes to exit.*)

ELLIE   COME BACK HERE, BOY!

JUNIE   (*Stopping at door.*) What? To watch you blubber over Massa? No, thanks!

ELLIE   I said come here, you hear me talking to you!

VI   You still ain't too big to git yourself slapped down!

ELLIE   Your ma gave us right any time we saw fit! (*He returns reluctantly. Stands aside. An uneasy silence pre-*

vails. They commence a sweet, sly, needling attack.) . . .
Better git yourself somp'um to eat. (*Rises, taking off coat.*)

JUNIE   (*Sulking.*)   I lost my appetite.

ELLIE   (*Hanging coat up.*)   What you want?

JUNIE   I told you I'm not hungry anymore.

VI   *We* made you lose your appetite . . . ? (*He doesn't reply.*)

ELLIE   What did you crave befo' you lost it?

JUNIE   Anything you had cooked. Didn't have anything special in mind. . . .

ELLIE   (*Off-handedly.*)   Steak? . . . T-Bone? . . . Porter-house? . . . Filet . . . ?

JUNIE   No. . . . I didn't particularly have steak in mind.

VI   Been eating too many lately, huh? (*Stands at table exchanging goods from* ELLIE'S *shopping bag into her own.*)

JUNIE   Just kinda tired of 'em, that's all.

ELLIE   How 'bout some chicken then . . . ? Roast beef? . . . Lobster? . . . Squab? Duck, or something?

JUNIE   (*Nettled.*)   All I wanted was some food, Ellie! . . . In fact, I really had a hankering for some plain ole collard greens, neck bones or ham hocks. . . .

ELLIE   Good eatin', boy. Glad to hear that. Means that high-class digestion hasn't spoiled your taste buds yet. . . . But if you want that rich, choice food, you welcome to it—

JUNIE   I know that, Ellie!

ELLIE   It's in the freezer for you, go and look.

JUNIE   I don't hafta, Ellie, I know—

ELLIE   Go look anyway.

JUNIE   (*Goes and opens refrigerator door.*)   It's there, Ellie, I didn't need look.

VI   Come here for a second, Junie, got something on your pants leg. (*He obeys. She picks a piece of lint off trousers, then rubs material admiringly.*) Pants to your suit, ain't they? . . . Sure is a fine suit to be trotting off to the unemployment office. . . . Which one-'r the other you gon' wear tonight when you try to con that girl out her virginity—if she still got it?—The gray one? Brown one? The tweed? Or maybe you go'n' git sporty and strut that snazzy plaid jacket and them tight light pants? If not—which jacket and which pants?

ELLIE   Slept good last night, nephew? Or maybe you gitting tired of that foam rubber mattress and sheep-fur blanket?

VI   How do them fine college queens and snooty office girls like the furniture they half-see when you sneak 'em in here late at night? Surprised to see such fancy stuff in a beat-up ole flat, ain't they? But it helps you put 'em at ease, don't it? I bet even those sweet li'l' white ones are impressed by your class?

JUNIE   (*Indignantly.*)   That's not fair, Vi—

ELLIE   When last time you bought any food in this house, boy?

JUNIE   Ellie, you know—

ELLIE   When, Junie?

JUNIE   Not since I been here, but—

VI   And your last piece of clothes?

JUNIE   (*More indignant.*)   I bought some underwear last week, Vi!

VI   I mean clothes you wear on top, Junie. Shirts, pants, jackets, coats?

JUNIE   (*Squirming.*)   You—you know I haven't, Vi—

ELLIE   (*Resits.*)   Buy anything else in your room besides that tiny, midget frame for your ma's picture?

JUNIE   All right. I know I'm indebted to ya. You don't
          have to rub it in. I'll make it up to you when I git on my
          feet and *fulfill* my potential. . . . But that's not the point!

ELLIE   You ain't indebted to us, Junie.

JUNIE   Yes, I am, I know it, I thank you for it.

ELLIE   Don't hafta thank us—

JUNIE   But that's not the issue! Despite your benevolence,
          I refuse to let you blackmail my principle, slapping me in
          the face wit' how good you been to me during my tempo-
          rary outta work period! I'm talking to you now, 'bout
          something above our personal relationship. Pride—Race—
          Dignity—

ELLIE   What's go'n' happen to me and Vi's dignity if Mr.
          Harrison throws Mrs. Harrison out on her nose as you
          put it?

JUNIE   Git another job! You not dependent on them. You
          young, healthy, in the prime of life. . . . In fact—I've
          always wondered why you stagnate as domestics when
          you're trained and qualified to do something better and
          more dignified.

ELLIE   Glad you brought that up. Know why I'm not break-
          ing my back as a practical nurse and Vi's not frying hair—
          'cept on the side? . . . 'Cause the work's too hard, the
          money ain't worth it and there's not much room for ad-
          vancement—

JUNIE   Where kin you advance as a domestic? From kitchen
          to closet?! (VI *has moved to fridge to deposit meats etc.*)

ELLIE   (*Refusing to be provoked, continuing evenly.*) Be-
          sides, when I started working for the Harrisons, Junie, Mr.
          Harrison vowed that he would support me for life if I
          stayed with 'em until his daughter Sandy, his oldest child,
          reached ten years old.

JUNIE   Bully for him! He'll build ya a little cottage backa
          the penthouse garage!

ELLIE (*Still unruffled.*) Mr. Harrison is strictly a man of his word, Junie. Which means that even if I left one day after Sandy made ten, he owes me some money every week or every month as long as I live. . . . Sandy is *nine*, Junie, EN-EYE-EN-EE! If I don't last another year, the deal is off.

JUNIE Don't need no handouts! Even hearing you say you want any, makes me shame!

ELLIE Done used that word quite a lot, boy. You shamed of us? . . . Well, git slapped in the face wit' this? How shame you go'n' be when you hafta git outta here and hustle yourself a job?—ANY JOB?!!!

JUNIE Huh?

ELLIE How shame you go'n' be when you start gitting raggedy and all them foxy girls are no longer impressed 'bout how slick, smooth and pretty you look? When you stop being one-'r the best-dressed black boys in New York City?

JUNIE Don't get you, Ellie?

ELLIE I know you went to college for a coupler years, boy, but I thought you still had some sense, or I woulda told you. . . .

VI (*Standing at* JUNIE's *right as* ELLIE *sits to his left.*) Every time you bite into one of them big tender juicy steaks and chaw it down into your belly, ever think where it's coming from?

ELLIE The Harrisons.

VI Every time you lay one of them young gals down in that plush soft bed of yours and hear her sigh in luxury, ever think 'bout who you owe it to?

ELLIE The Harrisons.

VI When you swoop down home to that rundown house your ma and pa rent, latch eyes on all that fine furniture there, you ever think who's responsible?

ELLIE   The Harrisons.

VI   You ain't bought a suit or piece of clothes in five years
and none of the other four men in this family have. . . .
Why not?

ELLIE   Mr. Harrison.

VI   Junie, you is a fine, choice hunk of chocolate pigmeat,
pretty as a new-minted penny and slick 'nuff to suck sugar
outta gingerbread wit'out it losing its flavor—but the Harrisons ain't hardly elected you no favorite pin-up boy to
introduce to Santa Claus. Took a heap of pow'ful coaxing
to win you such splendid sponsorship and wealthy com-
missions, 'cause waiting for the Harrisons to voluntarily
donate their Christian charity is one sure way of landing
head-first in the poor-house dungeon. . . . Who runs the
Harrisons' house, Junie?   (*Moves to sit at table.*)

JUNIE   ???. . . Ellie . . . I guess . . . ?

ELLIE   *From top to bottom.* I cook the food, scrub the floor,
open the doors, serve the tables, answer the phones, dust
the furniture, raise the children, lay out the clothes, greet
the guests, fix the drinks and dump the garbage—all for
bad pay as you said. . . . You right, Junie, money I git in
my envelope ain't worth the time 'n' the headache. . . .
But—God Helps Those Who Help Themselves. . . . I also
ORDER the food, estimate the credit, PAY the bills and
BALANCE the budget. Which means that each steak I
order for them, befo' butcher carves cow, I done reserved
TWO for myself. Miss Harrison wouldn't know how much
steak cost and Mr. Harrison so loaded, he writes me a
check wit'out even looking. . . . Every once in a full moon
they git so good-hearted and tell me take some left-overs
home, but by that time my freezer and pantry is already
fuller than theirs. . . . Every one of them high price suits I
lay on you haven't been worn more than once and some
of 'em not at all. You lucky to be same size as Mr. Harrison, Junie. He don't know how much clothes he got in his

wardrobe, which is why *yours* is as big as *his*. Jim, Roy, Arthur and Ben can't even fit into the man's clothes, but that still don't stop 'em from cutting, shortening, altering and stretching 'em to fit. Roy almost ruined his feet trying to wear the man's shoes. . . . Now, I've had a perfect record keeping y'all elegantly dressed and stylishly-fashion-plated—'cept that time Mr. Harrison caught me off-guard asking: "Ellie, where's my brown suit?" "In the cleaners," I told him and had to snatch it off your hanger and smuggle it back—temporarily.

VI   If y'all warn't so lucky and *Mrs. Harrison* so tacky flashy Ellie and I would also be best dressed domestics of the year.

ELLIE   Which, if you didn't notice, is what your Aunt Doris was—rest her soul—when we laid her in her grave, decked out in the costliest, ritziest, most expensest nightgown the good Lord ever waited to feast his eyes on. . . . As for furniture, we could move out his whole house in one day if we had to.

VI   Which is what we did when they moved from the old penthouse and we hired us a moving van to haul 'nuff pieces to furnish both our own apartments and still had enough to ship a living room set down home to your ma. Mr. Harrison told us to donate the stuff to charity. We did—US!

ELLIE   Add all *our* bills I add on to *their* bills—Jim even tried to git me to sneak in his car note, but that was going too far—all the deluxe plane tickets your ma jets up here on every year, weekly prescriptions filled on their tab, tons of laundry cleaned along wit' theirs and a thousand other services and I'm earning me quite a bonus along with my bad pay. It's the BONUS that counts, Junie. Total it up for nine years and I'd be losing money on any other job. Now Vi and I, after cutting cane, picking rice and shucking corn befo' we could braid our hair in pigtails, figure we just gitting back what's owed us. . . . But, if Mr. Harrison boots Mrs. Harrison out on her tocus, the party's over. He's not go'n' need us. Miss Harrison ain't got a copper cent of her own. Anyway, the set-up won't be as ripe for picking. My bonus is suddenly cut off and out the window go my pension.

VI   Suppose we did git us another job wit' one-'r them penny-pinching old misers hiding behind cupboards watching whether you stealing sugar cubes? Wit' our fringe benefits choked off, we'd fall down so quick to a style of living we ain't been used to for a long time, it would make your head swim. I don't think we could stand it. . . . Could you?

ELLIE   So when me and Vi saw our pigeons scampering out the window for good today, tears started flowing like rain. The first tear trickle out my eyes had a roast in it.

VI   Mine was a chicken.

ELLIE   Second had a crate of eggs.

VI   Mine a whole pig.

ELLIE   Third an oriental rug.

VI   A continental couch.

ELLIE   An overcoat for Arthur.

VI   A bathrobe for Ben.

ELLIE   My gas, electric and telephone bills in it.

VI   Three months' rent, Lord!

ELLIE   The faster the stream started gushing, the faster them nightmares crowded my eyes until I coulda flooded 'em 'nuff water to swim in. Every time I pleaded "Think of your love!—"

VI   She meant think 'bout our bills.

ELLIE   Every time I begged "Don't crack up the home!—"

VI   It meant please keep *ours* cemented together!

ELLIE   "Don't victim the chillun!—"

VI   By all means insure the happiness of *our* li'l' darlings!

ELLIE   They didn't know 'bout these eyeball visions—they only see what they see 'n' hear what they hear—and that's okey-doke wit' me—but I was gitting these watery pictures in my mind 'n' feeling a giant-size sickness in my gut! Few seconds longer and I woulda been down on my knees wit'out even thinking 'bout it!

VI   If I didn't beat ya to the floor!

ELLIE   Junie—maybe we shoulda given a little more thought to that—watchamacallit?—"image" of yours. Maybe we did dishonor Africa, embarrass the NAACP, are hopelessly behind time and scandalously outdated. But we didn't have too much time to think. . . . Now that you know the whole truth, you have a right to disown us. We hardly worthy of your respect. . . . But when I thought 'bout that new topcoat wit' the velvet-trimmed collar I just packed to bring you . . . (*Tears begin to re-form.*) . . . coupler new cashmere sweaters, brand-new slacks, a shiny new attache case for your appointments, and a scrumptous new collapsible swimming pool I promised your ma for her backyard—I couldn't help but cry. (VI *has joined her in a double torrent.*)

JUNIE   (*Who has been standing stoically throughout, says.*) . . . Vi?

VI   . . . What?

JUNIE   . . . Pass me the handkerchief. . . . (*He receives it and joins the table—a moist-faced trio.* ARTHUR, ELLIE'S *husband, walks in, finding them thus.*)

ARTHUR   (*Beelining for bathroom.*) Even', everybody. . . . (*Hearing no response, stops before entering john.*) Hey, what's the matter? What you three looking like somebody died for?

ELLIE   It's the Harrisons, Arthur. Mr. Harrison gitting a divorce.

ARTHUR   Aww, not ag'in!

VI   He really means it this time, Arthur.

ARTHUR   . . . He does?

ELLIE   Yes, Jesus.

ARTHUR   You sure?

VI   Caught her dead to rights.

ARTHUR   (*Indignant.*)   But he can't do that!

VI   He is.

ARTHUR   What 'bout us?!

JUNIE   What you think we grieving 'bout?

ARTHUR   Well, just don't sit there! What we go'n' do?

ELLIE   Done it, didn't work.

ARTHUR   Not at all.

ELLIE   Nope.

ARTHUR   Not even a little bit?

ELLIE   Not one lousy inch.

ARTHUR   (*Crestfallen.*)   Make room for me.   (*They provide space. He sits, completing the depressed quartet.*)

JUNIE   (*Suddenly jolted with an idea.*)   Ellie! Wait! Why don't you tell him to take her on a private ocean cruise, just the two of 'em, so they kin recapture the thrill for one another!

ELLIE   He did that already, until somebody told him she was cuddling up with the ship stoker in the engine room.

JUNIE   (*Undaunted.*)   Advise him to spend less time wit' his business and more with her. She wouldn't need look outside for satisfaction!

ELLIE   Tried that too, but his business like to fell apart and he caught her making eyes at the messenger bringing him the news.

JUNIE   (*Desperate.*)   Convince him she's sick! It's not her fault, he should send her to a psychiatrist!

ELLIE   Already did . . . till he found out she was doing more than talking on the couch.

JUNIE   What 'bout a twenty-four hour guard on her? That won't give her so many opportunities?!

ELLIE   What about guards? They men, too.

JUNIE   (*In angry frustration.*)   Well, damn, git her a chastity belt and lock her up!

ELLIE   Locks, also, have been known to be picked.

ARTHUR   (*Inspired by a brilliant solution.*)   WAIT! *I GOT IT! I GOT IT!* . . . Tell him you know of some steady-ready goofer dust . . . or jooger-mooger saltpeter to cool her down. And you'll slip it in her food every day!

ELLIE   Wouldn't work. . . . Way her glands function, probably jazz her up like a Spanish fly.

VI   Let's face it, it's all over. We just gotta tuck in our belts, stare the future square in the eye and git ready for a depression. It's not go'n' do us no good to whine over spilt clabber. . . . You jist better start scrounging 'round for that job, Junie. Befo' you git a chance to sneeze, we will have had it. And call up— NO! Write your ma and tell her not to come up this year.

ELLIE   Arthur, best you scrape up another job to moonlight wit' the one you got. We facing some scuffling days 'head us.

VI   Well. . . . I better git out of here and go warn my own crew 'bout Satan's retribution. . . . Well . . . it was good while it lasted, Ellie. . . .

ELLIE   Real good. (*They glance at each other and another deluge starts. The phone interrupts, but no one bothers to answer. Finally,* ARTHUR *rises and exits in the direction of peals. During his absence, the disconsolate trio remains silent.*)

ARTHUR   (*Reentering slowly, treading each step with the deliberateness of a man fearful of cracking eggs.*)   That —was—Mr. Harrison—he said—thank both of you for desperately trying to—shock him to his senses—pry open his eyes to the light—and rescue his house from collapsing —he and Mrs. Harrison, after stren'ous consideration, are gonna stick it out together! (*A stunned moment of absolute silence prevails, finally broken by an ear-splitting, exultant whoop which erupts simultaneously from each member of the quartet. They spring to feet, embracing and prancing around the room, crying through laughter.* AR-THUR *simmers down first, shhushes to recapture their attention.*)   ELLIE . . . Ellie, Mr. Harrison requests if it's not too much trouble, he'd like for you to come over and stay wit' Sandy and Snookie while he and Mrs. Harrison go out and celebrate their reunion and it's too late to git a baby-sitter.

ELLIE   If it's all right?!!!! . . . Tell him I'm climbing on a broomstick, then shuttling to a jet! (ARTHUR *starts to exit.*)   Wait a minute! Waaaait a minute! Hold on!—I must be crazy! Don't tell him that. . . . Tell him he knows very well it's after my working hours and I'm not paid to baby-sit and since I've already made plans for the evening, I'll be glad to do it for double-overtime, two extra days' pay and triple-time off to recuperate from the imposition. . . . And, Arthur! . . . Kinda suggest that *you* is a little peeved 'cause he's interrupting me from taking care of something important for you. He might toss in a day for your suffering.

ARTHUR   He'll swear he was snatching you away from my

death-bed, guarding my door 'gainst Lucifer busting through! (*Exits.*)

ELLIE   I'd better throw on some more clothes. (*Exits.*)

JUNIE   Vi, what you s'pose grandpa would say 'bout his chillun if he got a breathing-spell in between dodging pitchforks and side-stepping the fiery flames?

VI   Shame on you, boy, Papa ain't near'bouts doing no ducking 'n' dodging. Why, he's right up there plunked down safe, snuggled up tight beside the good Lord's righteous throne.

ARTHUR   (*Reentering.*)   He was real sorry. "If it wasn't such a special occasion, he wouldn't bother us!" (*They guffaw heartily.*)

JUNIE   This IS a special occasion! . . . (*Grandly.*)   Arthur, break out a flagon of the latest champagne Ellie brought us.

ARTHUR   At your service, massa Junie.

JUNIE   The nineteen-forty-seven! That was a good year. Not the fifty, which was bad!

ARTHUR   No kidding?! (ARTHUR *moves to refrigerator.* ELLIE *returns, ready to depart.*)

JUNIE   Wait for a drink, auntie. We've gotta celebrate OUR resurrection. A Toast of Deliverance. (ARTHUR *presents* JUNIE *with champagne, points out '47 label, then gets goblets from shelf.* JUNIE *pours, they lift goblets.*) First! . . . To the victors and the vanquished, top-dog and the bottom-dog! Sometimes it's hard to tell which is which . . . !

VI   If nothing else, boy, education did teach you how to sling around some GAB.

ARTHUR   Ain't hardly the way I heard the slinging described. (*They all laugh.*)

JUNIE   Second! . . . To my two cagey aunts. May they continue to prevail in times of distress!

ARTHUR   May they!

JUNIE   . . . Third! . . . To the Harrisons! . . . May they en-
dure forever in marital bliss! Cheers to 'em! (*All cheer.
After finishing drink,* ELLIE *moves to exit through hallway
door.* JUNIE *stops her.*)   Oh, Ellie . . . why don't you
start fattening Mr. Harrison up? Please slip some more
potatoes and starch onto his menu. I've gained a few
pounds and the clothes are gitting a little tight. Don't you
think it's time for him to plumpen up a bit, stick on a little
weight? . . .

ELLIE   Would ten pounds do?

JUNIE   Perfect! (*Another round of laughter. Again she
moves to exit.*)   . . . AND ELLIE! . . . Kinda hint 'round
to him that fashions is changing. I wouldn't want him to
fall behind in the latest styles. . . .

VI   (*Lifting goblet, along with* ARTHUR *and* ELLIE, *in a final
toast.*)   There's hope, Junie. You'll make it, boy, you'll
make it. . . .   (*Laughter rings as lights fade.*)

CURTAIN

FUNNYHOUSE
OF A NEGRO

A One Act Play

Adrienne Kennedy

ADRIENNE KENNEDY was born in Pittsburgh in 1931 and reared in Cleveland. Her father was a YMCA social worker for twenty-five years and her mother, a school teacher. Miss Kennedy attended Ohio State University where she first began to write.

When she moved to New York she became a member of Edward Albee's Playwright's Workshop. *Funnyhouse of a Negro* was first produced at The Cricket Theatre on January 18, 1964, to high critical acclaim. A Village Voice Obie Award was given the play at the end of the season.

Another play, *The Rat's Mass*, was performed in 1966 by the Theatre Company of Boston. An earlier work, *The Owl Answers*, was in 1969 part of a double bill under the title *Cities in Bizique* at the Public Theatre of the New York Shakespeare Festival. Unlike other Black writers Adrienne Kennedy forgoes a realistic style in her plays; instead she forms the dramatic action out of the tools of the expressionistic playwright. Character is fractured and multi-faceted. Thus the central action is based not on the clash of characters but on the internal conflict within a central character.

Funnyhouse of a Negro embodies all of the elements of expressionistic drama, the extravagant use of symbol, the tricks of stagecraft and the substitution of theme for plot as a structural form. The reality of the play is beyond the here and now; it is the hallucinatory world of the black-white "funnyhouse," inhabited by the different selves of Sarah, in which the anguish of discovering selfhood is played out in the fantasy of racial dreams. Like all expressionistic plays, *Funnyhouse of a Negro* gains dimension in production when the poetic use of light, sound and color in staging can be manifested. Even so, the rich imagery, the imaginative use of language and the emotional power of this short play can be experienced in the reading.

Miss Kennedy has taken residence in London and is at work on a major three act play about a character like her brother, an ex-college student permanently hospitalized.

FUNNYHOUSE OF A NEGRO

Characters

SARAH *Negro*

DUCHESS OF HAPSBURG *One of Herselves*

QUEEN VICTORIA *One of Herselves*

PATRICE LUMUMBA *One of Herselves*

JESUS *One of Herselves*

THE MOTHER

LANDLADY *Funnylady*

RAYMOND *Funnyman*

BEGINNING   *Before the closed curtain a woman dressed in a white nightgown walks across the stage carrying before her a bald head. She moves as one in a trance and is mumbling something inaudible to herself. She appears faceless, wearing a yellow whitish mask over her face, with no apparent eyes. Her hair is wild, straight and black and falls to her waist. As she moves, holding her hands before her, she gives the effect of one in a dream. She crosses the stage from right to left. Before she has barely vanished, the curtain opens. It is a white satin curtain of a cheap material and a ghastly white, a material that brings to mind the interior of a cheap casket; parts of it are frayed and it looks as if it has been gnawed by rats.*

THE SCENE   *Two women are sitting in what appears to be a queen's chamber. It is set in the middle of the stage in a strong white light, while the rest of the stage is in strong unnatural blackness. The quality of the white light is unreal and ugly. The monumental bed resembling an ebony tomb, a low dark chandelier with candles and wine-colored walls. Flying about are great black ravens. Queen Victoria is standing before her bed, holding a small mirror in her hand. On the white pillow of her bed is a dark indistinguishable object. The Duchess of Hapsburg is standing at the foot of her bed. Her back is to us as is the Queen's. Throughout the entire scene they do not move. Both women are dressed in royal gowns of white, a white similar to the white of the curtain, the material cheap satin. Their headpieces are white and of a net that falls over their faces. From beneath both their headpieces springs a headful of wild kinky hair. Although in this scene we do not see their faces, they look exactly alike and will wear masks or be made up to appear a whitish yellow. It is an alabaster face, the skin drawn tightly over the high cheekbones, great dark eyes that seem gouged out of the head, a high forehead, a full red mouth and a head of frizzy hair. If the characters do not wear a mask, the face must be highly powdered and possess a hard expressionless quality and a stillness as in the fact of death.*

The text printed here is from *The International Library of Negro Life and History*, Vol III, *Anthology of the American Negro in the Theatre* (New York: Publisher's Company, 1967).

(*We hear a knocking.*)

VICTORIA   (*listening to the knocking*).   It is my father. He
     is arriving again for the night.   (*The* DUCHESS *makes no*
     reply.)   He comes through the jungle to find me. He
     never tires of his journey.

DUCHESS   How dare he enter the castle, he who is the dark-
     est of them all, the darkest one. My mother looked like a
     white woman, hair as straight as any white woman's. And
     at least I am yellow, but he is black, the blackest one of
     them all. I hoped he was dead. Yet he still comes through
     the jungle to find me.   (*The knocking is louder.*)

VICTORIA   He never tires of the journey, does he, Duchess?
     (*Looking at herself in the mirror.*)

DUCHESS   How dare him enter the castle of Queen Vic-
     toria Regina, Monarch of England. It is because of him
     that my mother died. The wild black beast put his hands
     on her. She died.

VICTORIA   Why does he keep returning? He keeps returning
     forever, coming back ever and keeps coming back for-
     ever. He is my father.

DUCHESS   He is a black Negro.

VICTORIA   He is my father. I am tied to the black Negro. He
     came when I was a child in the south, before I was born
     he haunted my conception, diseased my birth.

DUCHESS   Killed my mother.

VICTORIA   My mother was the light. She was the lightest
     one. She looked like a white woman.

DUCHESS   We are tied to him unless, of course, he should
     die.

VICTORIA   But he is dead.

DUCHESS   And he keeps returning.   (*The knocking is*
     louder, blackout. Onto the stage from the left comes the

figure in the white nightgown carrying the bald head. This time we hear her speak.)

MOTHER   Black man, black man, I never should have let a black man put his hands on me. The wild black beast raped me and now my skull is shining.

> *(She disappears to the right. Now the light is focused on a single white square wall that is to the left of the stage that is suspended and stands alone, of about five feet in dimension and width. It stands with the narrow part facing the audience. A character steps through. She is a faceless dark character with a hangman's rope about her neck and red blood on the part that would be her face. She is the Negro. On first glance she might be a young person but at a closer look the impression of an ancient character is given. The most noticeable aspect of her looks is her wild kinky hair, part of which is missing. It is a ragged head with a patch of hair missing from the crown which the Negro carries in her hand. She is dressed in black. She steps slowly through the wall, stands still before it and begins her monologue.)*

NEGRO   Part of the time I live with Raymond, part of the time with God, Prince Charlies and Albert Saxe Coburg. I live in my room. It is a small room on the top floor of a brownstone in the West Nineties in New York, a room filled with my dark old volumes, a narrow bed and on the wall old photographs, castles and monarchs of England. It is also Victoria's chamber, Queen Victoria Regina's. Partly because it is consumed by a gigantic plaster statue of Queen Victoria, who is my idol, and partly for other reasons; three steps that I contrived out of boards lead to the statue which I have placed opposite the door as I enter the room. It is a sitting figure, a replica of one in London, and a thing of astonishing whiteness. I found it in a dusty shop on Morningside Heights. Raymond says it is a thing of terror, possessing the quality of nightmares, suggesting large and probable deaths. And of course he is right. When I am the Duchess of Hapsburg, I sit opposite Victoria in my headpiece and we talk. The other times I wear the dress of a student, dark clothes and dark stockings. Victoria always wants me to tell her of whiteness. She wants me to tell her of a royal world where everything and everyone is white and there are no unfortunate black ones. For as we of royal blood know, black is evil and has been from the beginning. Even before my mother's hair started to fall out. Before she was raped by a wild black beast. Black was evil.

When I am not the Duchess of Hapsburg I am myself. As for myself, I long to become even a more pallid Negro than I am now, pallid like Negroes on the covers of American Negro magazines; soulless, educated and irreligious. I want to possess no moral value, particularly value as to my being. I want not to be. I ask nothing except anonymity.

I am an English major, as my mother was when she went to school in Atlanta. My father majored in social work. I am graduated from a city college and have occasional work in libraries, but mostly spend my days preoccupied with the placement and geometric position of words on paper. I write poetry, filling white page after white page with imitations of Edith Sitwell. It is my dream to live in rooms with European antiques and my Queen Victoria, photographs of Roman ruins, walls of books, a piano, oriental carpets, and to eat my meals on a white glass table. I will visit my friends' apartments which will contain books, photographs of Roman ruins, pianos, and oriental carpets. My friends will be white. I need them as an embankment to keep me from reflecting too much upon the fact that I am a Negro. For, like all educated Negroes

—out of life and death essential—I find it necessary to maintain a stark fortress against recognition of myself. My white friends like myself will be shrewd, intellectual and anxious for death. Anyone's death. I will mistrust them, as I do myself. But if I had not wavered in my opinion of myself then my hair would never have fallen out. And if my hair hadn't fallen out, I wouldn't have bludgeoned my father's head with an ebony mask.

In appearance I am good-looking in a boring way; no glaring Negroid features, medium nose, medium mouth and pale yellow skin. My one defect is that I have a head of frizzy hair, unmistakably Negro kinky hair; and it is indisguisable. I would like to lie and say I love Raymond. But I do not. He is a poet and is Jewish. He is very interested in Negroes.

> (*The Negro stands by the wall and throughout her following speech, the following characters come through the wall, disappearing off into the varying directions in the darkened night of the stage —* DUCHESS, QUEEN VICTORIA, JESUS, PATRICE LUMUMBA. JESUS *is a hunchback, yellow-skinned dwarf, dressed in white rags and sandals.* PATRICE LUMUMBA *is a black man. His head appears to be split in two with blood and tissue in eyes. He carries an ebony mask.*)

The characters are myself: the Duchess of Hapsburg, Queen Victoria Regina, Jesus, Patrice Lumumba. The rooms are my rooms; a Hapsburg chamber, a chamber in a Victorian castle, the hotel where I killed my father, the jungle. These are the places myselves exist in. I know no places. That is I cannot believe in places. To believe in places is to know hope and to know the emotion of hope is to know beauty. It links us across a horizon and connects us to the world. I find there are no places, only my funnyhouse. Streets are rooms, cities are rooms, eternal rooms. I try to create a space for myself in cities. New York, the midwest, a southern town but it becomes a lie. I try to give myselves a logical relationship but that too is a lie. For relationships was one of my last religions. I clung loyally to the lie of relationships, again and again seeking to establish a connection between my characters. Jesus is Victoria's son. Mother loved my father before her hair fell out. A loving relationship exists between myself and Jesus but they are lies. You will assume I am trifling with you, teasing your intellect, dealing in subtleties, denying connection then suddenly at a point reveal a startling heartbreaking connection. You are wrong. For the days are past when there are places and characters with connections with themes as in stories you pick up on the shelves of public libraries.

Too, there is no theme. No statements. I might borrow a statement, struggle to fabricate a theme, borrow one from my contemporaries, renew one from the master, hawkishly scan other stories searching for statements, consider the theme then deceive myself that I held such a statement within me, refusing to accept the fact that a statement has to come from an ordered force. I might try to join horizontal elements such as dots on a horizontal line, or create a centrifugal force, or create causes and effects so that they would equal a quantity but it would be a lie. For the statement is the characters and the characters are myself.

> (*Blackout—then to the right front of the stage comes the white light. It goes to a suspended stairway. At the foot of it stands the* LANDLADY. *She is a tall, thin woman dressed in a black hat with red and appears to be talking to someone in a suggested open doorway in a corridor of a rooming house. She laughs like a mad character in a funnyhouse throughout her speech.*)

LANDLADY   (*looking up the stairway*).   Ever since her father hung himself in a Harlem hotel when Patrice Lumumba was murdered, she hides in her room. Each night she repeats; he keeps returning. How dare he enter the castle walls, he who is the darkest of them all, the darkest one. My mother looked like a white woman, hair as straight as any white woman's. And I am yellow but he, he is black, the blackest one of them all. I hoped he was dead. Yet still he comes through the jungle.

I tell her: Sarah, honey, the man hung himself. It's not your blame. But, no, she stares at me: No, Mrs. Conrad, he did not hang himself, that is only the way they understand it, they do, but the truth is that I bludgeoned his head with an ebony skull that he carries about with him. Wherever he goes, he carries out black masks and heads.

She's suffering so till her hair has fallen out. But then she did always hide herself in that room with the walls of books and her statues. I always did know she thought she was somebody else, a Queen or something, somebody else.

(*Blackout.* FUNNYMAN'S *place. The next scene is enacted with the* DUCHESS *and* RAYMOND. RAYMOND'S *place is suggested as being above the* NEGRO'S *room, and is etched in with a prop of blinds and a bed . . . behind the blinds are mirrors and when the blinds are opened and closed by* RAYMOND, *this is revealed.* RAYMOND *turns out to be the* FUNNYMAN *of the funnyhouse. He is tall, white and ghostly thin and dressed in a black shirt and black trousers in attire suggesting an artist. Throughout his dialogue he laughs. The* DUCHESS *is partially disrobed and it is implied from their attitudes of physical intimacy—he is standing and she is sitting before him clinging to his leg. During the scene,* RAYMOND *keeps opening and closing the blinds. His face has black sores on it and he is wearing*

*a black hat. Throughout the scene he strikes her as in
affection when he speaks to her.*

DUCHESS   (*carrying a red paper bag*).   My father is arriving, and what am I to do?

> (RAYMOND *walks about the place opening the blinds
> and laughing.*)

FUNNYMAN   He is arriving from Africa, is he not?

DUCHESS   Yes, yes, he is arriving from Africa.

FUNNYMAN   I always knew your father was African.

DUCHESS   He is an African who lives in the jungle. He is
an African who has always lived in the jungle. Yes, he is
a nigger who is an African, who is a missionary teacher
and is now dedicating his life to the erection of a Christian
mission in the middle of the jungle. He is a black man.

FUNNYMAN   He is a black man who shot himself when they
murdered Patrice Lumumba.

DUCHESS   (*goes on wildly*).   Yes, my father is a black man
who went to Africa years ago as a missionary teacher, got
mixed up in politics, was reviled and is now devoting his
foolish life to the erection of a Christian mission in the
middle of the jungle in one of those newly freed countries.
Hide me. (*Clinging to his knees.*)   Hide me here so the
nigger will not find me.

FUNNYMAN   (*laughing*).   Your father is in the jungle dedicating his life to the erection of a Christian mission.

DUCHESS   Hide me here so the jungle will not find me.
Hide me.

FUNNYMAN   Isn't it cruel of you?

DUCHESS   Hide me from the jungle.

FUNNYMAN   Isn't it cruel?

DUCHESS   No, no.

FUNNYMAN   Isn't it cruel of you?

DUCHESS   No. (*She screams and opens her red paper bag and draws from it her fallen hair. It is a great mass of dark wild. She holds it up to him. He appears not to understand. He stares at it.*) It is my hair. (*He continues to stare at her.*)   When I awakened this morning it had fallen out, not all of it but a mass from the crown of my head that lay on the center of my pillow. I rose and in the greyish winter morning light of my room I stood staring at my hair, dazed by my sleeplessness, still shaken by nightmares of my mother. Was it true, yes, it was my hair. In the mirror I saw that, although my hair remained on both sides, clearly on the crown and at my temples my scalp was bare. (*She removes her black crown and shows him the top of her head.*)

RAYMOND (FUNNYMAN)   (*staring at her*). Why would your hair fall out? Is it because you are cruel? How could a black father haunt you so?

DUCHESS   He haunted my very conception. He was a black wild beast who raped my mother.

RAYMOND (FUNNYMAN).   He is a black Negro. (*Laughing.*)

DUCHESS   Ever since I can remember he's been a nigger pose of agony. He is the wilderness. He speaks niggerly, grovelling about wanting to touch me with his black hand.

FUNNYMAN   How tormented and cruel you are.

DUCHESS   (*as if not comprehending*). Yes, yes, the man's dark, very dark skinned. He is the darkest, my father is the darkest, my mother is the lightest. I am between. But my father is the darkest. My father is a nigger who drives me to misery. Any time spent with him evolves itself into suffering. He is a black man and the wilderness.

FUNNYMAN   How tormented and cruel you are.

DUCHESS   He is a nigger.

FUNNYMAN   And your mother, where is she?

DUCHESS   She is in the asylum. In the asylum bald. Her
father was a white man. And she is in the asylum. (*He
takes her in his arms. She responds wildly.*)

(*Blackout. Knocking is heard, it continues, then
somewhere near the center of the stage a figure appears in the darkness, a large dark faceless man carrying a mask in his hand.*)

HE SPEAKS   It begins with the disaster of my hair. I awaken.
My hair has fallen out, not all of it, but a mass from the
crown of my head that lies on the center of my white pillow. I arise and in the greyish winter morning light of my
room I stand staring at my hair, dazed by sleeplessness,
still shaken by nightmares of my mother. Is it true? Yes. It
is my hair. In the mirror I see that although my hair remains on both sides, clearly on the crown and at my temples my scalp is bare. And in my sleep I had been visited
by my bald crazy mother who comes to me crying, calling
me to her bedside. She lies on the bed watching the strands
of her own hair fall out. Her hair fell out after she married
and she spent her days lying on the bed watching the
strands fall from her scalp, covering the bedspread until
she was bald and admitted to the hospital. Black man,
black man, my mother says I never should have let a black
man put his hands on me. She comes to me, her bald skull
shining. Black diseases, Sarah, she says. Black diseases. I
run. She follows me, her bald skull shining. That is the
beginning.

(*Several women with white nightgowns on, waist-
length black hair, all identical, emerge from the sides
of the stage and run into the darkness, toward him
shouting—black man, black man. They are carrying
bald heads. Blackout.*)

(*Queen's Chamber: Her hair is in a small pile on the
bed and in a small pile on the floor, several other small*

*piles of hair are scattered about her and her white
gown is covered with fallen out hair.)*

(QUEEN VICTORIA *acts out the following scene: She
awakens [in pantomime] and discovers her hair
has fallen. It is on her pillow. She arises and stands at
the side of the bed with her back toward us staring at
her hair. She opens the red paper bag that she is carrying and takes out her hair, attempting to place it
back on her head [for unlike* VICTORIA, *she does not
wear her headpiece now]. Suddenly the women in
white gowns come carrying their skulls before them
screaming.)*

(*The unidentified* MAN *returns out of the darkness
and speaks. He carries the mask.)*

MAN   I am a nigger of two generations. I am Patrice Lumumba.

PATRICE LUMUMBA   I am a nigger of two generations. I am
the black shadow that haunted my mother's conception.
I belong to the generation born at the turn of the century and the generation born before the depression. At
present I reside in New York City in a brownstone in the
West Nineties. I am an English major at a city college. My
nigger father majored in social work, so did my mother.
I am a student and have occasional work in libraries. But
mostly I spend my vile days preoccupied with the placement and geometric position of words on paper. I write
poetry filling white page after white page with imitations
of Sitwell. It is my vile dream to live in rooms with European antiques and my statues of Queen Victoria, photographs of Roman ruins, pianos and oriental carpets. My
friends will be white. I need them as an embankment to
keep me from reflecting too much upon the fact that I am
Patrice Lumumba who haunted my mother's conception.
They are necessary for me to maintain recognition against
myself. My white friends, like myself, will be shrewd intel-

lectuals and anxious for death. Anyone's death. I will despise them as I do myself. For if I did not despise myself
then my hair would not have fallen and if my hair had
not fallen then I would not have bludgeoned my father's
face with the ebony mask.

> (*Then another wall is dropped, larger than the first
> one was. This one is near the front of the stage facing
> thus.*
> *Throughout the following monologue the characters*
> DUCHESS, VICTORIA *and* JESUS *go back and forth. As
> they go in their backs are to us but the* NEGRO *faces
> us speaking.*)

NEGRO   I always dreamed of a day when my mother would
smile at me. My father—his mother wanted him to be
Christ. From the beginning in the lamp of their dark
room she said—I want you to be Jesus, to walk in Genesis
and save the race. You must return to Africa, find revelation in the midst of golden savannas, nim and white frankopenny trees, white stallions roaming under a blue sky, you
must walk with a white dove and heal the race, heal the
misery, take us off the cross . . . at dawn he watched her
rise, kill a hen for him to eat at breakfast, then go to
work, down at the big house till dusk, till she died.

His father told him the race was no damn good. He
hated his father and adores his mother. His mother didn't
want him to marry my mother and sent a dead chicken
to the wedding. I *don't* want you marrying that child, she
wrote, she's not good enough for you, I want you to go to
Africa. When they first married they lived in New York.

Then they went to Africa where my mother fell out of
love with my father. She didn't want him to save the black
race and spent her days combing her hair. She would not
let him touch her in their wedding bed and called him
black. He is black of skin with dark eyes and a great dark
square brow. Then in Africa he started to drink and came

home drunk one night and raped my mother. The child
from the union is me. I clung to my mother. Long after
she went to the asylum I wove long dreams of her beauty,
her straight hair and fair skin and gray eyes, so identical
to mine. How it anguished him. I turned from him, nailing
him to the cross, he said, dragging him through grass and
nailing him on a cross until he bled. He pleaded with me
to help him find Genesis, search for Genesis in the minds
of golden savannas, nim and white frankopenny trees and
white stallions roaming under a blue sky, help him search
for the white dove; he wanted the black man to make a
pure statement, he wanted the black man to rise from
colonialism. But I sat in the room with my mother, sat
by her bedside and helped her comb her straight black
hair and wove long dreams of her beauty. She had long
since begun to curse the place and spoke of herself trapped
in blackness. She preferred the company of night owls.
Only at night did she rise, walking in the garden among
the trees with the owls. When I spoke to her she saw I was
a black man's child and she preferred speaking to owls.
Nights my father came from his school in the village struggling to embrace me. But I fled and hid under my mother's
bed while she screamed of remorse. Her hair was falling
badly and after a while we had to return to this country.

He tried to hang himself once. After my mother went to
the asylum he had hallucinations, his mother threw a dead
chicken at him, his father laughed and said the race was
no damn good, my mother appeared in her nightgown
screaming she had trapped herself in blackness. No white
doves flew. He had left Africa and was again in New York.
We lived in Harlem and no white doves flew. Sarah, Sarah,
he would say to me, the soldiers are coming and a cross
they are placing high on a tree and are dragging me
through the grass and nailing me upon the cross. My blood
is gushing. I wanted to live in Genesis in the midst of
golden savannas, nim and white frankopenny trees and

white stallions roaming under a blue sky. I wanted to walk
with a white dove. I wanted to be a Christian. Now I am
Judas, I betrayed my mother. I sent your mother to the
asylum. I created a yellow child who hates me. And he
tried to hang himself in a Harlem hotel.

> (*Blackout. A bald head is dropped on a string. We
> hear laughing.*)
>
> (DUCHESS'S *place: The next scene is done in the
> DUCHESS of HAPSBURG'S place which is a chandelier
> ballroom with snow falling, a black and white marble
> floor, a bench decorated with white flowers, all of this
> can be made of obviously fake materials as they would
> be in a funnyhouse. The DUCHESS is wearing a white
> dress and as in the previous scene a white headpiece
> with her kinky hair springing out from under it. In the
> scene are the DUCHESS and JESUS. JESUS enters the
> room which is at first dark, then suddenly brilliant, he
> starts to cry out at the DUCHESS who is seated on a
> bench under the chandelier, and pulls his hair from
> the red paper bag holding it up for the DUCHESS to
> see.*)

JESUS   My hair! (*The DUCHESS does not speak, JESUS
again screams.*)   My hair. (*Holding the hair up, waiting
for a reaction from the DUCHESS.*)

DUCHESS   (*as if oblivious*).   I have something I must show
you. (*She goes quickly to shutters and darkens the room,
returning standing before JESUS. She then slowly removes
her headpiece and from under it takes a mass of her hair.*)
When I awakened I found it fallen out, not all of it
but a mass that lay on my white pillow. I could see, although my hair hung down at the sides, clearly on my
white scalp it was missing. (*Her baldness is identical to
JESUS'S.*)

> (*A blackout. Then the light comes back up. They are
> both sitting on the bench examining each other's hair,*

running it through their fingers, then slowly the
DUCHESS *disappears behind the shutters and returns*
with a long red comb. She sits on the bench next to
JESUS *and starts to comb her remaining hair over her*
baldness. (This is done slowly.) JESUS *then takes*
the comb and proceeds to do the same to the DUCHESS
of HAPSBURG'S *hair. After they finish they place the*
DUCHESS'S *headpiece back on and we can see the*
strands of their hair falling to the floor. JESUS *then*
lies down across the bench while the DUCHESS *walks*
back and forth, the knocking does not cease.)

(They speak in unison as the DUCHESS *walks and*
JESUS *lies on the bench in the falling snow, staring*
at the ceiling.)

DUCHESS and JESUS *(their hair is falling more now, they
are both hideous).* My father isn't going to let us alone.
(Knocking.) Our father isn't going to let us alone, our
father is the darkest of us all, my mother was the fairest,
I am in between, but my father is the darkest of them all.
He is a black man. Our father is the darkest of them all.
He is a black man. My father is a dead man. *(Then they
suddenly look up at each other and scream, the lights go
to their heads and we see that they are totally bald.)*

(There is a knocking. Lights go to the stairs and the
LANDLADY.)

LANDLADY   He wrote to her saying he loved her and asked
for forgiveness. He begged her to take him off the cross.
(He had dreamed she would.) Stop them for tormenting
him, the one with the chicken and his cursing father. Her
mother's hair fell out, the race's hair fell out because he
left Africa, he said. He had tried to save them. She must
embrace him. He said his existence depended on her embrace. He wrote her from Africa where he is creating his
Christian center in the jungle and that is why he came
here. I know that he wanted her to return there with him

and not desert the race. He came to see her once before he tried to hang himself, appearing in the corridor of my apartment. I had let him in. I found him sitting on a bench in the hallway. He put out his hand to her, tried to take her in his arms, crying out—Forgiveness, Sarah, Is it that you will never forgive me for being black. I know you were a child of torment. But forgiveness. That was before his breakdown. Then, he wrote her and repeated that his mother hoped he would be Christ but he failed. He had married his mother because he could not resist the light. Yet, his mother from the beginning in the kerosene lamp of their dark rooms in Georgia said—I want you to be Jesus, to walk in Genesis and save the race, return to Africa, find revelation in the black. He went away.

But Easter morning, she got to feeling badly and went into Harlem to see him; the streets were filled with vendors selling lilies. He had checked out of that hotel. When she arrived back at my brownstone he was there, dressed badly, rather drunk. I had let him in again. He sat on a bench in the dark hallway, put out his hand to her, trying to take her in his arms, crying out—Forgiveness, Sarah. Forgiveness for my being black, Sarah. I know you are a child of torment. I know on dark winter afternoons you sat alone, weaving stories of your mother's beauty. But, Sarah, answer me, don't turn away, Sarah. Forgive my blackness. She would not answer. He put out his hand to her. She ran past him on the stairs, left him there with his hands out to me, repeating his past, saying his mother hoped he would be Christ. From the beginning in the kerosene lamp of their dark room, she said—Wally, I want you to be Jesus, to walk in Genesis and save the race. You must re-turn to Africa, Wally, find revelation in the midst of golden savannas, nim and white frankopenny trees and white stal-lions roaming under a blue sky. Wally, you must find the white dove and heal the pain of the race, heal the misery of the black man, Wally, take us off the cross, Wally. In the kerosene light she stared at him anguished from her old Negro face . . . but she ran past him leaving him. And now he is dead, she says, now he is dead. He left Africa and now Patrice Lumumba is dead.

(*The next scene is enacted back in the* DUCHESS *of* HAPSBURG's *place.* JESUS *is still in the* DUCHESS's *chamber, apparently he has fallen asleep and we see him awakening with the* DUCHESS *by his side, and then sitting as in a trance. He rises terrified and speaks.*)

JESUS   (*He is awakening*).   Through my apocalypses and my raging sermons I have tried so to escape him, through God Almighty I have tried to escape being black.   (*He then appears to rouse himself from his thoughts and calls.*) Duchess, Duchess   (*He looks about for her, there is no answer. He gets up slowly, walks back into the darkness and there we see that she is hanging on the chandelier, her bald head suddenly drops to the floor and she falls upon* JESUS. *He screams.*)   I am going to Africa and kill this black man named Patrice Lumumba. Why? Because all my life I believed my Holy Father to be God, but now I know that my father is a black man. I have no fear for whatever I do I will do in the name of God, I will do in the name of Albert Saxe Godburg, in the name of Victoria, Queen Victoria Regina, the monarch of England, I will.

(*Blackout.*)

(*Next scene. In the jungle, red run, flying things, wild black grass. The effect of the jungle is that it, unlike the other scenes, is over the entire scene. In time this is the longest scene in the play and is played the slow-est as the slow, almost standstill, stages of a dream. By lighting the desired effect would be—suddenly the jungle has overgrown the chambers and all the other places with a violence and a dark brightness, a grim yellowness.*)

(JESUS *is the first to appear in the center of the jungle
darkness. Unlike in previous scenes, he has a nimbus
above his head. As they each successively appear, they
all too have nimbuses atop their heads in a manner to
suggest that they are saviours.*)

JESUS   I always believed my father to be God.

(*Suddenly they all appear in various parts of the
jungle.* PATRICE LUMUMBA, *the* DUCHESS, VICTORIA,
*wandering about speaking at once. Their speeches
are mixed and repeated by one another.*)

He never tires of the journey, he who is the darkest one,
the darkest one of them all. My mother looked like a white
woman, hair as straight as any white woman's. I am yellow but he is black, the darkest one of us all. How I hoped
he was dead, yet he never tired of the journey. It was because of him that my mother died because she let a black
man put his hands on her. Why does he keep returning?
He keeps returning forever, keeps returning and returning
and he is my father. He is a black Negro. They told me
my father was God but my father is black. He is my father.
I am tied to a black Negro. He returned when I lived in
the south back in the twenties, when I was a child, he returned. Before I was born at the turn of the century, he
haunted my conception, diseased my birth . . . killed my
mother. He killed the light. My mother was the lightest
one. I am bound to him unless, of course, he should die.
But he is dead.
And he keeps returning. Then he is not dead.
Then he is not dead.
Yes, he is dead, but dead he comes knocking at my door.

(*This is repeated several times, finally reaching a loud
pitch and then all rushing about the grass. They stop
and stand perfectly still. All speaking tensely at various times in a chant.*)

I see him. The black ugly thing is sitting in his hallway, surrounded by his ebony masks, surrounded by the blackness of himself. My mother comes into the room. He is there with his hand out to me, groveling, saying—Forgiveness, Sarah, is it that you will never forgive me for being black.

Forgiveness, Sarah. I know you are a nigger of torment. Why? Christ would not rape anyone.

You will never forgive me for being black.

Wild beast. Why did you rape my mother?

Black beast, Christ would not rape anyone.

He is in grief from that black anguished face of his. Then at once the room will grow bright and my mother will come toward me smiling while I stand before his face and bludgeon him with an ebony head.

Forgiveness, Sarah, I know you are a nigger of torment.

(SILENCE—VICTORY: *Then they suddenly begin to laugh and shout as though they are in. They continue for some minutes running about laughing and shouting.*)

(*Blackout.*)

(*Another wall drops. There is a white plaster of* QUEEN VICTORIA *which represents the* NEGRO'S *room in the brownstone, the room appears near the staircases highly lit and small. The main prop is the statue but a bed could be suggested. The figure of* VICTORIA *is a sitting figure, one of astonishing repulsive whiteness, possessing the quality of nightmares and terror.* SARAH'S *room could be further suggested by dusty volumes of books and old yellowed walls. The* NEGRO SARAH *is standing perfectly still, we hear the knocking, the lights come on quickly, her father's black figures with bludgeoned hands rush upon her, the lights black and we see her hanging in the room.*)

(*Lights come on the laughing* LANDLADY. *At the same time remain on the hanging figure of the* NEGRO.)

LANDLADY   The poor bitch has hung herself.

(FUNNYMAN RAYMOND *appears from his room at the commotion.*)

LANDLADY   The poor bitch has hung herself.

RAYMOND   (*observing her hanging figure*). She was a funny little liar.

LANDLADY   (*informing him*). Her father hung himself in a Harlem hotel when Patrice Lumumba died.

RAYMOND   She was a funny little liar.

LANDLADY   Her father hung himself in a Harlem hotel when Patrice Lumumba died.

RAYMOND   Her father never hung himself in a Harlem hotel when Patrice Lumumba was murdered.
    I know the man. He is a doctor, married to a white whore. He lives in the city in a room with European antiques, photographs of Roman ruins, walls of books and oriental carpets. Her father is a nigger who eats his meals on a white glass table.

CURTAIN

PURLIE VICTORIOUS

A Comedy in Three Acts

Ossie Davis

OSSIE DAVIS was born in Cogdell, Georgia, in 1917. He attended Howard University and later made his theatrical debut as an actor with the Rose McClendon's Players, appearing in *Joy, Exceeding Glory* in 1941. During his army service he wrote and directed plays, and on his return from service he made his Broadway debut in the title role of *Jeb* at the Martin Beck Theatre on February 21, 1946. Subsequently he became one of the leading Black actors in the New York theatre, appearing in such plays as the revival of *Green Pastures, No Time for Sergeants, The Wisteria Trees, Jamaica*, and eventually playing the Walter Lee Younger part in *A Raisin in the Sun.*

In 1961 he wrote and played the title role in *Purlie Victorious* which opened at the Court Theatre on September 28, 1961, and ran for 261 performances. Appearing opposite him was his wife, Ruby Dee, in the role of Lutiebelle. A boisterous film of *Purlie Victorious* was adapted by Davis and he and Ruby Dee performed in it. Ossie Davis continues to be a leading actor in television, films and on the stage.

Although Harold Cruse, in *The Crisis of the Negro Intellectual*, can accuse Ossie Davis of integrating his blackness into the commercialization of Broadway, *Purlie Victorious* is a deft comic "put-down" and "put-on" of both black and white. In accepting the clichés by which we separate ourselves one from another, and the stereotypes which we attach to each other's character and action, Davis has constructed a brilliant comedy containing the most inventive humor of any modern American play. It is humor born of a keen, intellectual mind tempered by the passion for justice for all men. *Purlie Victorious* is unique not alone in accomplishing its aesthetic aims, but as a play creating new fictions that may become the material stuff of our lives.

PURLIE VICTORIOUS

Characters

PURLIE VICTORIOUS JUDSON
LUTIEBELLE GUSSIEMAE JENKINS
MISSY JUDSON
GITLOW JUDSON
CHARLIE COTCHIPEE
IDELLA LANDY
OL' CAP'N COTCHIPEE
THE SHERIFF
THE DEPUTY

"Our churches will say segregation is immoral because it makes per-fectly wonderful people, white and black, do immoral things; . . .

Our courts will say segregation is illegal because it makes perfectly wonderful people, white and black, do illegal things; . . .

And finally our Theatre will say segregation is ridiculous because it makes perfectly wonderful people, white and black, do ridiculous things!"

—From "Purlie's I.O.U."

Act I

Scene 1

PLACE   *The cotton plantation country of the Old South*

TIME   *The recent past*

SCENE   *The setting is the plain and simple interior of an antiquated, run-down farmhouse such as Negro sharecroppers still live in, in South Georgia. Threadbare but warm-hearted, shabby but clean. In the Center is a large, rough-hewn table with three homemade chairs and a small bench. This table is the center of all family activities. The main entrance is a door in the Upstage Right corner, which leads in from a rickety porch which we cannot see. There is a small archway in the opposite corner, with some long strips of gunny-sacking hanging down to serve as a door, which leads off to the kitchen. In the center of the Right wall is a window that is wooden, which opens outward on hinges. Downstage Right is a small door leading off to a bedroom, and opposite, Downstage Left, another door leads out into the backyard, and on into the cotton fields beyond. There is also a smaller table and a cupboard against the wall. An old dresser stands against the Right wall, between the window and the Downstage door. There is a shelf on the Left wall with a pail of drinking water, and a large tin dipper. Various cooking utensils, and items like salt and pepper are scattered about in appropriate places.*

AT RISE   *The CURTAIN rises on a stage in semi-darkness. After a moment, when the LIGHTS have come up, the door in the Up Right corner bursts open: Enter* PURLIE JUDSON. PURLIE JUDSON *is tall, restless, and commanding. In his middle or late thirties, he wears a wide-brim, ministerial black hat, a string tie, and a claw hammer coat, which, though far from new, does not fit him too badly. His arms are loaded with large boxes and parcels, which must have come fresh from a department store.* PURLIE *is a man consumed with that divine impatience, without which nothing truly good, or truly bad, or even truly ridiculous, is ever accomplished in this world—with rhetoric and flourish to match.*

The text printed here is from the Samuel French Acting Edition (New York: Samuel French, Inc., 1961).

279

PURLIE   (*Calling out loudly.*)   Missy!   (*No answer.*)   Gitlow!—It's me—Purlie Victorious!   (*Still no answer.* PUR-
LIE *empties his overloaded arms, with obvious relief, on
top of the big Center table. He stands, mops his brow, and
blows.*)   Nobody home it seems.   (*This last he says to
someone he assumes has come in with him. When there is
no answer he hurries to the door through which he entered.*)   Come on—come on in!

> (*Enter* LUTIEBELLE JENKINS, *slowly, as if bemused.
> Young, eager, well-built: though we cannot tell it at
> the moment. Clearly a girl from the backwoods, she
> carries a suitcase tied up with a rope in one hand, and
> a greasy shoebox with what's left of her lunch, to-
> gether with an out-moded, out-sized handbag, in the
> other. Obviously she has traveled a great distance, but
> she still manages to look fresh and healthy. Her hat is
> a horror with feathers, but she wears it like a banner.
> Her shoes are flat-heeled and plain white, such as a
> good servant girl in the white folks' kitchen who knows
> her place absolutely is bound to wear. Her fall coat is
> dowdy, but well-intentioned with a stingy strip of rab-
> bit fur around the neck.* LUTIEBELLE *is like thousands
> of Negro girls you might know. Eager, desirous—even
> anxious, keenly in search for life and for love, trem-
> bling on the brink of self-confident and vigorous
> young womanhood—but afraid to take the final leap:
> because no one has ever told her it is no longer neces-
> sary to be white in order to be virtuous, charming, or
> beautiful.*)

LUTIEBELLE   (*Looking around as if at a museum of great
importance.*)   Nobody home it seems.

PURLIE   (*Annoyed to find himself so exactly echoed, looks
at her sharply. He takes his watch from his vest pocket,
where he wears it on a chain.*)   Cotton-picking time in

Georgia it's against the law to be home. Come in—unload yourself. (*Crosses and looks out into the kitchen.* LUTIE-BELLE *is so enthralled, she still stands with all her bags and parcels in her arm.*)   Set your suitcase down.

LUTIEBELLE   What?

PURLIE   It's making you lopsided.

LUTIEBELLE   (*Snapping out of it.*)   It is? I didn't even notice. (*Sets suitcase, lunch box, and parcels down.*)

PURLIE   (*Studies her for a moment; goes and gently takes off her hat.*)   Tired?

LUTIEBELLE   Not stepping high as I am!

PURLIE   (*Takes the rest of her things and sets them on the table.*)   Hungry?

LUTIEBELLE   No, sir. But there's still some of my lunch left if you—

PURLIE   (*Quickly.*)   No, thank you. Two ham-hock sandwiches in one day is my limit. (*Sits down and fans himself with his hat.*)   Sorry I had to walk you so far so fast.

LUTIEBELLE   (*Dreamily.*)   Oh, I didn't mind, sir. Walking's good for you, Miz Emmylou sez—

PURLIE   Miz Emmylou can afford to say that: Miz Emmylou got a car. While all the transportation we got in the world is tied up in second-hand shoe leather. But never mind, my sister, never-you-mind! (*Rises, almost as if to dance, exaltation glowing in his eyes.*)   And toll the bell, Big Bethel—toll that big, black, fat and sassy liberty bell! Tell Freedom the bridegroom cometh; the day of her deliverance is now at hand! (PURLIE *catches sight of* MISSY *through door Down Left.*)   Oh, there she is. (*Crosses to door and calls out.*)   Missy!—Oh, Missy!

MISSY   (*From a distance.*)   Yes-s-s-s-!

PURLIE   It's me!—Purlie!

MISSY   Purlie Victorious?

PURLIE   Yes. Put that battling stick down and come on in here!

MISSY   All right!

PURLIE   (*Crosses hurriedly back to above table at Center.*) That's Missy, my sister-in-law I was telling you about. (*Clears the table of everything but one of the large cartons, which he proceeds to open.*)

LUTIEBELLE   (*Not hearing him. Still awe-struck to be in the very house, in perhaps the very same room that* PURLIE *might have been born in.*) So this is the house where you was born and bred at.

PURLIE   Yep! Better'n being born outdoors.

LUTIEBELLE   What a lovely background for your home-life.

PURLIE   I wouldn't give it to my dog to raise fleas in!

LUTIEBELLE   So clean—and nice—and warm-hearted!

PURLIE   The first chance I get I'ma burn the damn thing down!

LUTIEBELLE   But—Reb'n Purlie!—It's yours, and that's what counts. Like Miz Emmylou sez—

PURLIE   Come here! (*Pulls her across to the window, flings it open.*) You see that big white house, perched on top of that hill with them two windows looking right down at us like two eyeballs: that's where Ol' Cap'n lives.

LUTIEBELLE   Ol' Cap'n?

PURLIE   Stonewall Jackson Cotchipee. He owns this dump, not me.

LUTIEBELLE   Oh—

PURLIE   And that ain't all: hill and dale, field and farm, truck and tractor, horse and mule, bird and bee and bush and tree—and cotton!—cotton by bole and by bale—every bit o' cotton you see in this county!—Everything and everybody he owns!

LUTIEBELLE   Everybody? You mean he owns people?

PURLIE   (*Bridling his impatience.*) Well—look!—ain't a man, woman or child working in this valley that ain't in debt to that ol' bastard!— (*Catches himself.*) bustard!— (*This still won't do.*) buzzard!—And that includes Gitlow and Missy—everybody—except me.—

LUTIEBELLE   But folks can't own people no more, Reb'n Purlie. Miz Emmylou sez that—

PURLIE   (*Verging on explosion.*) You ain't working for Miz Emmylou no more, you're working for me—Purlie Victorious. Freedom is my business, and I say that ol' man runs this plantation on debt: the longer you work for Ol' Cap'n Cotchipee, the more you owe at the commissary; and if you don't pay up, you can't leave. And I don't give a damn what Miz Emmylou nor nobody else sez—that's slavery!

LUTIEBELLE   I'm sorry, Reb'n Purlie—

PURLIE   Don't apologize, wait!—Just wait!—til I get my church;—wait til I buy Big Bethel back— (*Crosses to window and looks out.*) Wait til I stand once again in the pulpit of Grandpaw Kincaid, and call upon my people and talk to my people— About Ol' Cap'n, that miserable son-of-a—

LUTIEBELLE   (*Just in time to save him.*) Wait—!

PURLIE   Wait, I say! And we'll see who's gonna dominize this valley!—him or me! (*Turns and sees* MISSY *through door Down Left.*) Missy—!

(*Enter* MISSY, *ageless, benign, and smiling. She wears a ragged old straw hat, a big house apron over her faded gingham, and low-cut, dragged-out tennis shoes on her feet. She is strong and of good cheer—of a cer-*

(*tain shrewdness, yet full of the desire to believe. Her eyes light on* LUTIEBELLE, *and her arms go up and outward automatically.*)

MISSY   Purlie!

PURLIE   (*Thinks she is reaching for him.*)   Missy!

MISSY   (*Ignoring him, clutching* LUTIEBELLE, *laughing and crying.*)   Well—well—well!

PURLIE   (*Breaking the stranglehold.*)   For God's sake, Missy, don't choke her to death!

MISSY   All my life—all my life I been praying for me a daughter just like you. My prayers is been answered at last. Welcome to our home, whoever you is!

LUTIEBELLE   (*Deeply moved.*)   Thank you, m'am.

MISSY   "M'am—m'am." Listen to the child, Purlie. Everybody down here calls me Aunt Missy, and I'd be much obliged if you would, too.

LUTIEBELLE   It would make me very glad to do so—Aunt Missy.

MISSY   Uhmmmmmm! Pretty as a pan of buttermilk biscuits. Where on earth did you find her, Purlie?   (PURLIE *starts to answer.*)   Let me take your things—now, you just make yourself at home— Are you hungry?

LUTIEBELLE   No, m'am, but cheap as water is, I sure ain't got no business being this thirsty!

MISSY   (*Starts forward.*)   I'll get some for you—

PURLIE   (*Intercepts her; directs* LUTIEBELLE.)   There's the dipper. And right out yonder by the fence just this side of that great big live oak tree you'll find the well—sweetest water in Cotchipee county.

LUTIEBELLE   Thank you, Reb'n Purlie. I'm very much obliged.   (*Takes dipper from water pail and exits Down Left.*)

MISSY   Reb'n who?

PURLIE   (*Looking off after* LUTIEBELLE.) Perfection—absolute Ethiopian perfect. Hah, Missy?

MISSY   (*Looking off after* LUTIEBELLE.) Oh, I don't know about that.

PURLIE   What you mean you don't know? This girl looks more like Cousin Bee than Cousin Bee ever did.

MISSY   No resemblance to me.

PURLIE   Don't be ridiculous; she's the spitting image—

MISSY   No resemblance whatsoever!

PURLIE   I ought to know how my own cousin looked—

MISSY   But I was the last one to see her alive—

PURLIE   Twins, if not closer!

MISSY   Are you crazy? Bee was more lean, loose, and leggy—

PURLIE   Maybe so, but this girl makes it up in—

MISSY   With no chin to speak of—her eyes: sort of fickle one to another—

PURLIE   I know, but even so—

MISSY   (*Pointing off in* LUTIEBELLE'S *direction.*) Look at her head—it ain't nearly as built like a rutabaga as Bee's own was!

PURLIE   (*Exasperated.*) What's the difference! White folks can't tell one of us from another by the head!

MISSY   Twenty years ago it was, Purlie, Ol' Cap'n laid bull whip to your natural behind—

PURLIE   Twenty years ago I swore I'd see his soul in hell!

MISSY   And I don't think you come full back to your senses yet—That ol' man ain't no fool!

PURLIE   That makes it one "no fool" against another.

MISSY   He's dangerous, Purlie. We could get killed if that old man was to find out what we was trying to do to get that church back.

PURLIE   How can he find out? Missy, how many times must I tell you, if it's one thing I am foolproof in it's white folks' psychology.

MISSY   That's exactly what I'm afraid of.

PURLIE   Freedom, Missy, that's what Big Bethel means. For you, me and Gitlow. And we can buy it for five hundred dollars, Missy. Freedom!—You want it, or don't you?

MISSY   Of course I want it, but— After all, Purlie, that rich ol' lady didn't exactly leave that $500 to us—

PURLIE   She left it to Aunt Henrietta—

MISSY   Aunt Henrietta is dead—

PURLIE   Exactly—

MISSY   And Henrietta's daughter Cousin Bee is dead, too.

PURLIE   Which makes us next in line to inherit the money by law!

MISSY   All right, then, why don't we just go on up that hill man-to-man and tell Ol' Cap'n we want our money?

PURLIE   Missy! You have been black as long as I have—

MISSY   (*Not above having her own little joke.*) Hell, boy, we could make him give it to us.

PURLIE   Make him—how? He's a white man, Missy. What you plan to do, sue him?

MISSY   (*Drops her teasing; thinks seriously for a moment.*) After all, it is our money. And it was our church.

PURLIE   And can you think of a better way to get it back than that girl out there?

MISSY   But you think it'll work, Purlie? You really think she can fool Ol' Cap'n?

PURLIE   He'll never know what hit him.

MISSY   Maybe—but there's still the question of Gitlow.

PURLIE   What about Gitlow?

MISSY   Gitlow has changed his mind.

PURLIE   Then you'll have to change it back.

GITLOW   (*Offstage.*)   Help, Missy; help, Missy; help, Missy; help, Missy!   (GITLOW *runs on.*)

MISSY   What the devil's the matter this time?

GITLOW   There I was, Missy, picking in the high cotton, twice as fast as the human eye could see. All of a sudden I missed a bole and it fell—it fell on the ground, Missy! I stooped as fast as I could to pick it up and—   (*He stoops to illustrate. There is a loud tearing of cloth.*)   ripped the seat of my britches. There I was, Missy, exposed from stem to stern.

MISSY   What's so awful about that? It's only cotton.

GITLOW   But cotton is white, Missy. We must maintain respect. Bring me my Sunday School britches.

MISSY   What!

GITLOW   Ol' Cap'n is coming down into the cotton patch today, and I know you want your Gitlow to look his level best.   (MISSY *starts to answer.*)   Hurry, Missy, hurry!   (GITLOW *hurries her off.*)

PURLIE   Gitlow— have I got the girl!

GITLOW   Is that so—what girl?

PURLIE   (*Taking him to the door.*)   See? There she is! Well?

GITLOW   Well what?

PURLIE   What do you think?

GITLOW   Nope; she'll never do.

PURLIE   What you mean, she'll never do?

GITLOW   My advice to you is to take that girl back to Florida as fast as you can!

PURLIE   I can't take her back to Florida.

GITLOW   Why can't you take her back to Florida?

PURLIE   'Cause she comes from Alabama. Gitlow, look at her: she's just the size—just the type—just the style.

GITLOW   And just the girl to get us all in jail. The answer is no! (*Crosses to kitchen door.*) MISSY! (*Back to* PUR- LIE.) Girl or no girl, I ain't getting mixed up in no more of your nightmares—I got my own. Dammit, Missy, I said let's go!

MISSY   (*Entering with trousers.*) You want me to take my bat to you again?

GITLOW   No, Missy, control yourself. It's just that every sec- ond Gitlow's off the firing line-up, seven pounds of Ol' Cap'n's cotton don't git gotten. (*Snatches pants from* MISSY, *but is in too much of a hurry to put them on—starts off.*)

PURLIE   Wait a minute, Gitlow. . . . Wait! (GITLOW *is off in a flash.*) Missy! Stop him!

MISSY   He ain't as easy to stop as he used to be. Especially now Ol' Cap'n's made him Deputy-For-The-Colored.

PURLIE   Deputy-For-The-Colored? What the devil is that?

MISSY   Who knows? All I know is Gitlow's changed his mind.

PURLIE   But Gitlow can't change his mind!

MISSY   Oh, it's easy enough when you ain't got much to start with. I warned you. You don't know how shifty ol' Git can git. He's the hardest man to convince and keep convinced I ever seen in my life.

PURLIE   Missy, you've got to make him go up that hill, he's got to identify this girl—Ol' Cap'n won't believe nobody else.

MISSY   I know—

PURLIE   He's got to swear before Ol' Cap'n that this girl is the real Cousin Bee—

MISSY   I know.

PURLIE   Missy, you're the only person in this world ol' Git'll really listen to.

MISSY   I know.

PURLIE   And what if you do have to hit him a time or two—it's for his own good!

MISSY   I know.

PURLIE   He'll recover from it, Missy. He always does—

MISSY   I know.

PURLIE   Freedom, Missy—Big Bethel; for you; me; and Gitlow—!

MISSY   Freedom—and a little something left over—that's all I ever wanted all my life. (*Looks out into the yard.*) She do look a little somewhat like Cousin Bee—about the feet!

PURLIE   Of course she does—

MISSY   I won't guarantee nothing, Purlie—but I'll try.

PURLIE   (*Grabbing her and dancing her around.*) Everytime I see you, Missy, you get prettier by the pound!

    (LUTIEBELLE *enters.* MISSY *sees her.*)

MISSY   Stop it, Purlie, stop it! Stop it. Quit cutting the fool in front of company!

PURLIE   (*Sees* LUTIEBELLE, *crosses to her, grabs her about the waist and swings her around too.*)
    How wondrous are the daughters of my people,
    Yet knoweth not the glories of themselves!

    (*Spins her around for* MISSY'S *inspection. She does look better with her coat off, in her immaculate blue and white maid's uniform.*)

Where do you suppose I found her, Missy—
This Ibo prize—this Zulu Pearl—
This long lost lily of the black Mandingo—
Kikuyu maid, beneath whose brown embrace
Hot suns of Africa are burning still: where—where?
A drudge; a serving wench; a feudal fetch-pot:
A common scullion in the white man's kitchen.
Drowned is her youth in thankless Southern dishpans;
Her beauty spilt for Dixiecratic pigs!
This brown-skinned grape! this wine of Negro vintage—

MISSY   (*Interrupting.*)   I know all that, Purlie, but what's
her name?
          (PURLIE *looks at* LUTIEBELLE *and turns abruptly
          away.*)

LUTIEBELLE   I don't think he likes my name so much—it's
Lutiebelle, ma'am—Lutiebelle Gussiemae Jenkins!

MISSY   (*Gushing with motherly reassurance.*)   Lutiebelle
Gussiemae Jenkins! My, that's nice.

PURLIE   Nice! It's an insult to the Negro people!

MISSY   Purlie, behave yourself!

PURLIE   A previous condition of servitude, a badge of in-
feriority, and I refuse to have it in my organization!—
change it!

MISSY   You want me to box your mouth for you!

PURLIE   Lutiebelle Gussiemae Jenkins! What does it mean
in Swahili? Cheap labor!

LUTIEBELLE   Swahili?

PURLIE   One of the thirteen silver tongues of Africa: Swahili, Bushengo, Ashanti, Baganda, Herero, Yoruba, Bam-
bora, Mpongwe, Swahili: a language of moons, of velvet
drums; hot days of rivers, red-splashed, and bird-song
bright!, black fingers in rice white at sunset red!—ten
thousand Queens of Sheba—

MISSY   (*Having to interrupt.*)   Just where did Purlie find you, honey?

LUTIEBELLE   It was in Dothan, Alabama, last Sunday, Aunt Missy, right in the junior choir!

MISSY   The junior choir—my, my, my!

PURLIE   (*Still carried away.*)

Behold! I said, this dark and holy vessel,
In whom should burn that golden nut-brown joy
Which Negro womanhood was meant to be.
Ten thousand queens, ten thousand Queens of Sheba:

    (*Pointing at* LUTIEBELLE.)

Ethiopia herself—in all her beauteous wonder,
Come to restore the ancient thrones of Cush!

MISSY   Great Gawdamighty, Purlie, I can't hear myself think—!

LUTIEBELLE   That's just what I said last Sunday, Aunt Missy, when Reb'n Purlie started preaching that thing in the pulpit.

MISSY   Preaching it!?

LUTIEBELLE   Lord, Aunt Missy, I shouted clear down to the Mourners' Bench.

MISSY   (*To* PURLIE.)   But last time you was a professor of Negro Philosophy.

PURLIE   I told you, Missy: my intention is to buy Big Bethel back; to reclaim the ancient pulpit of Grandpaw Kincaid, and preach freedom in the cotton patch—I told you!

MISSY   Maybe you did, Purlie, maybe you did. You got yourself a license?

PURLIE   Naw!—but—

MISSY   (*Looking him over.*)   Purlie Victorious Judson: Self-made minister of the gospel-claw-hammer coattail, shoe-string tie and all.

PURLIE   (*Quietly but firmly holding his ground.*)   How else can you lead the Negro people?

MISSY   Is that what you got in your mind: leading the
     Negro people?

PURLIE   Who else is they got?

MISSY   God help the race.

LUTIEBELLE   It was a sermon, I mean, Aunt Missy, the likes
     of which has never been heard before.

MISSY   Oh, I bet that. Tell me about it, son. What did you
     preach?

PURLIE   I preached the New Baptism of Freedom for all
     mankind, according to the Declaration of Independence,
     taking as my text the Constitution of the United States of
     America, Amendments First through Fifteenth, which
     readeth as follows: "Congress shall make no law—"

MISSY   Enough—that's enough, son—I'm converted. But it
     is confusing, all the changes you keep going through. (*To*
     LUTIEBELLE.)   Honey, every time I see Purlie he's some-
     body else.

PURLIE   Not any more, Missy; and if I'm lying may the good
     Lord put me down in the book of bad names: Purlie is
     put forever!

MISSY   Yes. But will he stay put forever?

PURLIE   There is in every man a finger of iron that points
     him what he must and must not do—

MISSY   And your finger points up the hill to that five hun-
     dred dollars with which you'll buy Big Bethel back, preach
     freedom in the cotton patch, and live happily ever after!

PURLIE   The soul-consuming passion of my life! (*Draws
     out watch.*)   It's 2:15, Missy, and Gitlow's waiting. Missy,
     I suggest you get a move on.

MISSY   I already got a move on. Had it since four o'clock
     this morning!

PURLIE   Time, Missy—exactly what the colored man in this
     country ain't got, and you're wasting it!

MISSY   (*Looks at* PURLIE, *and decides not to strike him dead.*)   Purlie, would you mind stepping out into the cotton patch and telling your brother Gitlow I'd like a few words with him? (PURLIE, *overjoyed, leaps at* MISSY *as if to hug and dance her around again, but she is too fast.*) Do like I tell you now—go on! (PURLIE *exits singing.* MISSY *turns to* LUTIEBELLE *to begin the important task of sizing her up.*)   Besides, it wouldn't be hospitable not to set and visit a spell with our distinguished guest over from Dothan, Alabama.

LUTIEBELLE   (*This is the first time she has been called anything of importance by anybody.*)   Thank you, ma'am.

MISSY   Now. Let's you and me just set back and enjoy a piece of my potato pie. You like potato pie, don't you?

LUTIEBELLE   Oh, yes, ma'am, I like it very much.

MISSY   And get real acquainted.   (*Offers her a saucer with a slice of pie on it.*)

LUTIEBELLE   I'm ever so much obliged. My, this looks nice! Uhm, uhn, uhn!

MISSY   (*Takes a slice for herself and sits down.*)   You know —ever since that ol' man— (*Indicates up the hill.*)   took after Purlie so unmerciful with that bull whip twenty years ago—he fidgets! Always on the go; rattling around from place to place all over the country: one step ahead of the white folks—something about Purlie always did irritate the white folks.

LUTIEBELLE   Is that the truth!

MISSY   Oh, my yes. Finally wound up being locked up a time or two for safekeeping— (LUTIEBELLE *parts with a loud, sympathetic grunt. Changing her tack a bit.*)   Always kept up his schooling, though. In fact that boy's got one of the best second-hand educations in this country.

LUTIEBELLE   (*Brightening considerably.*)   Is that a fact!

MISSY   Used to read everything he could get his hands on.

LUTIEBELLE   He did? Ain't that wonderful!

MISSY   Till one day he finally got tired, and threw all his books to the hogs—not enough "Negro" in them, he said. After that he puttered around with first one thing then another. Remember that big bus boycott they had in Montgomery? Well, we don't travel by bus in the cotton patch, so Purlie boycotted mules!

LUTIEBELLE   You don't say so?

MISSY   Another time he invented a secret language, that Negroes could understand but white folks couldn't.

LUTIEBELLE   Oh, my goodness gracious!

MISSY   He sent it C.O.D. to the NAACP but they never answered his letter.

LUTIEBELLE   Oh, they will, Aunt Missy; you can just bet your life they will.

MISSY   I don't mind it so much. Great leaders are bound to pop up from time to time 'mongst our people—in fact we sort of look forward to it. But Purlie's in such a hurry I'm afraid he'll lose his mind.

LUTIEBELLE   Lose his mind—no! Oh, no!

MISSY   That is unless you and me can do something about it.

LUTIEBELLE   You and me? Do what, Aunt Missy? You tell me—I'll do anything!

MISSY   (*Having found all she needs to know.*) Well, now; ain't nothing ever all that peculiar about a man a good wife—and a family—and some steady home cooking won't cure. Don't you think so?

LUTIEBELLE   (*Immensely relieved.*) Oh, yes, Aunt Missy, yes. (*But still not getting* MISSY's *intent.*) You'd be surprised how many tall, good-looking, great big, ol' handsome looking mens—just like Reb'n Purlie—walking around, starving theyselves to death! Oh, I just wish I had one to aim my pot at!

MISSY Well, Purlie Judson is the uncrowned appetite of the age.

LUTIEBELLE He is! What's his favorite?

MISSY Anything! Anything a fine-looking, strong and healthy—girl like you could put on the table.

LUTIEBELLE Like me? Like ME! Oh, Aunt Missy—!

MISSY (PURLIE'S *future is settled.*) Honey, I mind once at the Sunday School picnic Purlie et a whole sack o' pullets!

LUTIEBELLE Oh, I just knowed there was something— something—just reeks about that man. He puts me in the mind of all the good things I ever had in my life. Picnics, fish-fries, corn-shuckings, and love-feasts, and gospel-sing-ings—picking huckleberries, roasting groundpeas, quilt-ing-bee parties and barbecues; that certain kind of—wel-come—you can't get nowhere else in all this world. Aunt Missy, life is so good to us—sometimes!

MISSY Oh, child, being colored can be a lotta fun when ain't nobody looking.

LUTIEBELLE Ain't it the truth! I always said I'd never pass for white, no matter how much they offered me, unless the things I love could pass, too.

MISSY Ain't it the beautiful truth!

(PURLIE *enters again; agitated.*)

PURLIE Missy—Gitlow says if you want him come and get him!

MISSY (*Rises, crosses to door Down Left; looks out.*) Lawd, that man do take his cotton picking seriously. (*Comes back to* LUTIEBELLE *and takes her saucer.*) Did you get enough to eat, honey?

LUTIEBELLE   Indeed I did. And Aunt Missy, I haven't had potato pie like that since the senior choir give—

MISSY   (*Still ignoring him.*)   That's where I met Gitlow, you know. On the senior choir.

LUTIEBELLE   Aunt Missy! I didn't know you could sing!

MISSY   Like a brown-skin nightingale. Well, it was a Sunday afternoon—Big Bethel had just been—

PURLIE   Dammit, Missy! The white man is five hundred years ahead of us in this country, and we ain't gonna ever gonna catch up with him sitting around on our non-Caucasian rumps talking about the senior choir!

MISSY   (*Starts to bridle at this sudden display of passion, but changes her mind.*)   Right this way, honey.   (*Heads for door Down Right.*)   Where Cousin Bee used to sleep at.

LUTIEBELLE   Yes, ma'am.   (*Starts to follow* MISSY.)

PURLIE   (*Stopping her.*)   Wait a minute—don't forget your clothes!   (*Gives her a large carton.*)

MISSY   It ain't much, the roof leaks, and you can get as much September inside as you can outside any time; but I try to keep it clean.

PURLIE   Cousin Bee was known for her clothes!

MISSY   Stop nagging, Purlie—   (*To* LUTIEBELLE.)   There's plenty to eat in the kitchen.

LUTIEBELLE   Thank you, Aunt Missy.   (*Exits Down Right.*)

PURLIE   (*Following after her.*)   And hurry! We want to leave as soon as Missy gets Gitlow in from the cotton patch!

MISSY   (*Blocking his path.*)   Mr. Preacher—   (*She pulls him out of earshot.*)   If we do pull this thing off—   (*Studying him a moment.*)   what do you plan to do with her after that—send her back where she came from?

PURLIE   Dothan, Alabama? Never! Missy, there a million things I can do with a girl like that, right here in Big Bethel!

MISSY   Yeah! Just make sure they're all legitimate. Anyway, marriage is still cheap, and we can always use another cook in the family! (PURLIE *hasn't the slightest idea what* MISSY *is talking about.*)

LUTIEBELLE   (*From Offstage.*)   Aunt Missy.

MISSY   Yes, honey.

LUTIEBELLE   (*Offstage.*)   Whose picture is this on the dresser?

MISSY   Why, that's Cousin Bee.

LUTIEBELLE   (*A moment's silence. Then she enters hastily, carrying a large photograph in her hand.*)   Cousin Bee!

MISSY   Yes, poor thing. She's the one the whole thing is all about.

LUTIEBELLE   (*The edge of panic.*)   Cousin Bee— Oh, my! —Oh, my goodness! My goodness gracious!

MISSY   What's the matter?

LUTIEBELLE   But she's pretty—she's so pretty!

MISSY   (*Takes photograph; looks at it tenderly.*)   Yes—she was pretty. I guess they took this shortly before she died.

LUTIEBELLE   And you mean—you want me to look like her?

PURLIE   That's the idea. Now go and get into your clothes. (*Starts to push her off.*)

MISSY   They sent it down to us from the college. Don't she look smart? I'll bet she was a good student when she was living.

LUTIEBELLE   (*Evading* PURLIE.)   Good student!

MISSY   Yes. One more year and she'd have finished.

LUTIEBELLE   Oh, my gracious Lord have mercy upon my poor soul!

PURLIE   (*Not appreciating her distress or its causes.*)
Awake, awake! Put on thy strength, O, Zion—put on thy
beautiful garments. (*Hurries her Offstage.*)   And hurry!
(*Turning to* MISSY.)   Missy, Big Bethel and Gitlow is
waiting. Grandpaw Kincaid gave his life. (*Gently places
the bat into her hand.*)   It is a far greater thing you do
now, than you've ever done before—and Gitlow ain't never
got his head knocked off in a better cause. (MISSY *nods
her head in sad agreement, and accepts the bat.* PURLIE
*helps her to the door Down Left, where she exits, a most
reluctant executioner.* PURLIE *stands and watches her off
from the depth of his satisfaction. The door Down Right
eases open, and* LUTIEBELLE, *her suitcase, handbag, fall
coat and lunch box firmly in hand, tries to sneak out the
front door.* PURLIE *hears her, and turns just in time.*)
Where do you think you're going?

LUTIEBELLE   Did you see that, Reb'n Purlie? (*Indicating
bedroom from which she just came.*)   Did you see all them
beautiful clothes—slips, hats, shoes, stockings? I mean ny-
lon stockings like Miz Emmylou wears—and a dress, like
even Miz Emmylou don't wear. Did you look at what was
in that big box?

PURLIE   Of course I looked at what was in that big box—
I bought it—all of it—for you.

LUTIEBELLE   For me!

PURLIE   Of course! I told you! And as soon as we finish you
can have it!

LUTIEBELLE   Reb'n Purlie, I'm a good girl. I ain't never
done nothing in all this world, white, colored or otherwise,
to hurt nobody!

PURLIE   I know that.

LUTIEBELLE   I work hard; I mop, I scrub, I iron; I'm clean
and polite, and I know how to get along with white folks'
children better'n they do. I pay my church dues every

second and fourth Sunday the Lord sends; and I can cook catfish—and hushpuppies— You like hushpuppies, don't you, Reb'n Purlie?

PURLIE   I love hushpuppies!

LUTIEBELLE   Hushpuppies—and corn dodgers; I can cook you a corn dodger would give you the swimming in the head!

PURLIE   I'm sure you can, but—

LUTIEBELLE   But I ain't never been in a mess like this in all my life!

PURLIE   Mess—what mess?

LUTIEBELLE   You mean go up that hill, in all them pretty clothes, and pretend—in front of white folks—that—that I'm your Cousin Bee—somebody I ain't never seen or heard of before in my whole life!

PURLIE   Why not? Some of the best pretending in the world is done in front of white folks.

LUTIEBELLE   But Reb'n Purlie, I didn't know your Cousin Bee was a student at the college; I thought she worked there!

PURLIE   But I told you on the train—

LUTIEBELLE   Don't do no good to tell ME nothing, Reb'n Purlie! I never listen. Ask Miz Emmylou and 'em, they'll tell you I never listen. I didn't know it was a college lady you wanted me to make like. I thought it was for a sleep-in like me. I thought all that stuff you bought in them boxes was stuff for maids and cooks and— Why, I ain't never even been near a college!

PURLIE   So what? College ain't so much where you been as how you talk when you get back. Anybody can do it; look at me.

LUTIEBELLE   Nawsir, I think you better look at me like Miz Emmylou sez—

PURLIE   (*Taking her by the shoulders, tenderly.*) Calm
down—just take it easy, and calm down. (*She subsides a
little, her chills banished by the warmth of him.*) Now
—don't tell me, after all that big talking you done on the
train about white folks, you're scared.

LUTIEBELLE   Talking big is easy—from the proper distance.

PURLIE   Why—don't you believe in yourself?

LUTIEBELLE   Some.

PURLIE   Don't you believe in your own race of people?

LUTIEBELLE   Oh, yessir—a little.

PURLIE   Don't you believe the black man is coming to power
some day?

LUTIEBELLE   Almost.

PURLIE   Ten thousand Queens of Sheba! What kind of a
Negro are you! Where's your race pride?

LUTIEBELLE   Oh, I'm a great one for race pride, sir, believe
me—it's just that I don't need it much in my line of work!
Miz Emmylou sez—

PURLIE   Damn Miz Emmylou! Does her blond hair and blue
eyes make her any more of a woman in the sight of her
men folks than your black hair and brown eyes in mine?

LUTIEBELLE   No, sir!

PURLIE   Is her lily-white skin any more money-under-the-
mattress than your fine fair brown? And if so, why does
she spend half her life at the beach trying to get a sun tan?

LUTIEBELLE   I never thought of that!

PURLIE   There's a whole lotta things about the Negro question you ain't thought of! The South is split like a fat man's
underwear; and somebody beside the Supreme Court has
got to make a stand for the everlasting glory of our people!

LUTIEBELLE   Yessir.

PURLIE   Snatch Freedom from the jaws of force and fili-
buster!

LUTIEBELLE   Amen to that!

PURLIE   Put thunder in the Senate—!

LUTIEBELLE   Yes, Lord!

PURLIE   And righteous indignation back in the halls of
Congress!

LUTIEBELLE   Ain't it the truth!

PURLIE   Make Civil Rights from Civil Wrongs; and bring
that ol' Civil War to a fair and a just conclusion!

LUTIEBELLE   Help him, Lord!

PURLIE   Remind this white and wicked world there ain't
been more'n a dime's worth of difference twixt one man
and another'n, irregardless of race, gender, creed, or color
—since God Himself Almighty set the first batch out to
dry before the chimneys of Zion got hot! The eyes and ears
of the world is on Big Bethel!

LUTIEBELLE   Amen and hallelujah!

PURLIE   And whose side are you fighting on this evening,
sister?

LUTIEBELLE   Great Gawdamighty, Reb'n Purlie, on the
Lord's side! But Miss Emmylou sez—

PURLIE   (*Blowing up.*) This is outrageous—this is a ca-
tastrophe! You're a disgrace to the Negro profession!

LUTIEBELLE   That's just what she said all right—her exactly words.

PURLIE   Who's responsible for this? Where's your Maw and
Paw at?

LUTIEBELLE   I reckon I ain't rightly got no Maw and Paw,
wherever they at.

PURLIE   What!

LUTIEBELLE   And nobody else that I knows of. You see, sir—
I been on the go from one white folks' kitchen to another
since before I can remember. How I got there in the first
place—whatever became of my Maw and Paw, and my
kinfolks—even what my real name is—nobody is ever
rightly said.

PURLIE   (*Genuinely touched.*)   Oh. A motherless child—

LUTIEBELLE   That's what Miz Emmylou always sez—

PURLIE   But—who cared for you—like a mother? Who
brung you up—who raised you?

LUTIEBELLE   Nobody in particular—just whoever happened
to be in charge of the kitchen that day.

PURLIE   That explains the whole thing—no wonder; you've
missed the most important part of being somebody.

LUTIEBELLE   I have? What part is that?

PURLIE   Love—being appreciated, and sought out, and
looked after; being fought to the bitter end over even.

LUTIEBELLE   Oh, I have missed that, Reb'n Purlie, I really
have. Take mens—all my life they never looked at me the
way the other girls get looked at!

PURLIE   That's not so. The very first time I saw you—right
up there in the junior choir—I give you that look!

LUTIEBELLE   (*Turning to him in absolute ecstasy.*)   You
did! Oh, I thought so!—I prayed so. All through your
sermon I thought I would faint from hoping so hard so.
Oh, Reb'n Purlie—I think that's the finest look a person
could ever give a person— Oh, Reb'n Purlie! (*She closes
her eyes and points her lips at him.*)

PURLIE   (*Starts to kiss her, but draws back shyly.*)   Lutiebelle—

LUTIEBELLE   (*Dreamily, her eyes still closed.*)   Yes, Reb'n
Purlie—

PURLIE   There's something I want to ask you—something I never—in all my life—thought I'd be asking a woman— Would you—I don't know exactly how to say it—would you—

LUTIEBELLE   Yes, Reb'n Purlie?

PURLIE   Would you be my disciple?

LUTIEBELLE   (*Rushing into his arms.*) Oh, yes, Reb'n Purlie, yes!

> (*They start to kiss, but are interrupted by a NOISE coming from Offstage.*)

GITLOW   (*Offstage; in the extremity of death.*) No, Missy. No—no!—NO!— (*This last plea is choked off by the sound of some solid object brought smartly into contact with sudden flesh. "CLUNK!"* PURLIE *and* LUTIEBELLE *stand looking off Left, frozen for the moment.*)

LUTIEBELLE   (*Finally daring to speak.*) Oh, my Lord, Reb'n Purlie, what happened?

PURLIE   Gitlow has changed his mind. (*Grabs her and swings her around bodily.*) Toll the bell, Big Bethel!— toll that big, fat, black and sassy liberty bell. Tell Freedom— (LUTIEBELLE *suddenly leaps from the floor into his arms and plants her lips squarely on his. When finally he can come up for air.*) Tell Freedom—tell Freedom— WOW!

CURTAIN

Act I

Scene 2

TIME   *It is a little later the same afternoon.*

SCENE   *We are now in the little business office off from the commissary, where all the inhabitants of Cotchipee Valley buy food, clothing, and supplies. In the back a traveler has been drawn with just enough of an opening left to serve as the door to the main part of the store. On Stage Left and on Stage Right are simulated shelves where various items of reserve stock are kept: A wash tub, an axe, sacks of peas, and flour; bolts of gingham and calico, etc. Downstage Right is a small desk, on which an ancient typewriter, and an adding machine, with various papers and necessary books and records of commerce are placed. There is a small chair at this desk. Downstage Left is a table, with a large cash register, that has a functioning drawer. Below this is an entrance from the street.*

AT RISE   *As the CURTAIN rises, a young white* MAN *of 25 or 30, but still gawky, awkward, and adolescent in outlook and behavior, is sitting on a high stool Downstage Right Center. His face is held in the hands of* IDELLA, *a Negro cook and woman of all work, who has been in the family since time immemorial. She is the only mother* CHARLIE, *who is very much oversized even for his age, has ever known.* IDELLA *is as little as she is old and as tough as she is tiny, and is busily applying medication to* CHARLIE'S *black eye.*

CHARLIE   Ow, Idella, ow!—Ow!

IDELLA   Hold still, boy.

CHARLIE   But it hurts, Idella.

IDELLA   I know it hurts. Whoever done this to you musta meant to knock your natural brains out.

CHARLIE   I already told you who done it— OW!

IDELLA   Charlie Cotchipee, if you don't hold still and let me put this hot poultice on your eye, you better! (CHARLIE *subsides and meekly accepts her ministrations.*) First the milking, then the breakfast, then the dishes, then the washing, then the scrubbing, then the lunch time, next the dishes, then the ironing—and now; just where the picking and plucking for supper ought to be—you!

CHARLIE   You didn't tell Paw?

IDELLA   Of course I didn't—but the sheriff did.

CHARLIE   (*Leaping up.*)   The sheriff!

IDELLA   (*Pushing him back down.*)   Him and the deputy come to the house less than a hour ago.

CHARLIE   (*Leaping up again.*)   Are they coming over here!

IDELLA   Of course they're coming over here—sooner or later.

CHARLIE   But what will I do, Idella, what will I say?

IDELLA   (*Pushing him down.* CHARLIE *subsides.*)   "He that keepeth his mouth keepeth his life—"

CHARLIE   Did they ask for me?

IDELLA   Of course they asked for you.

CHARLIE   What did they say?

IDELLA   I couldn't hear too well; your father took them into the study and locked the door behind them.

CHARLIE   Maybe it was about something else.

IDELLA   It was about YOU: that much I could hear! Charlie—you want to get us both killed!

CHARLIE   I'm sorry, Idella, but—

IDELLA   (*Overriding; finishing proverb she had begun.*) "But he that openeth wide his lips shall have destruction!"

CHARLIE   But it was you who said it was the law of the land—

IDELLA   I know I did—

CHARLIE   It was you who said it's got to be obeyed—

IDELLA   I know it was me, but—

CHARLIE   It was you who said everybody had to stand up and take a stand against—

IDELLA   I know it was me, dammit! But I didn't say take a stand in no barroom!

CHARLIE   Ben started it, not me. And you always said never to take low from the likes of him!

IDELLA   Not so loud; they may be out there in the commissary! (*Goes quickly to door Up Center and peers out; satisfied no one has overheard them she crosses back down to* CHARLIE.) Look, boy, everybody down here don't feel as friendly towards the Supreme Court as you and me do —you big enough to know that! And don't you ever go outta here and pull a fool trick like you done last night again and not let me know about it in advance. You hear me!

CHARLIE   I'm sorry.

IDELLA   When you didn't come to breakfast this morning, and I went upstairs looking for you, and you just setting there, looking at me with your big eyes, and I seen that they had done hurt you—my, my, my! Whatever happens to you happens to me—you big enough to know that!

CHARLIE   I didn't mean to make trouble, Idella.

IDELLA   I know that, son, I know it. (*Makes final adjustments to the poultice.*) Now. No matter what happens when they do come I'll be right behind you. Keep your nerves calm and your mouth shut. Understand?

CHARLIE   Yes.

IDELLA   And as soon as you get a free minute come over to the house and let me put another hot poultice on that eye.

CHARLIE   Thank you, I'm very much obliged to you. Idella—

IDELLA   What is it, son?

CHARLIE   Sometimes I think I ought to run away from home.

IDELLA   I know, but you already tried that, honey.

CHARLIE   Sometimes I think I ought to run away from home —again!

> (OL' CAP'N *has entered from the Commissary just in time to hear this last remark.*)

OL' CAP'N   Why don't you, boy—why don't you? (OL' CAP'N COTCHIPEE *is aged and withered a bit, but by no means infirm. Dressed in traditional southern linen, the wide hat, the shoestring tie, the long coat, the twirling moustache of the Ol' Southern Colonel. In his left hand he carries a cane, and in his right a coiled bull whip: his last line of defense. He stops long enough to establish the fact that he means business, threatens them both with a mean cantankerous eye, then hangs his whip—the definitive answer to all who might foolishly question his Confederate power and glory—upon a peg.* CHARLIE *freezes at the sound of his voice.* IDELLA *tenses but keeps working on* CHARLIE'S *eye.* OL' CAP'N *crosses down, rudely pushes her hand aside, lifts up* CHARLIE'S *chin so that he may examine the damage, shakes his head in disgust.*) You don't know, boy, what a strong stomach it takes to stomach you. Just look at you, sitting there—all slopped over like something the horses dropped; steam, stink and all!

IDELLA   Don't you dare talk like that to this child!

OL' CAP'N   (*This stops him—momentarily.*) When I think of his grandpaw, God rest his Confederate soul, hero of the battle of Chicamauga— (*It's too much.*) Get outta my sight! (CHARLIE *gets up to leave.*) Not you—you! (*Indicates* IDELLA. *She gathers up her things in silence and starts to leave.*) Wait a minute— (IDELLA *stops.*) You been closer to this boy than I have, even before his ma died—ain't a thought ever entered his head you didn't know 'bout it first. You got anything to do with what my boy's been thinking lately?

IDELLA   I didn't know he had been thinking lately.

OL' CAP'N   Don't play with me, Idella—and you know what I mean! Who's been putting these integrationary ideas in my boy's head? Was it you—I'm asking you a question, dammit! Was it you?

IDELLA   Why don't you ask him?

OL' CAP'N   (*Snorts.*) Ask him! ASK HIM! He ain't gonna say a word unless you tell him to, and you know it. I'm asking you again, Idella Landy, have you been talking integration to my boy!?

IDELLA   I can't rightly answer you any more on that than he did.

OL' CAP'N   By God, you will answer me. I'll make you stand right there—right there!—all day and all night long, till you do answer me!

IDELLA   That's just fine.

OL' CAP'N   What's that! What's that you say?

IDELLA   I mean I ain't got nothing else to do—supper's on the stove; rice is ready, okra's fried, turnip's simmered, biscuits' baked, and stew is stewed. In fact them lemon pies you wanted special for supper are in the oven right now, just getting ready to burn—

OL' CAP'N   Get outta here!

IDELLA   Oh—no hurry, Ol' Cap'n—

OL' CAP'N   Get the hell out of here! (IDELLA *deliberately takes all the time in the world to pick up her things. Following her around trying to make his point.*) I'm warning both of you; that little lick over the eye is a small skimption compared to what I'm gonna do.   (IDELLA *pretends not to listen.*)   I won't stop till I get to the bottom of this! (IDELLA *still ignores him.*)   Get outta here, Idella Landy, before I take my cane and—   (*He raises his cane but* IDELLA *insists on moving at her own pace to exit Down Left.*)   And save me some buttermilk to go with them lemon pies, you hear me!   (*Turns to* CHARLIE; *not knowing how to approach him.*)   The sheriff was here this morning.

CHARLIE   Yessir.

OL' CAP'N   Is that all you got to say to me: "Yessir"?

CHARLIE   Yessir.

OL' CAP'N   You are a disgrace to the southland!

CHARLIE   Yessir.

OL' CAP'N   Shut up! I could kill you, boy, you understand that? Kill you with my own two hands!

CHARLIE   Yessir.

OL' CAP'N   Shut up! I could beat you to death with that bull whip—put my pistol to your good-for-nothing head—my own flesh and blood—and blow your blasted brains all over this valley!   (*Fighting to retain his control.*)   If—if you wasn't the last living drop of Cotchipee blood in Cotchipee County, I'd—I'd—

CHARLIE   Yessir.   (*This is too much.* OL' CAP'N *snatches* CHARLIE *to his feet. But* CHARLIE *does not resist.*)

OL' CAP'N   You trying to get non-violent with me, boy? (CHARLIE *does not answer, just dangles there.*)

CHARLIE   (*Finally.*)   I'm ready with the books, sir—that is—whenever you're ready.

OL' CAP'N   (*Flinging* CHARLIE *into a chair.*)   Thank you— thank you! What with your Yankee propaganda, your

barroom brawls, and all your other non-Confederate activities, I didn't think you had the time.

CHARLIE   (*Picks up account book; reads.*) "Cotton report.
Fifteen bales picked yesterday and sent to the cotton gin;
bringing our total to 357 bales to date."

OL' CAP'N   (*Impressed.*) 357—boy, that's some picking.
Who's ahead?

CHARLIE   Gitlow Judson, with seventeen bales up to now.

OL' CAP'N   Gitlow Judson; well I'll be damned; did you ever
see a cotton-pickinger darky in your whole life?!

CHARLIE   Commissary report—

OL' CAP'N   Did you ever look down into the valley and
watch ol' Git a-picking his way through that cotton patch?
Holy Saint Mother's Day! I'll bet you—

CHARLIE   Commissary report!

OL' CAP'N   All right!—commissary report.

CHARLIE   Yessir—well, first, sir, there's been some complaints: the flour is spoiled, the beans are rotten, and the
meat is tainted.

OL' CAP'N   Cut the price on it.

CHARLIE   But it's also a little wormy—

OL' CAP'N   Then sell it to the Negras— Is something wrong?

CHARLIE   No, sir—I mean, sir . . . , we can't go on doing
that, sir.

OL' CAP'N   Why not? It's traditional.

CHARLIE   Yessir, but times are changing—all this debt—
(*Indicates book.*) According to this book every family in
this valley owes money they'll never be able to pay back.

OL' CAP'N   Of course—it's the only way to keep 'em working. Didn't they teach you nothin' at school?

CHARLIE   We're cheating them—and they know we're cheating them. How long do you expect them to stand for it?

OL' CAP'N   As long as they're Negras—

CHARLIE   How long before they start a-rearing up on their hind legs, and saying: "Enough, white folks—now that's enough! Either you start treating me like I'm somebody in this world, or I'll blow your brains out"?

OL' CAP'N   (*Shaken to the core.*)   Stop it—stop it! You're tampering with the economic foundation of the southland! Are you trying to ruin me? One more word like that and I'll kill—I'll shoot—   (CHARLIE *attempts to answer.*) Shut up! One more word and I'll—I'll fling myself on your Maw's grave and die of apoplexy. I'll—! I'll—! Shut up, do you hear me? Shut up!   (*Enter* GITLOW, *hat in hand, grin on face, more obsequious today than ever.*)   Now what the hell *you* want?

GITLOW   (*Taken aback.*)   Nothing, sir, nothing!—That is —Missy, my ol' 'oman—well, suh, to git to the truth of the matter, I got a little business—

OL' CAP'N   Negras ain't got no business. And if you don't get the hell back into that cotton patch you better. Git, I said!   (GITLOW *starts to beat a hasty retreat.*)   Oh, no— don't go. Uncle Gitlow—good ol' faithful ol' Gitlow. Don't go—don't go.

GITLOW   (*Not quite sure.*)   Well—you're the boss, boss.

OL' CAP'N   (*Shoving a cigar into* GITLOW'S *mouth.*)   Just the other day, I was talking to the Senator about you— What's that great big knot on your head?

GITLOW   Missy—I mean, a mosquito!

OL' CAP'N   (*In all seriousness, examining the bump.*)   Uh! Musta been wearin' brass knuck— And he was telling me, the Senator was, how hard it was—impossible, he said, to find the old-fashioned, solid, hard-earned, Uncle Tom type Negra nowadays. I laughed in his face.

GITLOW   Yassuh. By the grace of God, there's still a few of us left.

OL' CAP'N   I told him how you and me growed up together. Had the same mammy—my mammy was your mother.

GITLOW   Yessir! Bosom buddies!

OL' CAP'N   And how you used to sing that favorite ol' speritual of mine: (*Sings.*) "I'm a-coming . . . I'm a-coming, For my head is bending low," (GITLOW *joins in on harmony.*) "I hear the gentle voices calling, Ol' Black Joe. . . ." (*This proves too much for* CHARLIE; *he starts out.*) Where you going?

CHARLIE   Maybe they need me in the front of the store.

OL' CAP'N   Come back here! (CHARLIE *returns.*) Turn around—show Gitlow that eye. (CHARLIE *reluctantly exposes black eye to view.*)

GITLOW   Gret Gawdamighty, somebody done cold cocked this child! Who hit Mr. Charlie, tell Uncle Gitlow who hit you? (CHARLIE *does not answer.*)

OL' CAP'N   Would you believe it? All of a sudden he can't say a word. And just last night, the boys was telling me, this son of mine made hisself a full-fledged speech.

GITLOW   You don't say.

OL' CAP'N   All about Negras—NeGROES he called 'em— four years of college, and he still can't say the word right— seems he's quite a specialist on the subject.

GITLOW   Well, shut my hard-luck mouth!

OL' CAP'N   Yessireebob. Told the boys over at Ben's bar in town, that he was all for mixing the races together.

GITLOW   You go on 'way from hyeah!

OL' CAP'N   Said white children and darky children ought to go the same schoolhouse together!

GITLOW   Tell me the truth, Ol' Cap'n!

OL' CAP'N   Got hisself so worked up some of 'em had to cool him down with a co-cola bottle!

GITLOW   Tell me the truth—again!

CHARLIE   That wasn't what I said!

OL' CAP'N   You calling me a liar, boy!

CHARLIE   No, sir, but I just said, that since it was the law of the land—

OL' CAP'N   It is not the law of the land no sucha thing!

CHARLIE   I didn't think it would do any harm if they went to school together—that's all.

OL' CAP'N   That's all—that's enough!

CHARLIE   They do it up North—

OL' CAP'N   This is down South. Down here they'll go to school together over me and Gitlow's dead body. Right, Git?!

GITLOW   Er, you the boss, boss!

CHARLIE   But this is the law of the—

OL' CAP'N   Never mind the law! Boy—look! You like Gitlow, you trust him, you always did—didn't you?

CHARLIE   Yessir.

OL' CAP'N   And Gitlow here, would cut off his right arm for you if you was to ask him. Wouldn't you, Git?

GITLOW   (*Gulping.*) You the boss, boss.

OL' CAP'N   Now Gitlow ain't nothing if he ain't a Negra!— Ain't you, Git?

GITLOW   Oh—two-three hundred percent, I calculate.

OL' CAP'N   Now, if you really want to know what the Negra
    thinks about this here integration and all lackathat, don't
    ask the Supreme Court—ask Gitlow. Go ahead—ask him!

CHARLIE   I don't need to ask him.

OL' CAP'N   Then I'll ask him. Raise your right hand, Git.
    You solemnly swear to tell the truth, whole truth, nothing
    else but, so help you God?

GITLOW   (*Raising hand.*)   I do.

OL' CAP'N   Gitlow Judson, as God is your judge and maker,
    do you believe in your heart that God intended white folks
    and Negra children to go to school together?

GITLOW   Nawsuh, I do not!

OL' CAP'N   Do you, so help you God, think that white folks
    and black should mix and 'sociate in street cars, buses, and
    railroad stations, in any way, shape, form, or fashion?

GITLOW   Absolutely not!

OL' CAP'N   And is it not your considered opinion, God strike
    you dead if you lie, that all my Negras are happy with
    things in the southland just the way they are?

GITLOW   Indeed I do!

OL' CAP'N   Do you think ary single darky on my place would
    ever think of changing a single thing about the South, and
    to hell with the Supreme Court as God is your judge and
    maker?

GITLOW   As God is my judge and maker and you are my
    boss, I do not!

OL' CAP'N   (*Turning in triumph to* CHARLIE.)   The voice of
    the Negra himself! What more proof do you want!

CHARLIE   I don't care whose voice it is—it's still the law of
    the land, and I intend to obey it!

OL' CAP'N   (*Losing control.*)   Get outta my face, boy—get
    outta my face, before I kill you! Before I—

(CHARLIE *escapes into the commissary.* OL' CAP'N *collapses.*)

GITLOW   Easy, Ol' Cap'n, easy, suh, easy! (OL' CAP'N *gives out a groan.* GITLOW *goes to shelf and comes back with a small bottle and a small box.*) Some aspirins, suh . . . , some asaphoetida? (PURLIE *and* LUTIEBELLE *appear at door Left.*) Not now—later—later! (*Holds bottle to* OL' CAP'N'S *nose.*)

OL' CAP'N   Gitlow—Gitlow!

GITLOW   Yassuh, Ol' Cap'n—Gitlow is here, suh; right here!

OL' CAP'N   Quick, ol' friend—my heart. It's—quick! A few passels, if you please—of that ol' speritual.

GITLOW   (*Sings most tenderly.*) "Gone are the days, when my heart was young and gay . . ."

OL' CAP'N   I can't tell you, Gitlow—how much it eases the pain— (GITLOW *and* OL' CAP'N *sing a phrase together.*) Why can't he see what they're doing to the southland, Gitlow? Why can't he see it, like you and me? If there's one responsibility you got, boy, above all others, I said to him, it's these Negras—your Negras, boy. Good, honest, hard-working cotton choppers. If you keep after 'em.

GITLOW   Yes, Lawd. (*Continues to sing.*)

OL' CAP'N   Something between you and them no Supreme Court in the world can understand—and wasn't for me they'd starve to death. What's gonna become of 'em, boy, after I'm gone—?

GITLOW   Dass a good question, Lawd—you answer him. (*Continues to sing.*)

OL' CAP'N   They belong to you, boy—to you, evah one of 'em! My ol' Confederate father told me on his deathbed: feed the Negras first—after the horses and cattle—and I've done it evah time! (*By now* OL' CAP'N *is sheltered in*

GITLOW'S *arms. The LIGHTS begin slowly to fade away.*
GITLOW *sings a little more.*) Ah, Gitlow ol' friend—something, absolutely sacred 'bout that speritual—I live for the day you'll sing that thing over my grave.

GITLOW   Me, too, Ol' Cap'n, me, too! (GITLOW'S *voice rises to a slow, gentle, yet triumphant crescendo, as our LIGHTS fade away.*)

BLACKOUT
CURTAIN

Act II

Scene 1

TIME   *A short while later.*

SCENE   *The scene is the same: the little commissary office.*

AT RISE   *The Stage is empty. After a moment* GITLOW *hurries in from the commissary proper, crosses down to the little back door and opens it.*

PURLIE   (*Entering hurriedly.*)   What took you so long?

GITLOW   S-sh! Not so loud! He's right out there in the commissary! (PURLIE *crosses over and looks out into the commissary, then crosses back to the little back door and holds out his hands.* LUTIEBELLE *enters. She is dressed in what would be collegiate style. She is still full of awe and wonder, and—this time—of fear, which she is struggling to keep under cover.*)   Ain't she gonna carry no school books?

PURLIE   What are they doing out there?

GITLOW   The watermelon books don't balance.

PURLIE   What!

GITLOW   One of our melons is in shortage!

PURLIE   You tell him about Lutiebelle—I mean, about Cousin Bee?

GITLOW   I didn't have time. Besides, I wanted you to have one more chance to get out of here alive!

PURLIE   What's the matter with you!? Don't five hundred dollars of your own lawful money mean nothing to you? Ain't you got no head for business?

GITLOW   No! The head I got is for safekeeping, and—besides— (PURLIE *lifts* OL' CAP'N'S *bull whip down from its peg.*) don't touch that thing, Purlie! (GITLOW *races over, snatches it from him, replaces it, and pats it soothingly*

317

into place, while at the same time looking to see if OL'
CAP'N *is coming—and all in one continuous move.*)

PURLIE   Why not? It touched me!

GITLOW   (*Aghast.*)   Man, ain't nothing sacred to you!?

OL' CAP'N   (*Calling from Off in the commissary.*)   Gitlow,
come in here!

GITLOW   (*Racing off.*)   Coming, Ol' Cap'n, coming!

OL' CAP'N   (*Offstage.*)   Now! We are going to cross-exam-
ine these watermelons one more time—one watermelon—

GITLOW   (*Offstage.*)   One watermelon!

CHARLIE   (*Offstage.*)   One watermelon!

OL' CAP'N   Two watermelons—

GITLOW   Two watermelons—

CHARLIE   Two watermelons—

(*The sound of the watermelon count-down continues
in the background.* PURLIE, *finding he's got a moment,
comes over to reassure* LUTIEBELLE.)

PURLIE   Whatever you do, don't panic!

LUTIEBELLE   (*Repeating after him: almost in hypnotic
rote.*)   Whatever you do, don't panic!

PURLIE   Just walk like I taught you to walk, and talk like I
taught you to talk—

LUTIEBELLE   Taught like I walked you to—

PURLIE   (*Shaking her shoulders.*)   Lutiebelle!

LUTIEBELLE   Yes, Reb'n Purlie!

PURLIE   Wake up!

LUTIEBELLE   Oh my goodness, Reb'n Purlie—was I sleep?

PURLIE   Alert!

LUTIEBELLE   Alert!—

PURLIE   Wide awake!—

LUTIEBELLE   Wide awake!—

PURLIE   Up on your toes!

LUTIEBELLE   (*Starting to rise on toes.*) Up on your—

PURLIE   No. No, that's just a figure of speech. Now! You remember what I told you—?

LUTIEBELLE   No, sir. Can't say I do, sir.

PURLIE   Well—first: chit-chat—small-talk!

LUTIEBELLE   Yessir—how small?

PURLIE   Pass the time of day—you remember? The first thing I taught you on the train?

LUTIEBELLE   On the train— Oh! "Delighted to remake your acquaintance, I am sure."

PURLIE   That's it—that's it exactly! Now. Suppose he was to say to you: (PURLIE *imitates* OL' CAP'N.) "I bet you don't remember when you wasn't kneehigh to a grasshopper and Ol' Cap'n took you by the hand, and led you down on your first trip to the cotton patch?"

LUTIEBELLE   Just like you told me on the train?

PURLIE   Yes!

LUTIEBELLE   "I must confess—that much of my past life is vague and hazy."

PURLIE   (*Imitating.*) Doggone my hide—you're the cutest li'l' ol' piece of brown skin sugar I ever did see!

LUTIEBELLE   Oh, thank you, Reb'n Purlie!

PURLIE   I ain't exactly me, saying that—it's Ol' Cap'n. (*Continues imitation.*) And this is my land, and my cotton patch, and my commissary, and my bull whip—still here, just like you left us. And what might be your name, li'l gal?

LUTIEBELLE   (*Warming to the game.*) Beatrice Judson, sir.

PURLIE   And what is your daddy's name, li'l gal?

LUTIEBELLE   Horace Judson, sir.

PURLIE   And what did they teach you up in that college, li'l gal?

LUTIEBELLE   It was my major education, Ol' Cap'n.—

PURLIE   You mean you majored in education. (*Resumes imitation.*) Well—nothing wrong with Negras getting an education, I always say— But then again, ain't nothing right with it, either. Cousin Bee—heh, heh, heh—you don't mind if I call you Cousin Bee, do you, honey?

LUTIEBELLE   Oh, sir, I'd be delighted!

PURLIE   Don't! Don't be delighted until he puts the money in your hands. (*Resumes imitation.*) And where did you say your Maw worked at?

LUTIEBELLE   In North Carolina.

PURLIE   Where is your maw at now?

LUTIEBELLE   She's at the cemetery: she died.

PURLIE   And how much is the inheritance?

LUTIEBELLE   Five hundred dollars for the next of kin.

PURLIE   (*Delighted at her progress.*) Wonderful, just— just—wonderful! (*Enjoying his own imitation now.*) (OL' CAP'N *enters from the commissary, followed by* GITLOW. LUTIEBELLE *sees* OL' CAP'N, *but* PURLIE *is so wrapped up in his own performance he does not.*) Say, maybe you could teach a old dog like me some new tricks. (*He tries to get a rise out of* LUTIEBELLE *but she is frozen in terror.* OL' CAP'N *becomes aware of* PURLIE'S *presence, and approaches.*) By swickety—a gal like you could doggone well change a joker's luck if she had a mind to—see what I mean? (PURLIE *punches what he expects to be an invisible* GITLOW *in the ribs. His blow lands upon* OL' CAP'N *with such force, he falls onto a pile of sacks of chicken feed.*)

OL' CAP'N   (*Sputtering.*)   What! What in the name of—
(GITLOW *and* PURLIE *scramble to help him to his feet.*)

PURLIE   My compliments, sir—are only exceeded by my
humblest apologies. And allow me, if you please, to present my Aunt Henrietta's daughter, whom you remember
so well: Beatrice Judson—or as we call her—Cousin Bee.

OL' CAP'N   (*He is so taken by what he sees he forgets his
anger.*)   Well, I'll be switched!

PURLIE   Come, Cousin Bee. Say "howdo" to the man.

LUTIEBELLE   How do to the man. I mean—   (*Takes time
to correct herself, then.*)   Delighted to remake your acquaintance, I'm sure.

OL' CAP'N   What's that? What's that she's saying?

PURLIE   College, sir.

OL' CAP'N   College?

PURLIE   That's all she ever talks.

OL' CAP'N   You mean Henrietta's little ol' button-eyed
pickaninny was in college? Well bust my eyes wide open!
Just LOOK at that!   (*Gets closer, but she edges away.*)
You remember me, honey. I'm still the Ol' Cap'n round
here.

LUTIEBELLE   Oh, sir, it would not be the same without you
being the Ol' Cap'n around here.

OL' CAP'N   You don't say! Say, I'll bet you don't remember
a long time ago when—

LUTIEBELLE   When I wasn't but knee high to a hoppergrass,
and you took me by the hand, and led me on my very first
trip to the cotton patch.

OL' CAP'N   (*Ecstatic.*)   You mean you remember that!

LUTIEBELLE   Alert, wide awake, and up on my toes—if you
please, sir!   (*Rises up on her toes.*)

OL' CAP'N   (*Moving in.*)   Doggone my hide. You're the
cutest li'l ol' piece of brown sugar I ever did see—

LUTIEBELLE   (*Escaping.*)   And this is your land, and your
    cotton patch, and your commissary, and your bull whip—

OL' CAP'N   What's that?

LUTIEBELLE   Just a figure of speech or two—

OL' CAP'N   Well, Beatrice—you wouldn't mind if Ol' Cap'n
    was to call you Cousin Bee?

LUTIEBELLE   Oh, positively not, not!—since my mother's
    name was Henrietta Judson; my father's name was Hor-
    ace Judson—

OL' CAP'N   But most of all, I remember that little ol' dog
    of yours—"Spicey," wasn't it?

LUTIEBELLE   Oh, we wasn't much for eating dogs, sir—

OL' CAP'N   No, no! Spicey was the name—wasn't it?

    (LUTIEBELLE *looking to* PURLIE *for help, but* PURLIE
    cannot help. He looks to GITLOW, *who also cannot re-*
    member.)

LUTIEBELLE   You, er, really think we really called him
    "Spicey"?

OL' CAP'N   Not him—her!

PURLIE   HER!

LUTIEBELLE   Oh, her! Her! I am most happy to recollect
    that I do.

OL' CAP'N   You do! You don't say you do!

LUTIEBELLE   I did, as I recall it, have a fond remembrance
    of you and "Spicey," since you-all went so well together—
    and at the same time!

OL' CAP'N   You do? Well hush my mouth, eh, Git?

GITLOW   Hush your mouth indeed, sir.

LUTIEBELLE   Cose soon it is my sworn and true confession
    that I disremembers so many things out of my early pas-
    time that mostly you are haze and vaguey!

OL' CAP'N   Oh, am I now!

LUTIEBELLE   Oh, yes, and sir—indeedy.

OL' CAP'N   Doggone my hide, eh, Git?

GITLOW   Doggone your hide indeed, suh.

LUTIEBELLE   You see of coursely I have spount—

PURLIE   Spent—

LUTIEBELLE   Spunt so much of my time among the college that hardly all of my ancient maidenhead—

PURLIE   Hood.

LUTIEBELLE   Is a thing of the past!

OL' CAP'N   You don't say!

LUTIEBELLE   But yes, and most precisely.

OL' CAP'N   Tell me, Li'l Bee—what did they teach you up at that college?

LUTIEBELLE   Well, mostly they taught me an education, but in between I learned a lot, too.

OL' CAP'N   Is that a fact?

LUTIEBELLE   Reading, writing, 'rithmetic—oh, my Lord— just sitting out on the rectangular every evening after four o'clock home work and you have your regular headache—

OL' CAP'N   You know something, I been after these Negras down here for years: Go to school, I'd say, first chance you get—take a coupla courses in advanced cotton picking. But you think they'd listen to me? No sireebob. By swick-ety! A gal like you could doggone well change a joker's luck if she was a mind to. (*Gives* GITLOW *a broad wink and digs him in his ribs.* GITLOW *almost falls.*)   See what I mean?

LUTIEBELLE   Oh, most indo I deed.

OL' CAP'N   Look—anything! Ask me anything! Whatever you want—name it and it's yours!

LUTIEBELLE   You mean—really, really, really?

OL' CAP'N   Ain't a man in Cotchipee County can beat my time when I see something I want—name it! (*Indicates with a sweep the contents of the commissary.*) Some roasted peanuts; a bottle of soda water; a piece of pepmint candy?

LUTIEBELLE   Thank you, sir, but if it's all the same to you I'd rather have my money.

OL' CAP'N   (*As if shot.*) Your WHAT?

LUTIEBELLE   (*Frightened but determined to forge ahead under her own steam.*) Now I'm gonna tell you like it was, Your Honor: You see, Reb'n Purlie and Uncle Gitlow had one aunty between them, name of Harrietta—

PURLIE   Henrietta!

LUTIEBELLE   Henrietta—who used to cook for this rich ol' white lady up in North Carolina years ago; and last year this ol' lady died—brain tumor—

PURLIE   Bright's disease!

LUTIEBELLE   Bright's disease—leaving five hundred dollars to every servant who had ever worked on her place, including Henrietta. But Henrietta had already died, herself: largely from smallpox—

PURLIE   No!

LUTIEBELLE   Smally from large pox?

PURLIE   Influenza!

LUTIEBELLE   Influenza—and since Henrietta's husband Harris—

PURLIE   Horace!

LUTIEBELLE   Horace—was already dead from heart trouble—

PURLIE   Gunshot wounds!—

LUTIEBELLE   (*Exploding.*)   His heart stopped beating, didn't it?!

PURLIE   Yes, but—

LUTIEBELLE   Precisely, Reb'n Purlie, precisely! (*Turning back to* OL' CAP'N.)   Since, therefore and where-in-as Cousin Bee, her daughter, was first-in-line-for-next-of-kinfolks, the five hundred dollars left in your care and keep by Aunt Henrietta, and which you have been saving just for me all these lonesome years—

OL' CAP'N   I ain't been saving no damn sucha thing!

PURLIE   (*Stepping swiftly into the breach.*)   Oh, come out from behind your modesty, sir!

OL' CAP'N   What!

PURLIE   Your kindness, sir; your thoughtfulness, sir; your unflagging consideration for the welfare of your darkies, sir: have rung like the clean clear call of the clarion from Maine to Mexico. Your constant love for them is both hallmark and high water of the true gentility of the dear old South.

OL' CAP'N   Gitlow, Gitlow—go get Charlie. I want him to hear this. (GITLOW *exits Upstage Center.*)   Go on, boy, go on!

PURLIE   And as for your faithful ol' darkies themselves, sir— why, down in the quarters, sir, your name stands second only to God Himself Almighty.

OL' CAP'N   You don't mean to tell me!

PURLIE   Therefore, as a humble token of their high esteem and their deep and abiding affection, especially for saving that five hundred dollar inheritance for Cousin Bee, they have asked me to present to you ... this plaque! (PURLIE *unveils a "sheepskin scroll" from his inside coat pocket.* OL' CAP'N *reaches for it, but* PURLIE *draws it away.* CHARLIE *appears in the doorway Upstage Center followed by* GIT-

LOW.) Which bears the following citation to wit, and I quote: "Whereas Ol' Cap'n has kindly allowed us to remain on his land, and pick his cotton, and tend his cattle, and drive his mules, and whereas Ol' Cap'n still lets us have our hominy grits and fat back on credit and whereas Ol' Cap'n never resorts to bull whip except as a blessing and a benediction, therefore be it resolved, that Ol' Cap'n Cotchipee be cited as the best friend the Negro has ever had, and officially proclaimed Great White Father of the Year!"

OL' CAP'N   (*Stunned.*) I can't believe it—I can't believe it! (*Sees* CHARLIE.) Charlie, boy—did you hear it? Did you hear it, Charlie, my boy—GREAT WHITE FATHER OF THE YEAR!

PURLIE   (*Like a professional undertaker.*) Let me be the first to congratulate you, sir. (*They shake hands solemnly.*)

OL' CAP'N   Thank you, Purlie.

LUTIEBELLE   And me. (*They shake hands solemnly.*)

OL' CAP'N   Thank you, Cousin Bee.

GITLOW   And me, too, Ol' Cap'n.

OL' CAP'N   (*On the verge of tears, as they shake hands.*) Gitlow—Gitlow. I know this is some of your doings—my old friend. (*He turns expectantly to* CHARLIE.) Well, boy— (CHARLIE *is trapped.*) ain't you gonna congratulate your father?

CHARLIE   Yessir. (*Shakes his hand.*)

OL' CAP'N   This—is the happiest day of my life. My darkies —my Negras—my own— (*Chokes up; unable to continue.*)

PURLIE   Hear, hear!

GITLOW AND LUTIEBELLE   Hear, hear!

(CHARLIE *tries to sneak off again, but* OL' CAP'N *sees him.*)

OL' CAP'N   I am just too overcome to talk. Come back here, boy. (CHARLIE *comes back and stands in intense discomfort.*) Silent—speechless—dumb, my friends. Never in all the glorious hoary and ancient annals of all Dixie—never before— (*Chokes up with tears; blows nose with big red handkerchief, and pulls himself together.*) My friends, in the holy scripture—and I could cite you chapter and verse if I was a mind to—"In the beginning God created white folks and He created black folks," and in the name of all that's white and holy, let's keep it that way. And to hell with Abraham Lincoln and Martin Luther King!

PURLIE   I am moved, Ol' Cap'n—

GITLOW AND LUTIEBELLE   Uhn!

PURLIE   Moved beyond my jurisdiction; as for example, I have upon my person a certificate of legal tender duly affixed and so notarized to said itemized effect— (*Hands over an official-looking document.*) a writ of Habeas Corpus.

OL' CAP'N   (*Taking the document.*) Habeas who?

PURLIE   Habeas Corpus. It means I can have the body.

OL' CAP'N   Body—what body?

PURLIE   The body of the cash—the five hundred dollars—that they sent you to hold in trust for Cousin Bee.

OL' CAP'N   (*Pauses to study the eager faces in the room; then*) Charlie—

CHARLIE   Yessir.

OL' CAP'N   Bring me—five hundred dollars—will you? (CHARLIE *starts for safe.*) No, no, no—not that old stuff. Fresh money, clean money out of my private stock out back. Nothin's too good for my Negras.

CHARLIE   Yessir—yessir! (*Starts out, stops.*) And Paw?

OL' CAP'N   Yes, son?

CHARLIE   All I got to say is "Yessir!" (*Crosses to cash register.*)

OL' CAP'N   Just wait—wait till I tell the Senator: "Great White Father of the Year."

CHARLIE   (*Returns with roll of bills which he hands to his father.*) Here you are, Paw.

OL' CAP'N   Thank you, boy.

     (*Enter* IDELLA, *followed by the* SHERIFF *and the* DEPUTY.)

IDELLA   Here everybody is, back in the office.

OL' CAP'N   (*Overjoyed to see them.*) Just in time, Sheriff, for the greatest day of my life. Gentlemen—something has happened here today, between me and my Negras, makes me proud to call myself a Confederate: I have just been named Great White Father of the Year. (*To* PURLIE.) Right?

PURLIE   Right. And now if you'll just—

SHERIFF AND DEPUTY   Great White Father of the Year! Congratulations! (*They shake his hands warmly.*)

OL' CAP'N   True, there are places in this world where the darky is rebellious, running hog wild, rising up and sitting down where he ain't wanted, acting sassy in jail, getting plumb out of hand, totally forgetting his place and his manners—but not in Cotchipee County! (*To* PURLIE.) Right?

PURLIE   Right! And now perhaps we could get back to the business at hand.

OL' CAP'N   (*Finishing his count.*) All right—five hundred dollars. (PURLIE *impulsively reaches for the money, but* OL' CAP'N *snatches it back.*) Just a moment. There's still one small formality: a receipt.

PURLIE   A receipt? All right, I'll—

OL' CAP'N   Not you— You! (*Thrusts a printed form toward* LUTIEBELLE.) . . . just for the record. (*Offers her a fountain pen.*) Sign here. Your full and legal name— right here on the dotted line.

PURLIE   (*Reaching for the pen.*) I'll do it—I have her power of attorney.

LUTIEBELLE   (*Beating* PURLIE *to the pen.*) It's all right, Reb'n Purlie, I can write. (*Takes pen and signs paper with a flourish.*)

OL' CAP'N   (*Takes up paper and reads the signature.*) Sheriff, I want this woman arrested!

PURLIE   Arrested?! For what?

OL' CAP'N   She came into my presence, together with him— (*Indicates* PURLIE.) and with him— (*Indicates* GITLOW.) And they all swore to me that she is Beatrice Judson.

PURLIE   She IS Beatrice Judson!

OL' CAP'N   (*Pouncing.*) Then how come she to sign her name: Lutiebelle Gussiemae Jenkins!

PURLIE   Uhn-uhn!

GITLOW   Uhn-uhn!

LUTIEBELLE   Uhn-uhn!

GITLOW   (*Starting off suddenly.*) Is somebody calling my name out there—

OL' CAP'N   Come back here, Gitlow— (GITLOW *halts in his tracks.*) You'll go out of that door when the Sheriff takes you out. And that goes for all of you. (*The* SHERIFF *starts forward.*) Just a minute, Sheriff. Before you take 'em away there's something I've got to do. (*Crosses to where the whip is hung.*)

GITLOW   (*Horrified at the thought of the whip.*) I'll make it up to you in cotton, Ol' Cap'n—

OL' CAP'N   Shut up, Gitlow. (*Takes whip down, and starts to uncoil it.*) Something I started twenty years ago with this bull whip— (*Fastening his eyes on* PURLIE.) Something I intend to finish.

GITLOW   (*Drops to his knees and begins to sing.*) "Gone are the days—"

OL' CAP'N   (*Turning to* GITLOW.) Dammit! I told you to shut up! (*Then back to* PURLIE.) I'm gonna teach you to try to make a damn fool outta white folks; all right, boy, drop them britches.

PURLIE   The hell you preach!

OL' CAP'N   What's that you said?

LUTIEBELLE   He said, "The hell you preach!"

CHARLIE   Paw, wait, listen—!

OL' CAP'N   I thought I told you to shut up! (*Back to* PUR-LIE.) Boy, I'm gonna teach you to mind what I say!

> (PURLIE *doesn't move.* OL' CAP'N *takes a vicious cut at him with the bull whip, and* PURLIE, *leaping back to get out of the way, falls into the arms of the* SHERIFF.)

SHERIFF   I distinctly heard that gentleman order you to drop your britches. (*Spins* PURLIE *around, sets him up, and swings with all his might.* PURLIE *easily ducks and dances away.*)

DEPUTY   Save a little taste for me, Sheriff!

> (*The* SHERIFF *swings again; and, again,* PURLIE *dances away. He swings still again, but to no avail.*)

SHERIFF   (*Aggravated.*) Hold still, dammit! (*Swings again, and once more* PURLIE *ducks away.*) Confound it, boy! You trying to make me hurt myself?

DEPUTY   What's the matter, Sheriff—can't you find him?! (*Laughs.*)

SHERIFF   (*Desperate.*) Now, you listen to me, boy! Either you stand up like a man, so I can knock you down, or—

LUTIEBELLE   (*Stepping between the* SHERIFF *and* PURLIE.)
Don't you dare!

SHERIFF   What!

LUTIEBELLE   Insultin' Reb'n Purlie, and him a man of the
cloth! (*Grabs his gun arm and bites it.*)

SHERIFF   Owwww! (*She   kicks   him   in   the   shin.*)
Owwwwwww!

> (*The* DEPUTY *charges in to the rescue. He attempts
> to grab* LUTIEBELLE, *but she eludes him and steps
> down hard on his corns.*)

DEPUTY   Owwwwwwwwww!

PURLIE   (*Going for the* DEPUTY.)   Keep your hands off her,
you hypothetical baboon, keep your hands OFF her!
(*Grabs the* DEPUTY, *spins him around and knocks him
across the room, starts to follow, but the* SHERIFF *grabs
him and pins his arms behind him.*)

CHARLIE   (*Breaks   loose   from* IDELLA, *snatching   at   the
SHERIFF.)* You let him go, dammit, let him go! (*With
one arm the* SHERIFF *pushes* CHARLIE *away.*)

SHERIFF   (*Still holding* PURLIE'S *arms pinned back.*)   All
right, Dep, he's all yours. Throw him your fast ball—high,
tight and inside!

DEPUTY   Glad to oblige you, Sheriff! (*He draws back like
a big league baseball pitcher.*)

CHARLIE   (*Rushing into the breach.*)   Stop! Stop—stop in
the name of the—   (*The* DEPUTY *swings from the floor,*
PURLIE *ducks and rolls his head sharply to one side.* CHAR-
LIE *runs full into the force of the blow. Collapsing heavily.*)
Idella—aaaaaaa!

OL' CAP'N   (*Rushing to him.*)   Charlie—!

IDELLA   Charlie—!

> (PURLIE, *taking advantage of the confusion, snatches*
> LUTIEBELLE *by the arms and dashes with her out the
> back door.*)

OL' CAP'N   After them, you idiots, after them!

SHERIFF   (*To the* DEPUTY.)   After them, you idiot!   (*They both run off after* PURLIE *and* LUTIEBELLE.)

(OL' CAP'N *and* IDELLA *are kneeling beside the prostrate* CHARLIE. GITLOW, *after a moment, comes into the picture.*)

OL' CAP'N   His eyes, Idella, his eyes! Where are his eyes?

IDELLA   Gitlow, fetch me the asaphoetida, Ol' Cap'n, you rub his hands.

GITLOW   Yess'm.

IDELLA   (*Slapping his face.*)   Charlie, honey, wake up—wake up! It's me, Idella.

(OL' CAP'N *is too disorganized to be of any assistance.* GITLOW *has returned with a bottle which he hands to* IDELLA. *He then kneels and starts rubbing* CHARLIE'S *hands.*)

GITLOW   Mr. Charlie, wake up—

(*With* GITLOW *and* IDELLA'S *help,* CHARLIE *slowly rises to his feet. Still unsteady, his eyes glazed and vacant.*)

OL' CAP'N   (*Snapping his fingers in front of his eyes.*)   It's me, Charlie, me— It's your daddy, boy! Speak to me—talk to me—say something to me!

CHARLIE   (*Snaps suddenly into speech—but still out on his feet.*)   Fourscore and seven years ago, our fathers brought forth—

OL' CAP'N   Shut up!

CURTAIN

Act II

Scene 2

TIME   *Two days later.*

SCENE   *Back at the shack, outside in the yard area.*

AT RISE   MISSY *is discovered, busy working on some potted plants. She is preoccupied, but we feel some restlessness, some anticipation in the manner in which she works.* PURLIE *enters.*

PURLIE   (*The great prophet intones his sorrows.*) Toll the bell—Big Bethel; toll the big, black, ex-liberty bell; tell Freedom there's death in the family.

MISSY   Purlie—

PURLIE   All these wings and they still won't let me fly!

MISSY   Where you been these last two days, Purlie? We been lookin' for you. All this plotting and planning risking your dad-blasted neck like a crazy man! And for what —FOR WHAT! (IDELLA *enters.*)   Oh, come in, Miz Idella.

IDELLA   Is anybody here seen Charlie Cotchipee this morning?

MISSY   No, we haven't.

PURLIE   Is something wrong, Miz Idella?

IDELLA   He left home this morning right after breakfast— here it is after lunch and I ain't seen him since. I can't find Charlie—first time in forty-five years I been working up there in that house I ever misplaced anything! You don't suppose he'd run away from home and not take me—?

MISSY   Oh, no, Miz Idella! Not li'l Charlie Cotchipee.

IDELLA   Well, I guess I'd better be getting back. If you should see him—

MISSY   Miz Idella, we all want to thank you for keeping Purlie out of jail so kindly. (*Hands her flowers.*)

IDELLA   Oh, that was nothing; I just told that ol' man if he didn't stop all that foolishness about chain gangs and stuff, I would resign from his kitchen and take Charlie right along with me! But now I've lost Charlie. First time in forty-five years I ever misplaced anything! (*She exits.*)

MISSY   (*Turns to* PURLIE.)   Don't you know there's something more important in this world than having that broken down ol' ex-church of a barn to preach in?

PURLIE   Yeah—like what?

MISSY   Like asking Lutiebelle to marry you.

PURLIE   Asking Lutiebelle to marry me?

MISSY   She worships the ground you walk on. Talks about you all the time. You two could get married, settle down, like you ought to, and raise the cutest little ol' family you ever did see. And she's a cookin', po' child—she left you some of her special fritters.

PURLIE   Freedom, Missy, not fritters. The crying need of this Negro day and age is not grits, but greatness; not cornbread but courage; not fat-back, but fight-back; Big Bethel is my Bethel; it belongs to me and to my people; and I intend to have it back if I have to pay for it in blood!

MISSY   All right—come on in and I'll fix you some dinner.

GITLOW   (*Enters front door, singing.*)   "I'm comin', I'm comin'—"

MISSY   (*Entering house.*)   Not so loud, Gitlow. You want to wake up the mule?

GITLOW   Not on his day off. "For my head is bendin' low—" (GITLOW *sits, unfolds comic section and reads.*)

MISSY   Where's Lutiebelle, Gitlow?

GITLOW   "The history of the War Between the States will be continued next week." That sure is a good story—I wonder how that's gonna come out?

MISSY   Grown man, deacon in the church, reading the funny-paper. And your shirt. You sneaked outta here this morning in your clean white shirt, after I told you time and time again I was saving it!

GITLOW   Saving it for what?

MISSY   It's the only decent thing you got to get buried in! (*Exits side door.*)

GITLOW   Don't you know that arrangements for my funeral has been taken over by the white folks? (*To* PURLIE.) Besides, I got the money!

PURLIE   What kinda money?

GITLOW   The five hundred dollar kinda money.

PURLIE   Five hundred dollars! You mean Ol' Cap'n give the money to you?

GITLOW   "Gitlow," he said. "Ain't another man in this valley, black, white, or otherwise, I would trust to defend and protect me from the N double ACP but you."

PURLIE   Is that a fact?

GITLOW   Well, now. Whatever become of you? All them gretgawdamighty plans your mouth runneth over—all that white folks' psychology?

PURLIE   Gitlow! Er, Deacon Gitlow—Big Bethel is waiting!

GITLOW   So you're the good-for-nothing, raggedy ass high falute 'round here that goes for who-tied-the-bear!

PURLIE   Naw, Git, man—ain't nothing to me.

GITLOW   Always so high and mighty—can't nobody on earth handle white folks but you—don't pay no 'tention to Gitlow; naw—he's a Tom. Tease him—low-rate him—laugh at ol' Gitlow; he ain't nothing but a fool!

PURLIE   Aw, Git, man, you got me wrong. I didn't mean nothing like that!

GITLOW   Who's the fool now, my boy—who's the fool now?

PURLIE   Er—I'm the fool, Gitlow.

GITLOW   Aw, man, you can talk plainer than that.

PURLIE   I'm the fool, Gitlow.

GITLOW   Uh-huh! Now go over to that window, open it
wide as it will go and say it so everybody in this whole
damn valley can hear you! Go on! Go on, man—I ain't
got all day!

PURLIE   (*Goes to window.*)   I'm the fool, Gitlow!

GITLOW   Nice. Now beg me!

PURLIE   What!

GITLOW   I said if you want to see the money, beg me! Do it
like you do white folks.

PURLIE   I'd rather die and go to hell in a pair gasoline
drawers—   (GITLOW *starts to put money away.*)   No,
wait. Holy mackerel, dere, Massa Gitlow—hee, hee, hee.
Hey! Boss, could I possible have a look at that there five
hundred dollars dere, suh? Hyuh, hyuh, hyuh!

GITLOW   Man, you sure got style! You know together you
and me could make the big time!   (PURLIE *reaches for
money.*)   Come in and see me during office hours! As
Deputy-For-The-Colored, I guess I'll just sort of step outside for a minute and let that low September sun shine
down on a joker as rich as he is black!

PURLIE   Gitlow—Gitlow!   (GITLOW *starts for side door.*)
If slavery ever comes back I want to be your agent!

GITLOW   Now that was a snaggy-toothed, poverty-struck
remark if I ever heard one.

MISSY   (*Enters side door.*)   Youall wash your hands and
git ready—Gitlow! Where's Lutiebelle?

GITLOW   (*Evasive.*)   She didn't get back yet.

MISSY   We know she didn't get back yet.

PURLIE   Where is Lutiebelle, Gitlow?

GITLOW   What I mean is—on our way home from church, we stopped by Ol' Cap'n's awhile, and he asked me to leave her there to help with the Sunday dinner.

PURLIE   And you left her!

MISSY   With that frisky ol' man?

GITLOW   For goodness' sakes, she's only waiting on table.

PURLIE   The woman I love don't wait on table for nobody, especially Ol' Cap'n; I know that scoun'. I'm going and get her!

GITLOW   Wait a minute—you can't get her right now!

PURLIE   (*Studying him.*) What you mean, I can't get her right now?

GITLOW   Not right this minute—that'll spoil everything. Ol' Cap'n wouldn't like it.

MISSY   How low can you git, Gitlow!

GITLOW   I mean she's got to stay and bring us the $500.00.

MISSY   What 500 dollars?

PURLIE   I thought you already had the money?

GITLOW   Well, not exactly. But he promised me faithful to send it down by Lutiebelle.

PURLIE   I'm going and get Lutiebelle—

GITLOW   Wait a minute, wait a minute; you want to buy Big Bethel back or don't you?

PURLIE   (*A glimmering of truth.*) I hope I misunderstand you!

GITLOW   You said it yourself: It is meet that the daughters of Zion should sacrifice themselves for the cause.

PURLIE   (*Grabbing up* MISSY's *bat.*) Gitlow, I'll kill you—!

GITLOW   Wait a minute, wait a minute, wait a MINUTE!

(*The door opens suddenly, and there stands* LUTIE-
BELLE. *She, too, has on her Sunday best, but it is di-
sheveled. She has a work apron over her dress, with
her hat completely askew, the once proud feather now
hanging over her face. In her hands she still clutches
a rolling pin.*)

MISSY   Lutiebelle—Lutiebelle, honey!

LUTIEBELLE   I think I am going to faint. (*She starts to collapse, and they rush toward her to help; but suddenly she
straightens up and waves them off.*) No, I ain't, either—
I'm too mad! (*She shudders in recollection.*) I was
never so insulted in all my dad-blamed life!

PURLIE   Lutiebelle!

LUTIEBELLE   Oh, excuse me, Reb'n Purlie—I know I look
a mess, but—

MISSY   What happened up there?

LUTIEBELLE   (*Boiling again.*) I'm a maid first class, Aunt
Missy, and I'm proud of it!

MISSY   Of course you are.

LUTIEBELLE   I ain't had no complaints to speak of since first
I stepped into the white folks' kitchen. I'm clean; I'm
honest, and I work hard—but one thing: I don't stand for
no stuff from them white folks.

PURLIE   Of course you don't. You don't have to—

LUTIEBELLE   I mean, I KNOW my job, and I DO my job—
and the next ol' sweaty, ol' grimey, ol' drunkeny man puts
his hands on me—so much as touch like he got no business doing—God grant me strength to kill him! Excuse
me, Reb'n Purlie.

GITLOW   Well, Ol' Cap'n do get playful at times—did he
send the money?

LUTIEBELLE   Money! What money? There ain't none!

GITLOW   What! Naw, naw! He wouldn't do that to me—not to good ol', faithful ol' Gitlow, nawsir!

LUTIEBELLE   The whole thing was a trick—to get you out of the house—

GITLOW   Not to ME he didn't!

LUTIEBELLE   So he could—sneak up behind me in the pantry!

MISSY   What I tell you!—what I tell you!

LUTIEBELLE   I knowed the minute I— Come grabbing on me, Reb'n Purlie; come grabbing his dirty ol' hands on me!

PURLIE   He did!

LUTIEBELLE   And twisting me around, and—and pinching me, Reb'n Purlie!

PURLIE   Pinching you—where? Where?

LUTIEBELLE   Must I, Reb'n Purlie—?

PURLIE   I demand to know—where did he pinch you!

(LUTIEBELLE *diffidently locates a spot on her left cheek. They all examine it anxiously.*)

MISSY   That's him all right!

GITLOW   Aw, Missy—

MISSY   I'd know them fingerprints anywhere!

LUTIEBELLE   Right in the pantry—and then he, he—Oh, Reb'n Purlie, I'm so ashamed!

PURLIE   What did he do? Tell me, woman, tell me: what did he do? WHAT DID HE DO?

LUTIEBELLE   He kissed me!

PURLIE AND MISSY   No!

LUTIEBELLE   He kissed me—right here.

MISSY   (*Squinting, it is a very small spot indeed.*)   Right where?   (LUTIEBELLE *is so broken up, she can only point to her other cheek.*)

GITLOW   Aw, for Pete's sakes.

PURLIE   (*Almost out of control.*)   He kissed my woman, Gitlow—he kissed the woman I love!

GITLOW   So what!

PURLIE   So what do you mean, "So what"? No man kisses the woman I love and lives! (GITLOW *laughs.*)   Go ahead, laugh! Laugh. Let's have one last look at your teeth before I knock 'em down your throat!

GITLOW   Aw, man, git off my nerves.

PURLIE   I'm going up that hill, and I'm gonna call that buzzardly ol' bastard out, and I wouldn't be surprised if I didn't beat him until he died.

LUTIEBELLE   (*Suddenly not so sure.*)   Reb'n Purlie—

GITLOW   (*Also wondering about* PURLIE.)   Now looka here, Purlie—don't you be no fool, boy—you still in Georgia. If you just got to defend the honor of the woman you love, do it somewhere else.

PURLIE   Kissing my woman—kissing my woman! (*Runs to window, flings it open and shouts out.*)   Man, I'll break your neck off!

LUTIEBELLE   (*Helping* GITLOW *and* MISSY *to wrestle* PURLIE *away from the window.*)   Please, Reb'n Purlie!

PURLIE   (*Breaks away and goes to window and shouts again.*)   I'll stomp your eyeballs in!

LUTIEBELLE   (*They snatch him from the window again.*) Don't, Reb'n Purlie—oh my goodness!—

PURLIE   (*Breaks away still again and shouts from window.*) I'll snatch your right arm outta the socket, and beat the rest of you to death!

LUTIEBELLE   (*This time they get him away, and close the window.*)   Don't talk like that, Reb'n Purlie!

MISSY   (*Standing at the window, arms widespread to block him.*)   Have you gone crazy?

GITLOW   (*Still struggling with* PURLIE.)   You go up that hill tonight, boy, and they'll kill you!

PURLIE   Let 'em kill me, it won't be the first time.

LUTIEBELLE   Aunt Missy, stop him—

GITLOW   Listen, boy! This is your Deputy-For-The-Colored telling you you ain't gonna leave this house, and that's an order!

PURLIE   You try and stop me!

GITLOW   Good gracious a life, what's the matter with you? The man only kissed your woman.

PURLIE   Yeah! And what you suppose he'd a done to me if I'd a kissed his? (*The one question too obvious to answer.*)   And that's exactly what I'm gonna do to him!

LUTIEBELLE   Please, Reb'n Purlie. I beg you on bended knees. (*She throws her arms around him.*)

PURLIE   (*Holds her close.*)   For the glory and honor of the Negro National Anthem; for the glory and honor of brown-skin Negro womanhood; for the glory and honor of— (LUTIEBELLE *suddenly kisses him big and hard.*) —for LUTIEBELLE! (*His emotions explode him out of the door which slams shut behind him.*)

GITLOW   (*Singing.*)   "I hear them gentle bloodhounds callin'—Old Black Joe." . . .

(LUTIEBELLE *finds the deepest spot in* MISSY'S *shoulder to bury her head and cry, as:*)

CURTAIN

Act III

Scene 1

SCENE   *The shack.*

TIME   *Later that same night.*

AT RISE   *There is light only from a KEROSENE LAMP turned down low. The air of Sunday is gone from the room. The tablecloth has been changed, and things are as they were before.* LUTIEBELLE *enters Down Right.*

LUTIEBELLE   Is it him, Aunt Missy, is it him?

MISSY   No, honey, not yet.

LUTIEBELLE   Oh, I could have sworn I thought it was him. What time is it?

MISSY   About four in the morning from the sound of the birds. Now, why ain't you sleep after all that hot toddy I give you?

LUTIEBELLE   I can't sleep. The strangest thing. I keep hearing bells—

MISSY   Bells?

LUTIEBELLE   Wedding bells. Ain't that funny? Oh, Lord, please don't let him be hurt bad, please! Where can he be, Aunt Missy?

MISSY   Now don't you worry 'bout Purlie. My! You put on your pretty pink dress!

LUTIEBELLE   Yes, ma'am. It's the only thing I got fitting to propose in.

MISSY   Oh?

LUTIEBELLE   I thought, to sort of show my gratitude, I'd offer him my hand in matrimony—it's all I've got.

MISSY   It's a nice hand, and a nice dress—just right for matrimony.

LUTIEBELLE   You really think so, Aunt Missy: really, really, really?

MISSY   I know so, and wherever Reb'n Purlie is this morning, you can bet your bottom dollar he knows it, too.

LUTIEBELLE   Ten thousand Queens of Sheba! Aunt Missy—

MISSY   Yes—

LUTIEBELLE   (*Letting it out in a gush.*)   I wanted him to get mad; I wanted him to tear out up that hill; I wanted him to punch that sweaty ol' buzzard in his gizzard— You think I was wrong?

MISSY   I should say not!

LUTIEBELLE   Course I coulda punched him myself, I reckon.

MISSY   Why should you? Why shouldn't our men folks defend our honor with the white folks once in a while? They ain't got nothing else to do.

LUTIEBELLE   You really, really, really think so?

MISSY   (*Shrugs.*)   Ten thousand Queens of Sheba—

LUTIEBELLE   Oh, my goodness, when he walks through that door, I'm just gonna—

   (*Door Down Left suddenly swings open to reveal* GIT-LOW.)

GITLOW   (*Entering.*)   Well, well, Lutiebelle.

LUTIEBELLE   Did you find him, Uncle Git?

MISSY   Don't depend on Gitlow for nothing, honey— (*Exits to kitchen.*)

LUTIEBELLE   Where can he be, Uncle Gitlow, where can he be?

GITLOW   Oh—good wind like this on his tail oughta put him somewhere above Macon long 'bout now, if his shoes hold out!

LUTIEBELLE   You mean—running!

GITLOW   What's wrong with running? It emancipated more people than Abe Lincoln ever did.

LUTIEBELLE   How dare you! The finest, bravest man—

GITLOW   The finer they come, the braver they be, the deader these white folks gonna kill 'em when they catch 'em!

MISSY   (*Entering from the kitchen.*)   Gitlow, I'll skin you!

GITLOW   All that talk about calling that man out, and whipping him—

MISSY   A man is duty-bound to defend the honor of the woman he loves, and any woman worth her salt will tell you so.

LUTIEBELLE   Love can make you do things you really can't do—can't it, Aunt Missy?

GITLOW   Look. That man's got the president, the governor, the courthouse, and both houses of the congress—on his side!

MISSY   Purlie Judson is a man the Negro woman can depend on!

LUTIEBELLE   An honor to his race, and a credit to his people!

GITLOW   (*Not to be sidetracked.*)   The army, the navy, the marines; the sheriff, the judge, the jury, the police, the F.B.I.—all on his side. Not to mention a pair of brass knucks and the hungriest dogs this side of hell! Surely youall don't expect that po' boy to go up against all that caucasiatic power empty-handed!

MISSY   O, ye of little faith!

LUTIEBELLE   Didn't my Lord deliver Daniel?

GITLOW   Of course he did—but lions is one thing and white folks is another!

MISSY   Where there's a will there's a woman—

LUTIEBELLE   And where there's a woman there's a way!

GITLOW (*Exasperated.*) Great Gawdamighty! All right—go ahead and have it your way. But I'll lay you six bits 'gainst half my seat on the heavenly choir, Purlie ain't been up that hill. And the minute he walks in that door—if he ever shows up again around here—I'm gonna prove it! Oh, damn—I can make better time out there talkin' to that mule.

MISSY Why not—it's one jackass to another.

> (GITLOW *exits to the kitchen.* MISSY *and* LUTIEBELLE *look at each other, both determined not to give way to the very real fright they feel. There is a long, uncomfortable pause.*)

LUTIEBELLE It sure is a lovely year—for this time of morning, I mean. (*There is a pause.*) I can't tell you how much all this fresh air, wine-smoke, and apple-bite reminds me of Alabama.

MISSY Oh, yes—Ol' Georgia can sure smile pretty when she's of a mind to—

PURLIE (*Bursts in.*) "Arise and shine for thy light has come."

MISSY Purlie—Purlie Victorious! (*They embrace.*)

LUTIEBELLE Oh, you Reb'n Purlie you!

PURLIE "Truth and Mercy are met together, Righteousness and Peace have kissed each other!" (*They embrace.*)

MISSY Let me look at you—behold the man!—knee-deep in shining glory. Great day the righteous marching! What happened to you?

PURLIE Mine enemy hath been destroyed!

MISSY What!

PURLIE I told that ol' man twenty years ago, Missy, that over his dead body, Big Bethel would rise again!

MISSY Purlie—! You mean you done—

PURLIE   "Have I any pleasure that the wicked should die, saith the Lord, and not turn from his ways and live!" Lutiebelle, put on your hat and coat, and hurry!

LUTIEBELLE   Yessir!

PURLIE   Missy, throw us some breakfast into a paper sack, and quick!

MISSY   Yessir!

PURLIE   Gitlow, I'm calling on you and your fellow mule to write a new page in the annals of Negro History Week.

GITLOW   (*Entering.*) Well, if it ain't ol' little black riding hood, dere! How was the mean ol' peckerwolf tonight, dere, kingfish?

MISSY   Tell him, Purlie boy, what you told us: how you sashayed up that hill with force and fistfight!

GITLOW   Hallelujah!

MISSY   How you fit Ol' Cap'n to a halt and a standstill!

GITLOW   Talk that talk!

MISSY   And left him laying in a pool of his own Confederate blood!

GITLOW   For Pete sakes, Missy—quit lying!

MISSY   Don't you dare call Purlie Judson a liar!

LUTIEBELLE   No man calls Reb'n Purlie a liar and lives!

GITLOW   What's the matter with you people? Purlie ain't been up that hill; Purlie ain't seen Ol' Cap'n; Purlie ain't done doodley squat! And all that gabble about leaving somebody in a pool of his own Confederate blood ain't what the bull left in the barnyard!

PURLIE   Five hundred dollars says it is! (*Draws roll of bills from his pocket, for all to see.*)

ALL   Five hundred dollars!

PURLIE   In cool September cash!

GITLOW   Money! (*Lunges forward, but* PURLIE *slaps his hand.*)

PURLIE   And that ain't all I got— (*Opens bag he has brought. They look in.*)

GITLOW   (*Almost choking in awe.*) Oh, my goodness, Missy—great day in the morning time—Missy—Missy!

MISSY   (*Also impressed.*) Gitlow, that's *it!*

GITLOW   That's *it,* Missy—that's *it!*

MISSY   Of course that's *it!*—ain't nothing in the world but *it!* (PURLIE *slowly pulls out* OL' CAP'N'S *bull whip.*)

GITLOW   Ain't but one way—one way in all this world—for nobody to get that bull whip off'n Ol' Cap'n!

MISSY   And that's off'n his dead body!

GITLOW   And that's the everlovin' truth, so help me.

PURLIE   Here, take it—and burn it in a public place. Lutiebelle—

LUTIEBELLE   Yes, Reb'n Purlie.

PURLIE   This money belongs to the Negro people—

GITLOW   Reb'n Purlie, my boy, I apologize from the bottom of my knees. (*Kneels and starts to sing.*) "Gone are the days—"

MISSY   (*Snatching him to his feet.*) Get up and shut up!

PURLIE   (*Deliberately continuing to* LUTIEBELLE.) Take it, and wear it next to your heart.

LUTIEBELLE   (*Very conscious of the great charge laid upon her, turns her back to* GITLOW *and hides the money in her bosom.*) Until death us do part.

MISSY   (*To* GITLOW.) If I ever catch you with that song in your mouth again I'll choke you with it!

PURLIE   And go wake up the mule. We due in Waycross to buy Big Bethel.

GITLOW   I'm going, I'm going. (*Starts, but can't tear himself away.*) Cash—five hundred dollars in cash. And a bull whip, from Ol' Cap'n Cotchipee himself— Man, I'd give a pretty piece of puddin' to know how you did it!

MISSY   You go and wake up that mule! (*Turning back to* PURLIE.) Me, too! How did you do it, Purlie?

LUTIEBELLE   What happened when you first got there?

PURLIE   (*Almost laughing.*) Now wait a minute—don't rush me!

MISSY   That's what I say: don't rush him—let the man talk!

PURLIE   Talk! Missy, I told you. I haven't got time—

GITLOW   That's all right, Purlie, we'll listen in a hurry.

LUTIEBELLE   What happened when you called him out and whipped him?

PURLIE   I didn't call him out and whip him!

GITLOW   What!

MISSY   You didn't!

LUTIEBELLE   Reb'n Purlie—?

PURLIE   I mean, I did call him out—!

LUTIEBELLE   (*In ecstatic relief.*) Oh— You did call him out!

PURLIE   Yeah—but he didn't come.

ALL   What!

PURLIE   So—er—I went in to get him!

ALL   You did! Sure enough! What happened then?

PURLIE   (*Still seeking escape.*) Well, like I told you—

LUTIEBELLE   Tell us, Reb'n Purlie—please!

PURLIE   (*No escape.*) Well—here was me; and there was him—twisted and bent like a pretzel! Face twitchified like a pan of worms; eyes bugging out; sweat dreening down like rain; tongue plumb clove to the roof of his mouth! (*He looks to his audience, and is impelled to go on.*) Well—this thief! This murderer; this adulterer—this oppressor of all my people, just a sitting there: Stonewall Jackson Cotchipee, just a sitting there. (*Begins to respond to his own fantasy.*) "Go to, rich man, weep and howl, for your sorrows shall come upon you." And-a "Wherefore abhor yourself, and repent Ye in sackcloth and ashes!" cause ol' Purlie is done come to get you!

LUTIEBELLE   (*Swept away.*)   Oh, my Lord!

MISSY   What he do, Purlie—what he do!?

PURLIE   Fell down on bended knees and cried like a baby!

MISSY   Ol' Cap'n Cotchipee on his knees!?

GITLOW   Great day in the morning time!

PURLIE   (*Warming to the task.*)   Don't beg me, white folks, it's too late. "Mercy?" What do you know about mercy?! Did you have mercy on Ol' Uncle Tubb when he asked you not to cheat him out of his money so hard, and you knocked him deaf in his left ear? Did you have mercy on Lolly's boy when he sassed you back, and you took and dipped his head in a bucket of syrup! And twenty years ago when little Purlie, black and manly as he could be, stood naked before you and your bull whip and pleaded with tears in his li'l ol' eyes, did you have mercy!?

GITLOW   Naw!

PURLIE   —And I'll not have mercy now!

ALL   Amen! Help him, Lawd! Preach it, boy, preach it! (*Etc.*)

PURLIE   Vengeance is mine saith the Lord! (*Hallelujah!*) Ye serpents; ye vipers; ye low-down sons of—! (*Amen!*) How can ye escape the damnation of hell!

MISSY   Throw it at him, boy!

PURLIE   And then, bless my soul, I looked up—up from the blazing depths of my righteous indignation! And I saw tears spill over from his eyeballs; and I heard the heart be-clutching anguish of his outcry! His hands was both a-tremble; and slobber a-dribblin' down his lips!

GITLOW   Oh, my Lawd!

PURLIE   And he whined and whimpered like a ol' hound dog don't want you to kick him no more!

LUTIEBELLE   Great goodness a mighty!

PURLIE   And I commenced to ponder the meaning of this evil thing that groveled beneath my footstool—this no-good lump of nobody!—not fit to dwell on this earth beside the children of the blessed—an abomination to the Almighty and stench in the nostrils of his people! And yet— (*Pause for effect.*)   And yet—a man! A weak man; a scared man; a pitiful man; like the whole southland bogged down in sin and segregation crawling on his knees before my judgment seat—but still a MAN!

GITLOW   A man, Lawd!

PURLIE   He, too, like all the South, was one of God's creatures—

MISSY   Yes, Lawd!

PURLIE   He, too, like all the South, could never be beyond the reach of love, hope, and redemption.

LUTIEBELLE   Amen!

PURLIE   Somewhere for him—even for him, some father's heart was broken, some mother's tears undried.

GITLOW   Dry 'em, Lawd!

PURLIE   I am my brother's keeper!

ALL   Yes, Lawd.

PURLIE   And thinking on these things, I found myself to pause, and stumble in my great resolve—and sorrow squeezed all fury from my heart—and pity plucked all hatred from my soul—and the racing feet of an avenging anger slowed down to a halt and a standstill—and the big, black, and burly fist of my strong correction—raised on high like a stroke of God's own lightning—fell useless by my side. The book say, "Love one another."

MISSY   Love one another!

PURLIE   The book say, "Comfort ye one another."

LUTIEBELLE   Comfort ye one another.

PURLIE   The book say, "Forgive ye one another."

GITLOW   Forgive Ol' Cap'n, Lord.

PURLIE   Slowly I turned away—to leave this lump of human mess and misery to the infinite darkness of a hell for white folks only, when suddenly—

MISSY   Suddenly, Lord.

PURLIE   Suddenly I put on my brakes—Purlie Victorious Judson stopped dead in his tracks—and stood stark still, and planted his feet, and rared back, asked himself and all the powers—that—be some mighty important questions.

LUTIEBELLE   Yes, he did, Lawd.

MISSY   And that is the truth!

PURLIE   How come—I asked myself, it's always the colored folks got to do all the forgiving?

GITLOW   Man, you mighty right!

PURLIE   How come the only cheek gits turned in this country is the Negro cheek!

MISSY   Preach to me, boy!

PURLIE   What was this, this—man—Ol' Cap'n Cotchipee— that in spite of all his sins and evils, he still had dominion over me?

LUTIEBELLE   Ain't that the truth!

PURLIE   God made us all equal—God made us all brothers—

ALL   Amen, amen.

PURLIE   "And hath made of one blood all nations of men
for to dwell on the face of the earth."—Who changed all
that!?

GITLOW   (*Furious.*)   Who changed it, he said.

PURLIE   Who took it and twisted it around!

MISSY   (*Furious.*)   Who was it, he said!

LUTIEBELLE   (*Furious.*)   And where's that scoun' hiding?!

PURLIE   So that the Declarator of Independence himself
might seem to be a liar?

GITLOW   Who, that's what I want to know, who?

PURLIE   That a man the color of his face—   (*Pointing up
Cotchipee Hill.*)   could live by the sweat of a man the
color of mine!

LUTIEBELLE   Work with him, Lawd, work with him!

PURLIE   —Could live away up there in his fine, white mansion, and us down here in a shack not fitting to house the
fleas upon his dogs!

GITLOW   Nothing but fleas!

PURLIE   —Could wax hisself fat on the fat of the land;
steaks, rice, chicken, roastineers, sweet potato pies, hot
buttered biscuits and cane syrup anytime he felt like it and
never hit a lick at a snake! And us got to every day git-up-
and-git-with-it, sunup-to-sundown, on fatback and corn-
meal hoecakes—and don't wind up owning enough ground
to get buried standing up in!

MISSY   Do, Lord!

PURLIE   —And horses and cadillacs, bull whips and bour-
bon, and two for 'leven dollar seegars—and our fine young

men to serve at his table; and our fine young women to serve in his bed!

LUTIEBELLE   Help him, Lawd.

PURLIE   Who made it like this—who put the white man on top?

GITLOW   That's what I wants to know!

PURLIE   Surely not the Lord God of Israel who is a just God!

MISSY   Hah, Lord!

PURLIE   And no respecter of persons! Who proved in the American Revolution that all men are created equal!

GITLOW   Man, I was there when he proved it!

PURLIE   Endowed with Civil Rights and First Class Citizenship, Ku Klux Klan, White Citizens Council notwithstanding!

MISSY   Oh, yes, he did!

PURLIE   And when my mind commenced to commemorate and to reconsider all these things—

GITLOW   Watch him, Lawd!

PURLIE   And I thought of the black mother in bondage— (*Yes.*) and I thought of the black father in prison— (*IIa, Lawd!*) And of Momma herself—Missy can tell how pretty she was—

MISSY   Indeed I can!

PURLIE   How she died outdoors on a dirty sheet cause the hospital doors said—"For white folks only." And of Papa, God rest his soul—who brought her tender loving body back home—and laid her to sleep in the graveyard—and cried himself to death among his children!

MISSY   (*Crying.*) Purlie, Purlie—

PURLIE   (*Really carried away.*) Then did the wrath of a righteous God possess me; and the strength of the host and of ten thousand swept into my good right arm—and I arose and I smote Ol' Cap'n a mighty blow! And the wind from my fist ripped the curtains from the eastern walls— and I felt the weight of his ol' bull whip nestling in my hands—and the fury of a good Gawd-almighty was within me; and I beat him—I whipped him—and I flogged him —and I cut him—I destroyed him!

(IDELLA *enters.*)

GITLOW   Great day and the righteous marching— Whoeeeee! Man, I ain't been stirred that deep since the tree caught fire on a possum hunt and the dogs pushed Papa in the pot.

MISSY   Idella, you shoulda heard him!

IDELLA   I did hear him—all the way across the valley. I thought he was calling hogs. Well, anyway: all hell is broke loose at the big house. Purlie, you better get outta here. Ol' Cap'n is on the phone to the sheriff.

MISSY   Ol' Cap'n Cotchipee is dead.

IDELLA   The hell you preach.

ALL   What!

IDELLA   Ol' Cap'n ain't no more dead than I am.

LUTIEBELLE   That's a mighty tacky thing to say about your ex-fellow man.

MISSY   Mighty tacky.

LUTIEBELLE   Reb'n Purlie just got through preaching 'bout it. How he marched up Cotchipee hill—

GITLOW   (*Showing the bull whip.*) And took Ol' Cap'n by the bull whip—

MISSY   And beat that ol' buzzard to death!

IDELLA   That is the biggest lie since the devil learned to talk!

LUTIEBELLE   I am not leaving this room till somebody apologizes to Reb'n Purlie V. Judson, the gentleman of my intended.

IDELLA   Purlie Judson! Are you gonna stand there sitting on your behind, and preach these people into believing you spent the night up at the big house whipping Ol' Cap'n to death when all the time you was breaking into the commissary!

MISSY   Breaking into the commissary!

GITLOW   Something is rotten in the cotton!

PURLIE   It's all right, Miz Idella—I'll take it from there—

MISSY   It is not all right—!

PURLIE   While it is true that, maybe, I did not go up that hill just word for word, and call that ol' man out, and beat him to death so much on the dotted line—!

MISSY   (*Snatching up the paper bag.*)   I'm goin' to take back my lunch!

PURLIE   Missy! Wait a minute!

LUTIEBELLE   You know what, Aunt Missy?

MISSY   Yes, honey?

LUTIEBELLE   Sometimes I just wish I could drop dead for a while!

PURLIE   Wait, Lutiebelle, give me a chance to—

LUTIEBELLE   Here's your money!— (*Puts roll into* PURLIE'S *hand.*)   And that goes for every other great big ol' handsome man in the whole world!

PURLIE   What you want me to do? Go up that hill by myself and get my brains knocked out?

MISSY   It's little enough for the woman you love!

LUTIEBELLE   Why'd you have to preach all them wonderful things that wasn't so?

GITLOW   And why'd you have to go and change your mind?

PURLIE   I didn't mean for them not to be so: it was a—a parable! A prophecy! Believe me! I ain't never in all my

life told a lie I didn't mean to make come true, some day!
Lutiebelle—!

IDELLA   Purlie: unless you want to give heartbreak a headache, you better run!

PURLIE   Run—run for what!

MISSY   You want Ol' Cap'n to catch you here!?

PURLIE   Confound Ol' Cap'n! Dad-blast Ol' Cap'n! Damn,
damn, damn, and double-damn Ol' Cap'n!

(*The front door swings open and in walks* OL' CAP'N
steaming with anger.)

OL' CAP'N   (*Controlling himself with great difficulty.*)
Somebody—I say somebody—is calling my name!

GITLOW   Ol' Cap'n, you just in time to settle a argument: is
Rudolph Valentino still dead?

OL' CAP'N   Shut up!

GITLOW   (*To* MISSY.) See—I told you.

OL' CAP'N   One thing I have not allowed in my cotton patch
since am-I-born-to-die! And that's stealin'! Somebody
broke into my commissary tonight—took two cans of sar-
dines, a box of soda crackers, my bull whip!— (*Picks up
whip from table.*) And five hundred dollars in cash. And,
boy— (*Walking over to* PURLIE.) I want it back!

LUTIEBELLE   Stealing ain't all that black and white.

MISSY   And we certainly wasn't the ones that started it!

GITLOW   Who stole me from Africa in the first place?

LUTIEBELLE   Who kept me in slavery from 1619 to 1863,
working me to the bone without no social security?

PURLIE   And tonight—just because I went up that hill, and
disembezzled my own inheritance that you stole from
me—!

OL' CAP'N   (*Livid.*) I have had a belly full of your black
African sass—!

(*The door bursts open again; this time it is the* SHERIFF *who comes in with pistol drawn.*)

SHERIFF   All right, everybody, drop that gun!

PURLIE   Drop what gun?

OL' CAP'N   So there you are, you idiot—what kept you so long?

SHERIFF   Like you told us to do on the phone, suh, we was taking a good, long, slow snoop 'round and 'bout the commissary looking for clues! And dog-gone if one didn't, just a short while ago, stumble smack into our hands!

OL' CAP'N   What!

SHERIFF   We caught the culprit red-handed—bring in the prisoner, Dep!

DEPUTY   Glad to oblige you, Sheriff.

(*Enter* DEPUTY, *dragging* CHARLIE, *who has his hands cuffed behind him; wears heavy leg shackles, and has a large white gag stuck into his mouth.*)

SHERIFF   Southern justice strikes again!

OL' CAP'N   Charlie! oh, no!

IDELLA   Charlie, my baby!

OL' CAP'N   Release him, you idiots! Release him at once! (*Everybody pitches in to set* CHARLIE *free.*)   What have they done to you, my boy?

IDELLA   What have they done to you!

CHARLIE   (*Free from the gag.*)   Hello, Paw—Idella— Purlie—

OL' CAP'N   I'll have your thick, stupid necks for this!

SHERIFF   It was you give the orders, suh!

OL' CAP'N   Not my son, you idiot!

DEPUTY   It was him broke into the commissary.

OL' CAP'N   What!

SHERIFF   It was him stole the five hundred dollars—he confessed!

OL' CAP'N   Steal? A Cotchipee? Suh, that is biologically impossible! (*To* CHARLIE.) Charlie, my boy. Tell them the truth—tell them who stole the money. It was Purlie, wasn't it, boy?

CHARLIE   Well, as a matter of fact, Paw—it was mostly me that broke in and took the money, I'd say. In fact it WAS me!

OL' CAP'N   No!

CHARLIE   It was the only thing I could do to save your life, Paw.

OL' CAP'N   Save my life! Idella, he's delirious—!

CHARLIE   When Purlie come up that hill after you last night, I seen him, and lucky for you I did. The look he had on his face against you was not a Christian thing to behold! It was terrible! I had to get into that commissary, right then and there, open that safe, and pay him his inheritance —even then I had to beg him to spare your life!

OL' CAP'N   (*To* PURLIE.) You spare my life, boy? How dare you? (*To* CHARLIE.) Charlie, my son, I know you never recovered from the shock of losing your mother— almost before you were born. But don't worry—it was Purlie who stole that money and I'm going to prove it. (*Starts to take out gun.* GITLOW *grabs gun.*) Gitlow, my old friend, arrest this boy, Gitlow! As Deputy-For-The-Colored—I order you to arrest this boy for stealing!

GITLOW   (*With a brand new meaning.*) "Gone are the days—" (*Still twirls pistol safely out of* OL' CAP'N'S *reach.*)

PURLIE   "Stealin," is it? Well, I'm gonna really give you something to arrest me for. (*Snatches bull whip.*)

OL' CAP'N   Have a care, boy: I'm still a white man.

PURLIE   Congratulations! Twenty years ago, I told you this bull whip was gonna change hands one of these days!

MISSY   Purlie, wait—!

PURLIE   Stay out of my struggle for power!

MISSY   You can't do wrong just because it's right!

GITLOW   Never kick a man when he's down except in self-defense!

LUTIEBELLE   And no matter what you are, and always will be—the hero of Cotchipee Hill.

PURLIE   Am I?

LUTIEBELLE   Ten thousand queens!

PURLIE   I bow to the will of the Negro people. (*Throws whip away. Back to* OL' CAP'N.)   But one thing, Ol' Cap'n, I am released of you   the entire Negro people is released of you! No more shouting hallelujah! every time you sneeze, nor jumping jackass every time you whistle "Dixie"! We gonna love you if you let us and laugh as we leave if you don't. We want our cut of the Constitution, and we want it now: and not with no teaspoon, white folks—throw it at us with a shovel!

OL' CAP'N   Charlie, my boy—my own, lily-white, Anglo-Saxon, semi-confederate son. I know you never recovered from the shock of losing your mother, almost before you were born. But don't worry: there is still time to take these insolent, messy cotton-picking ingrates down a peg—and prove by word and deed that God is still a white man. Tell 'em! Boy, tell 'em!

CHARLIE   Tell 'em what, Paw?

OL' CAP'N   Tell 'em what you and me have done together. Nobody here would believe me. Tell 'em how you went to Waycross, Saturday night, in my name—

CHARLIE   Yes, sir— I did.

OL' CAP'N   Tell 'em how you spoke to Ol' Man Pelham in my name—

CHARLIE   Yes, sir—I spoke to him.

OL' CAP'N   And paid him cash for that ol' barn they used to call Big Bethel!

CHARLIE   Yes, sir; that's what I did, all right.

OL' CAP'N   And to register the deed in the courthouse in my name—

CHARLIE   Yes, sir, that's exactly what you told me to do—

OL' CAP'N   Then—ain't but one thing left to do with that ramshackle dung-soaked monstrosity—that's burn the damn thing down. (*Laughs aloud in his triumph.*)

CHARLIE   But, Paw—

OL' CAP'N   First thing, though—let me see the deed: I wouldn't want to destroy nothing that didn't—legally— belong to me. (*Snatches deed from* CHARLIE's *hand. Begins to mumble as he reads it.*)

IDELLA   Twenty years of being more than a mother to you!

CHARLIE   Wait, Idella, wait. I did go to Waycross, like Paw said; I did buy the barn—excuse me, Purlie: the church— like he said; and I registered the deed at the courthouse like he told me—but not in Paw's name—

OL' CAP'N   (*Startled by something he sees on the deed.*) What's this?

CHARLIE   (*To* IDELLA.)   I registered the deed in the name of—

OL' CAP'N   (*Reading, incredulous.*)   "Purlie Victorious Judson—" No!

IDELLA   PURLIE VICTORIOUS Judson?

OL' CAP'N   (*Choking on the words.*)   Purlie Victorious Judsssss—aaaarrrrgggghhhhh! (*The horror of it strikes him absolutely still.*)

CHARLIE   (*Taking the deed from* OL' CAP'N's *limp hand.*)
It was the only thing I could do to save your life.   (*Offering deed to* PURLIE.)   Well, Purlie, here it is.

PURLIE   (*Counting out the five hundred dollars.*) You did
a good job, Charlie—I'm much obliged!

CHARLIE   (*Refuses money; still holds out deeds to* PURLIE.)
Thank you, Purlie, but—

PURLIE   Big Bethel is my Bethel, Charlie: it's my responsibility. Go on, take it.

CHARLIE   No, no! I couldn't take your money, Purlie—

IDELLA   Don't be a fool, boy—business is business.   (*She
takes the deed from* CHARLIE *and gives it to* PURLIE, *while
at the same time taking the money from* PURLIE.)

CHARLIE   Idella—I can't do that!

IDELLA   I can! I'll keep it for you.

CHARLIE   Well—all right. But only, if—if—

IDELLA   Only if what?

CHARLIE   (*To* PURLIE.)   Would you let me be a member of
your church?

MISSY   You?

GITLOW   Li'l Charlie Cotchipee!

LUTIEBELLE   A member of Big Bethel?

CHARLIE   May I? That is—that is, if you don't mind—as
soon as you get it started?

PURLIE   Man, we're already started: the doors of Big Bethel,
Church of the New Freedom for all Mankind, are hereby
declared "Open for business!"

GITLOW   Brother Pastor, I move we accept Brother Charlie
Cotchipee as our first candidate for membership to Big
Bethel on a integrated basis—

MISSY   I second that motion!

PURLIE   You have heard the motion. Are you ready for the
question?

ALL   (*Except* OL' CAP'N.)   Question!

PURLIE   Those in favor will signify by saying "Aye."   (EV-
ERYBODY, *except* OL' CAP'N, *crowds around* CHARLIE, *saying*
"*Aye*" *over and over, in such a crescendo of welcome that*
PURLIE *has to ride over the noise.*)   Those opposed?
(*Looks at* OL' CAP'N, *who is still standing, as if frozen, as
we last saw him. He does not answer.*)   Those opposed will
signify by saying—

> (*He stops . . . all eyes focus on* OL' CAP'N *now, still
> standing in quiet, frozen-like immobility. There is a
> moment of silence, an unspoken suspicion in every-
> body's face. Finally,* GITLOW *goes over and touches* OL'
> CAP'N, *still standing rigid. Still he does not move.* GIT-
> LOW *feels his pulse, listens to his heart, and lifts up his
> eyelids. Nothing.*)

GITLOW   The first man I ever seen in all this world to drop
dead standing up!

BLACKOUT

Act III

Epilogue

TIME   *Immediately following.*

SCENE   *We are at Big Bethel at funeral services for* OL' CAP'N.

AT RISE   *We cannot see the coffin. We hear the ringing of the CHURCH BELL as we come out of the blackout.* PUR-LIE *is in the pulpit.*

PURLIE   And toll the bell, Big Bethel, toll the bell! Dearly beloved, recently bereaved, and friends, we welcome you to Big Bethel, Church of the New Freedom: part Baptist; part Methodist; part Catholic—with the merriness of Christmas and the happiness of Hanukkah; and to the first integrated funeral in the sovereign, segregated state of Georgia. Let there be no merriments in these buryments! Though you are dead, Ol' Cap'n, and in hell, I suspect— as post-mortal guest of honor, at our expense: it is not too late to repent. We still need togetherness; we still need each otherness—with faith in the futureness of our cause. Let us, therefore, stifle the rifle of conflict, shatter the scatter of discord, smuggle the struggle, tickle the pickle, and grapple the apple of peace!

GITLOW   This funeral has been brought to you as a public service.

PURLIE   Take up his bones. For he who was my skin's enemy, was brave enough to die standing for what he believed. . . . And it is the wish of his family—and his friends—that he be buried likewise— (*The* PALLBEARERS *enter, carrying* OL' CAP'N'S *ornate coffin just as he would have wished: standing up! It is draped in a Confederate flag; and his hat, his bull whip, and his pistol, have been fastened to the lid in appropriate places.*) Gently, gently. Put kindness in your fingers. He was a man—despite his own example.

363

Take up his bones. (*The* PALLBEARERS *slowly carry the upright coffin across the stage.*) Tonight, my friends—I find, in being black, a thing of beauty: a joy; a strength; a secret cup of gladness; a native land in neither time nor place—a native land in every Negro face! Be loyal to yourselves: your skin; your hair; your lips, your southern speech, your laughing kindness—are Negro kingdoms, vast as any other! Accept in full the sweetness of your blackness —not wishing to be red, nor white, nor yellow: nor any other race, or face, but this. Farewell, my deep and Africanic brothers, be brave, keep freedom in the family, do what you can for the white folks, and write me in care of the post office. Now, may the Constitution of the United States go with you; the Declaration of Independence stand by you; the Bill of Rights protect you; and the State Commission Against Discrimination keep the eyes of the law upon you, henceforth, now and forever. Amen.

CURTAIN

CONTRIBUTION

A One Act Play

Ted Shine

TED SHINE, born 19— in Dallas, Texas, whose interest in playwriting he traces back to elementary school, attended Howard University where, encouraged in Owen Dodson's playwriting class, he majored in drama and had two of his one-act plays performed: *Cold Day in August* and *Sho is Hot in the Cotton Patch*. After graduation, he spent two years at the Karamu Theatre in Cleveland, served in the army, and then studied under Dr. William Reardon at the University of Iowa, completed the requirements for an advanced degree and had his thesis play, *Epitaph for a Bluebird*, performed by the Iowa Drama Department.

Formerly a teacher of drama at both Dillard and Howard Universities, Mr. Shine is currently in the English Department of Prairie View College, Prairie View, Texas, where he is establishing a major in drama and continues to write. To date he is the author of fourteen plays.

Contribution was presented by the Negro Ensemble Company at the St. Marks Playhouse on March 25, 1969, and the production marked Mr. Shine's New York debut. Part of a bill of new works by Black authors, the play was the fourth offering in the second subscription season of the Negro Ensemble Company. Under the sure direction of Douglas Turner Ward, *Contribution* won special praise by Walter Kerr of the *New York Times*, who was impressed by "Mr. Shine's low-key sauciness, together with an uncanny knack for being warm-hearted and blood-curdling at once." Skillfully treading the borderline between farce and comedy, the play goes beyond the ingenuity of its central joke. For in the development of situation the character of the grandmother slowly unfolds to show her as a master of deception, a cunning, lovable, awesome woman who has mastered more than the art of baking. The humor and the horror do not detract from but underscore

moments of harsh truth spoken out of the agony of the characters' existence, while the skill with which the simple plot is
uncoiled sustains an undercurrent of militant outrage.

CONTRIBUTION

Characters

MRS. GRACE LOVE   *a Grandmother in her seventies*

KATY JONES   *a Neighbor*

EUGENE LOVE   *a College Student, Mrs. Love's Grandson*

SCENE   MRS. LOVE's *kitchen. Clean, neatly furnished, a door center leads into the backyard. A door, right, leads into the hall. In the center of the room is an ironing board with a white shirt resting on it to be ironed.*

TIME   *Sometime during the era of the sit-ins.*

PLACE   *A Southern Town.*

AT RISE   KATY *sits at the table drinking coffee. She is ill at ease.* MRS. LOVE *stands beside her mixing cornbread dough. Now and then she takes a drink of beer from the bottle resting on the table.*

MRS. LOVE   (*Singing*)
WHERE HE LEADS ME
IIIIIII SHALL FOLLOW!
WHERE HE LEADS ME
IIIIIII SHALL FOLLOW!
WHERE HE LEADS ME
IIIIIII SHALL FOLLOW!
IIIIIII'LLLLL GO WITH HIM—

EUGENE   (*Offstage.*)   GRANDMA, please! You'll wake the dead!

MRS. LOVE   I called you an hour ago. You dressed?

EUGENE   I can't find my pants.

MRS. LOVE   I pressed them. They're out here.
(EUGENE *enters in shorts and undershirt, unaware that* KATY *is present.*)

EUGENE   I just got those trousers out of the cleaners and they didn't need pressing. I'll bet you scorched them.   (*He sees* KATY *and conceals himself with his hands.*)

MRS. LOVE   You should wear a robe around the house, boy. You never know when I'm having company.   (*She tosses him the pants.*)

The text printed is from the author's typescript copy, Prairie View, Texas, 1969.

EUGENE   I'm sorry. 'Mornin', Miss Katy. (*He exits quickly.*)

KATY   Mornin', Eugene. (*To* MRS. LOVE.) He ran out of here like a skint cat. Like I ain't never seen a man in his drawers before.

MRS. LOVE   (*Pouring cornbread into pan.*) There, I'll put this bread in the oven and it'll be ready in no time. I appreciate your taking it down to the Sheriff for me. He'd bust a gut if he didn't have my cornbread for breakfast. (*Sings.*) I SING BECAUSE I'M HAPPY—I SING BE-CAUSE I'M FREE—

KATY   I'm only doing it because I don't want to see a woman your age out on the streets today—

MRS. LOVE   (*Singing.*) HIS EYE IS ON THE SPAR-ROW AND I KNOW HE WATCHES ME!

KATY   Just the same I'm glad you decided to take off. White folks have been coming into town since sun up by the truck loads. Mean white folks who're out for blood!

MRS. LOVE   They're just as scared as you, Katy Jones.

KATY   Ain't no sin to be scared. Ain't you scared for Eugene?

MRS. LOVE   Scared of what?

KATY   That lunch counter has been white for as long as I can remember—and the folks around here aim to keep it that way.

MRS. LOVE   Let 'em *aim* all they want to! The thing that tee's me off is they won't let me march.

KATY   Mrs. Love, your heart couldn't take it!

MRS. LOVE   You'd be amazed at what my heart's done took all these years, baby.

EUGENE   (*Entering.*) Where's my sport shirt? The green one?

MRS. LOVE   In the drawer where it belongs. I'm ironing this white shirt for you to wear.

EUGENE   A white shirt? I'm not going to a formal dance.

MRS. LOVE   I want you neat when you sit down at that counter. Newspaper men from all over the country'll be there and if they put your picture in the papers, I want folks to say, "my, ain't that a nice looking, neat, young man."

EUGENE   You ask your boss how long he'll let me stay neat?

MRS. LOVE   I ain't asked Sheriff Morrison nothin'.

EUGENE   He let you off today so you could nurse my wounds when I get back, huh?

MRS. LOVE   You ain't gonna get no wounds, son, and you ain't gonna get this nice white shirt ruined either. What's wrong with you anyway? You tryin' to—what yawl say—chicken out?

EUGENE   No, I'm not going to chicken out, but I *am* nervous.

KATY   I'm nervous too . . . for myself and for all you young folks. Like the Mayor said on TV last night the whites and the colored always get on well here. . .

EUGENE   So long as "we" stayed in our respective places.

KATY   He said if we want to eat in a drug store we ought to build our own.

EUGENE   Then why don't you build a drug store on Main Street with a lunch counter in it?

KATY   Where am I gonna get the money?

MRS. LOVE   Where is any colored person in this town gonna get the money? Even if we got it, you think they'd let us lease a building—let alone buy property on Main Street.

KATY   I know, Mrs. Love, but—

MRS. LOVE   But nothin'! If I was a woman your age I'd be joinin' them children!

KATY   I'm with yawl, Eugene, in mind—if not in body.

EUGENE   Um-huh.

KATY   But I have children to raise—and I have to think about my job.

MRS. LOVE   Why don't you think about your children's future? Them few pennies you make ain't worth it! And if things stay the same it'll be the same way for those children too; but Lord knows, if they're like the rest of the young folks today—they're gonna put you down real soon!

KATY   I provide for my children by myself—and they love me for it! We have food on our table each and every day!

MRS. LOVE   When's the last time you had steaks?

KATY   Well . . . at least we ain't starvin'!

EUGENE   Neither is your boss lady!

KATY   Mrs. Comfort say yawl are—*communists!*

EUGENE   I'LL BE DAMNED! How come every time a black person speaks up for himself he's got to be a communist?

KATY   That's what the white folks think!

EUGENE   Well ain't that somethin'! Here I am—old black me—trying to get this democracy to working like it oughta be working, and the democratic white folks say wait. Now tell me, why the hell would I want to join another bunch of white folks that I don't know nothin' about and expect them to put me straight?

MRS. LOVE   Here's your shirt, son. Wear a tie and comb that natural! Put a part in your hair!

EUGENE   Good Gracious! (*He exits.*)

KATY   "Militant!" That's what Mrs. Comfort calls us— "militants"!

MRS. LOVE   (*Removing bread from oven.*) What does that mean?

KATY   Bad! That's what it means—bad folks!

MRS. LOVE   I hope you love your children as much as you seem to love Miss Comfort.

KATY   I hate that woman! I hate all white folks—don't you?

MRS. LOVE   Katy Jones, I don't hate nobody. I get disgusted with 'em, but I don't hate 'em.

KATY   Well, you different from me.

MRS. LOVE   Ummmmmmmmm, just look at my cornbread!

KATY   It smells good!

MRS. LOVE   (*Buttering bread and wraps it.*)   Don't you dare pinch off it either!

KATY   I don't want that white man's food! I hope it chokes the hell outta that mean bastard!

MRS. LOVE   I see how come your boss lady is calling you militant, Katy.

KATY   Well, I don't like him! Patting me on the behind like I'm a dog. He's got that habit bad.

MRS. LOVE   You make haste with this bread. He likes it hot.

KATY   Yes'm. I ain't gonna be caught dead in the midst of all that ruckus.

MRS. LOVE   You hurry along now. (*Gives* KATY *the bread and* KATY *exits.* MRS. LOVE *watches her from the back door.*)   And don't you dare pinch off it! You'll turn to stone! (*She laughs to herself. She turns and moves to the hall door.*)   You about ready, son?

EUGENE   I guess so.

MRS. LOVE   Come out here and let me look at you.

EUGENE   Since when do I have to stand inspection?

MRS. LOVE   Since *now!*

(EUGENE *enters.*)

You look right smart. And I want you to stay that way.

EUGENE   How? You know the Sheriff ain't gonna stop at nothing to keep us out of that drug store.

MRS. LOVE   Stop worrying about Sheriff Morrison.

EUGENE   He's the one who's raisin' all the hell! The Mayor was all set to integrate until the Sheriff got wind of it.

MRS. LOVE   Yes, I know, but—Try to relax.

EUGENE   How can I relax?

MRS. LOVE   I thought most of you young "cats" had nerve today—

EUGENE   And I wish you'd stop embarrassing me using all that slang!

MRS. LOVE   I'm just tryin' to talk your talk, baby.

EUGENE   There's something wrong with a woman eighty years old trying to act like a teenager!

MRS. LOVE   What was it you was telling me the other day? 'Bout that gap—how young folks and old folks can't talk together?

EUGENE   The generation gap!

MRS. LOVE   Well, I done bridged it, baby! You dig?

EUGENE   You are ludicrous!

MRS. LOVE   Well, that's one up on me, but I'll cop it sooner or later.

EUGENE   I know you'll try!

MRS. LOVE   Damned right!

EUGENE   That's another thing—all this swearing you've been doing lately—

MRS. LOVE   Picked it up from you and your friends sitting right there in my living room under the picture of Jesus!

EUGENE   I. . . .

MRS. LOVE   Don't explain. Now you know how it sounds to me.

EUGENE   Why did you have to bring that up at a time like this?

MRS. LOVE   You brought it up, baby.

EUGENE   I wish you wouldn't call me baby—I'm a grown man.

MRS. LOVE   Ain't I heard you grown men callin' each other "baby"?

EUGENE   Well . . . that's different. And stop usin' "ain't" so much. You know better.

MRS. LOVE   I wish I was educated like you, Eugene, but I aren't!

EUGENE   Good gracious!

MRS. LOVE   Let me fix that tie.

EUGENE   My tie is all right!

MRS. LOVE   It's crooked.

EUGENE   Just like that phoney sheriff that you'd get up at six in the mornin' for to cook cornbread.

MRS. LOVE   The sheriff means well, son, in his fashion.

EUGENE   That bastard is one dimensional—all black!

MRS. LOVE   Don't let him hear you call him black!

EUGENE   What would he do? Beat me with his billy club like he does the rest of us around here?

MRS. LOVE   You have to try to understand folks like Mr. Morrison.

EUGENE   Turn the other cheek, huh?

MRS. LOVE   That's what the Bible says.

EUGENE   (*Mockingly.*)   That's what the Bible says!

MRS. LOVE   I sure do wish I could go with yawl!

EUGENE   To witness the slaughter?

MRS. LOVE   You young folks ain't the only militant ones, you know!

EUGENE   You work for the meanest paddy in town—and to hear you tell it, he adores the ground you walk on! Now you're a big militant!

MRS. LOVE   I try to get along with folks, son.

EUGENE   You don't have to work for trash like Sheriff Morrison! You don't have to work at all! You own this house. Daddy sends you checks which you tear up. You could get a pension if you weren't so stubborn—you don't have to work at your age! And you surely don't have to embarrass the family by working for trash!

MRS. LOVE   What am I supposed to do? Sit here and rot like an old apple? The minute a woman's hair turns gray folks want her to take to a rockin' chair and sit it out. Not this chick, baby. I'm keepin' active. I've got a long way to go and much more to do before I meet my maker.

EUGENE   Listen to you!

MRS. LOVE   I meant it! I want to be a part of this 'rights' thing—but no, yawl say I'm too old!

EUGENE   That's right, you are! Your generation and my generation are complete contrasts—we don't think alike at all! The grin and shuffle school is dead!

MRS. LOVE   (*Slaps him.*)   That's for calling me a "Tom"!

EUGENE   I didn't call you a "Tom," but I have seen you grinning and bowing to white folks and it made me sick at the stomach!

MRS. LOVE   And it put your daddy through college so he could raise you with comfort like he did—Northern comfort which you wasn't satisfied with. No, you had to come down here and "free" us soul brothers from bondage as if we can't do for ourselves! Now don't try to tell me that your world was perfect up there—I've been there and I've seen! Sick to your stomach! I get sick to my stomach everytime I see how disrespectful the world's gotten! I get sick to my stomach, baby, because the world is more ruined now than it ever was! You lookin' at me like that 'cause I shock you? *You* shock me! You know why? Your little secure behind is down here to make history in your own way—and you are scared "shitless!" I had dreams when I was your age too!

EUGENE   Times were different then. I know that—

MRS. LOVE   Maybe so, but in our hearts we knowed what was right and what was wrong. We knowed what this country was supposed to be and we knowed that we was a part of it—for better or for worse—like a marriage. We prayed for a better tomorrow—and that's why that picture of Jesus got dust on it in my front room right now—'cause the harder we prayed—the worse it got!

EUGENE   Things are better now, you always say.

MRS. LOVE   Let's hope they don't get no worse.

EUGENE   Thanks to *us*.

MRS. LOVE   If you don't take that chip off your shoulder I'm gonna blister your behind, boy! Sit down there and eat your breakfast!

EUGENE   I'm not hungry.

MRS. LOVE   Drink some juice then.

EUGENE   I don't want anything!

MRS. LOVE   Look at you—a nervous wreck at twenty-one—just because you've got to walk through a bunch of poor white trash and sit at a lunch counter in a musty old drug store!

EUGENE   I may be a little tense—it's only natural—you'd be too!

MRS. LOVE   I do my bit baby, and it don't affect me in the least! I've seen the blazing cross and hooded faces in my day. I've smelled black flesh burning with tar, and necks stretched like taffy.

EUGENE   Seeing those things was your contribution, I guess?

MRS. LOVE   You'd be surprised at *my* contribution!

EUGENE   Nothing that you'd do would surprise me. You're a hard headed old woman!

MRS. LOVE   Life ain't been pretty for me, son. Oh, I suppose I had some happiness-like when I married your grand-daddy or when I gave birth to your daddy, but as I watched him grow up I got meaner and meaner.

EUGENE   You may be evil, but not mean.

MRS. LOVE   I worked to feed and clothe him like Katy's doin' for her children, but I had a goal in mind. Katy's just doin' it to eat. I wanted something better for my son. They used to call me "nigger" one minute and swear that they loved me the next. I grinned and bore it like you said. Sometimes I even had to scratch my head and bow, but I got your daddy through college.

EUGENE   I know and I'm grateful—he's grateful. Why don't you go and live with him like he wants you to?

MRS. LOVE   'Cause I'm stubborn and independent! And I want to see me some more colored mens around here with pride and dignity!

EUGENE   So that Sheriff Morrison can pound the hell out of it every Saturday night?

MRS. LOVE   I've always worked for folks like that. I worked for a white doctor once, who refused to treat your grand-daddy. Let him die because he hated black folks. I worked for him and his family for 13 years and they grew to love me.

EUGENE   You are the *true* Christian lady!

MRS. LOVE   I held them white folk's hands when they was sick. Nursed their babies—and I sat back and watched 'em all die out year by year. Old Dr. Crawford was the last to go. He had worked around death all his life and death frightened him. He asked me—black me—to sit with him during his last hours.

EUGENE   I bet you hope they put me under the jail so that you can Tom up to your boss and say "I tried to tell him, but you know how—"

MRS. LOVE   (*Sharply.*)   I don't want to have to hit you again, boy!

EUGENE   I'm sorry.

MRS. LOVE   It ain't me that's nervous. You doin' all that huffin' and puffin'—the white folks are apt to blow you down with a hard stare. Now you scoot. Us Loves is known for our promptness.

EUGENE   If I die—remember I'm dying for Negroes like Miss Katy.

MRS. LOVE   You musta got that inferior blood from your mama's side of the family! You ain't gonna die, boy. You're coming back here to me just as pretty as you left.

EUGENE   Have you and the Sheriff reached a compromise?

MRS. LOVE   Just you go on.

EUGENE   (*Starts to the door. He stops.*)   I'll be back home, grandma.

MRS. LOVE   I know it, hon.   (*He turns to leave again.*)   Son!

EUGENE   Ma'am?

MRS. LOVE   The Bible says love and I does. I turns the other cheek and I loves 'til I can't love no more—   (EUGENE *nods.*)   Well . . . I reckon I ain't perfect— I ain't like Jesus was, I can only bear a cross so long. I guess I've "had it" as you say. Done been spit on, insulted, but I bore my cross.   (EUGENE *turns to go again.*)   Son, you've been a comfort to me. When you get to be my age you want someone to talk to who loves you, and I loves you from the bottom of my heart.

EUGENE   (*Embarrassed.*)   Ahh, granny . . . I know . . .
(*He embraces her tightly for a moment. She kisses him.*)
I'm sorry I said those things. I understand how you feel
and I understand why you—

MRS. LOVE   Don't try to understand me, son, 'cause you
don't even understand yourself yet. Gon' out there and get
yourself some dignity—be a man, then we can talk.

> (MRS. LOVE *watches him exit. She stands in the door-
> way for a moment, turns and takes the dishes to the
> sink. She takes another beer from her refrigerator and
> sits at the table and composes a letter.*)

(*Writing.*)   "Dear Eugene, your son has made me right
proud today. You ought to have seen him leaving here to
sit-in at the drug store with them other fine young colored
children." Lord, letter writin' can tire a body out! I'll let
the boy finish it when he gets back.

KATY   (*Offstage.*)   Miss Love! Miss Love!

MRS. LOVE   (*Rising.*)   Katy?

> (KATY *enters. She has been running and stops beside
> the door to catch her breath.*)

What's wrong with you child? They ain't riotin' are they?
(KATY *shakes her head.*)   Then what's the matter? You
give the Sheriff his bread?

KATY   Yes, when I got there I poked my head in through
the door and he said: "What you want, gal?" I told him I
brought him his breakfast. "Alright, bring it here," he says
and his eyes lit up at the sight of your cornbread!

MRS. LOVE   Didn't they!

KATY   He told me to go get him a quart of buttermilk from
the icebox, then started eatin' bread, yelling all the while
—"Hurry up, gal, 'fore I finish!"

MRS. LOVE   Then what happened?

KATY   When I got back with his milk he was half standin' and half-sittin' at his desk holding that big stomach of his'n, and cussin' to high heaven. "Gimmie that god-damned milk! Can't you see these ulcers is killin' the hell outta me?"

MRS. LOVE   He ain't got no ulcers.

KATY   He had something alright. His ol' blue eyes was just dartin' about in what looked like little pools of blood. His face was red as beet—

MRS. LOVE   Go on, child!

KATY   Panting and breathin' hard, he drank all the milk in one long gulp, then belched and told me to get my black ass outta his face. "Tell all the niggers," he said, "that today is the be all and end all day!"

MRS. LOVE   Indeed!

KATY   Then he flung the empty plate at me! I ran across the street and the street was full of white folks with sticks, rocks and things—old white folks and young 'uns—even children. *My* white folks was even there!

MRS. LOVE   What was they doin'?

KATY   Just standin'—that's all. They wasn't sayin' nothin'— just staring and watching. They'd look down the street towards the drug store, then turn and look towards the Sheriff office. Finally old Sheriff Morrison came out. He was sort of bent over in the middle, belching and his stomach growling! You could hear it clear across the street.

MRS. LOVE   Oh, I've seen it before, child! I've seen it! First Dr. Crawford—After his whole family had died out one by one—Called me to his own death bed and asked me to hold his hand. "I ain't got nobody else to turn to now, Auntie." "You related to me in some way?" I asked him. He laughed and the pain hit him like an axe. "Sing me a spiritual," he said. I told him I didn't know no spiritual. "Sing something Holy for me, I'm dyin'!" he says. (*She sings.*) "I'LL BE GLAD WHEN YOU'RE DEAD, YOU RASCAL, YOU! I'LL BE GLAD WHEN YOU'RE DEAD, YOU RASCAL, YOU!" Then I told him how come he was dyin'.

KATY   He was a doctor, didn't he know?

MRS. LOVE   Shoot! Dr. Crawford, didn't know his liver from his kidney. "Dr. Crawford," I said, "how come you didn't treat my husband? How come you let him die out there in the alley like an animal?" I gave him an earful and when I got through openin' his nose to what was happenin', he raised up—red just like the sheriff, his hands outstretched toward me and he fell right square off that bed onto the floor—dead. I spit on his body! Went down stairs, cooked me a steak, got my belongings and left.

KATY   You didn't call the undertaker?

MRS. LOVE   I left that bastard for the maggots. I wasn't his "auntie"!! A week later the neighbors found him stinking to hell. They came by to question me, but I was grieved, chile, so they left me alone. "You know how nigras is scared of death," they said. And now the sheriff. Oh, I have a great peace of mind, chile, cause I'm like my grandson in my own fashion. I'm too old to be hit and wet up, they say, but I votes and does my bit.

KATY   I reckon I'll get on. You think you oughta stay here by yourself?

MRS. LOVE   I'll be alright. You run along now. Go tend to your children before they get away from you.

KATY   Ma'am?

MRS. LOVE   Them kids got eyes, Katy, and they know what's happenin' and they ain't gonna be likin' their mama's attitude much longer. You're a young woman, Katy, there ain't no sense in your continuing to be such a fool.

KATY   I don't know what you're talkin' about, Mrs. Love!

MRS. LOVE   You'll find out one day—I just hope it ain't too late. I thank you for that favor.

KATY   Yes'm. (*She exits.*)

MRS. LOVE   (*Removes a small bag from her bosom.*)   Ain't much left. Lord!!!

EUGENE   (*Entering. He is dressed the same, but seems eager and excited now.*)   Grandma! They served us and didn't a soul do a thing! We've integrated!

MRS. LOVE   Tell me about it.

EUGENE   When I got there, every white person in the county was on that street! They had clubs and iron pipes, dogs and fire trucks with hoses. When we reached the drug store, old man Thomas was standing in the doorway. "What yawl want?" he asked. "Service," one of us said. The crowd started yelling and making nasty remarks, but none of us moved an inch. Then we saw the Sheriff down the street walking slowly like he was sick—

MRS. LOVE   Didn't he cuss none?

EUGENE   He swore up and down! He walked up to me and said, "Boy, what you and them other niggers want here?" "Freedom, baby!" I told him. "Freedom my ass," he said. "Yawl get on back where you belong and stop actin' up before I sic the dogs on you." "We're not leaving until we've been served!" I told him. He looked at me in complete amazement—

MRS. LOVE   Then he belched and started to foam at the mouth.

EUGENE   He was *mad*, grandma! He said he'd die before a nigger sat where a white woman's ass had been. "God is my witness!" he shouted. "May I die before I see this place integrated!" Then he took out his whistle—

MRS. LOVE   Put it to his lips and before he could get up the breath to blow, he fell on the ground—

EUGENE   He rolled himself into a tight ball, holding his stomach. Cussing, and moaning and thrashing around—

MRS. LOVE   And the foaming at the mouth got worse! He puked—a bloody puke, and his eyes looked like they'd popped right out of their sockets. He opened his mouth and gasped for breath.

EUGENE   In the excitement some of the kids went inside the drug store and the girl at the counter says, "Yawl can have anything you want—just don't put a curse on me!" While black faces were filling that counter, someone outside yelled—

MRS. LOVE   "Sheriff Morrison is *dead!*"

EUGENE   How do you know so much? You weren't there.

MRS. LOVE   No, son, I wasn't there, but I've seen it before. I've seen—

EUGENE   What?

MRS. LOVE   Death in the raw. Dr. Crawford's entire family went that-away.

EUGENE   Grandma . . . ?

MRS. LOVE   Some of them had it easier and quicker than the rest—dependin'.

EUGENE   "Dependin' " on what?

MRS. LOVE   How they had loved and treated their neighbor —namely *me*. (*Unconsciously she fumbles with the bag dangling from around her neck, which she removed from her bosom.*)

EUGENE   What's in that bag you're fumbling with?

MRS. LOVE   Spice.

EUGENE   You're lying to me. What is it?

MRS. LOVE   The spice of life, baby.

EUGENE   Did you . . . Did you do something to Sheriff Morrison?

MRS. LOVE   (*Singing.*)
IN THE SWEET BYE AND BYE
WE SHALLLLLLL MEET. . . . .

EUGENE   What did you do to Sheriff Morrison!??

MRS. LOVE   I helped yawl integrate—in my own fashion.

EUGENE   What did you do to that man?

MRS. LOVE   I gave him peace! Sent him to meet his maker! Sent him in grand style too. Tore his very guts out with my special seasoning! Degrading me! Callin' me "nigger"! Beating my men folks!

EUGENE   Why?

MRS. LOVE   Because I'm a tired old black woman who's been tired, and who ain't got no place and never had no place in this country. You talk about a "new Negro"—Hell, I was a new Negro seventy-six years ago. Don't you think I wanted to sip me a coke-cola in a store when I went out shoppin'? Don't you think I wanted to try on a dress or a hat when I bought it? Don't you think I wanted to have a decent job that would have given me some respect and enough money to feed my family and clothe them decently? I resented being called "girl" and "auntie" by folks who weren't even as good as me. I worked for nigger haters—made 'em love me, and I put my boy through school—and then I sent *them* to eternity with flying colors. I got no regrets, boy, just peace of mind and satisfaction. And I don't need no psychiatrist—I done vented my pent-up emotions! Ain't that what you always saying?

EUGENE   You can be sent to the electric chair!

MRS. LOVE   Who? Aunt Grace Love? Good old black auntie? Shoot! I know white folks, son, and I've been at this business for a long time now, and they know I know my place.

EUGENE   Oh, Grandma . . .

MRS. LOVE   Cheer up! I done what I did for all yawl, but if you don't appreciate it, ask some of the colored boys who ain't been to college, who's felt Ol' man Morrison's stick against their heads—they'd appreciate it. Liberation! Just like the underground railroad—Harriet Tubman—that's me, only difference is I ain't goin' down in history. Now you take off them clothes before you get them wrinkled.

EUGENE   Where you going?

MRS. LOVE   To shed a tear for the deceased and get me a train ticket.

EUGENE   You're going home to daddy?

MRS. LOVE   Your daddy don't need me no more, son. He's got your mama. No, I ain't going to your daddy.

EUGENE   Then where're you going?

MRS. LOVE   Ain't you said them college students is sittin' in in Mississippi and they ain't makin' much headway 'cause of the governor?

          (EUGENE *nods.*)

Well . . . I think I'll take me a little trip to Mississippi and see what's happenin'. You wouldn't by chance know the governor's name, would you?

EUGENE   What?

MRS. LOVE   I have a feeling he just might be needing a good cook.

EUGENE   Grandma!

MRS. LOVE   Get out of those clothes now.   (*She starts for the door.*)   And while I'm downtown I think I'll have me a cold ice cream soda at Mr. Thomas'.   (*She wanders to the apron of the stage.*)   . . . I wonder who will be next? I'll put me an ad in the paper. Who knows, it may be you or you, or you. . . .   (*Sings as she exits.*)

WHERE HE LEADS ME
I SHALLLLL FOLLOW
WHERE HE LEADS ME
I SHALLLLL FOLLOW

(EUGENE *sits stunned as the old woman's voice fades. . . .*)

CURTAIN

Bibliography

I. BLACK DRAMAS OF SIGNIFICANCE (1959–1969) NOT OTHERWISE TREATED IN THIS VOLUME.

BALDWIN, JAMES   *The Amen Corner.* Ethel Barrymore Theatre, April 15, 1965, 84 performances. Featured Bea Richards. Before opening in New York the play was staged in Los Angeles, Edinburgh, Tel Aviv, Vienna and London. Partially autobiographical, the play treats the spiritual and domestic problems of a woman pastor of a store-front Harlem church who rules her flock and her son with a despotic hand.

BALDWIN, JAMES   *Blues for Mr. Charlie.* ANTA Theatre, April 23, 1964, 148 performances. Produced by Actors Studio company. Featured Diana Sands, Al Freeman, Jr., Percy Rodriquez and Pat Hingle. The play is dedicated to the memory of Medgar Evers, and his widow and his children, and to the memory of the dead children of Birmingham. The play is a passionate telling of the murder of Negroes by whites and the fake justice which allows the white murderer to escape punishment.

BULLINS, ED   *The Electronic Nigger and Others.* American Place Theatre, March 6, 1968, 12 performances. Continued at the Martinique Theatre under the title *Three Plays by Ed Bullins.* The three plays included: *A Son, Come Home, The Electronic Nigger,* and *Clara's Ole Man.*

BURGIE, IRVING, and MITCHELL, LOFTEN   *Ballad for Bimshire.* Mayfair Theatre, October 15, 1963, 74 performances. Featured Frederic O'Neal and Ossie Davis. A boy-meets-girl musical set in Barbados, nicknamed "Bimshire" by the natives.

ELDER, LONNE   *Ceremonies in Dark Old Men.* St. Marks Playhouse, February 4, 1969, later transferred to the Pocket Theatre. Produced by the Negro Ensemble Company, with Douglas Ward and Rosalind Cash. A powerful, realistic drama of oppression that focuses for its tragic effects on an ex-vaudevillian and his poverty-stricken family in Harlem, and what results from the successful operation of a corn-whiskey still in the backroom of his barber shop.

GORDONE, CHARLES   *No Place to Be Somebody.* Public Theatre, May 4, 1969. Featured Nathan George and Ron O'Neal. A
comedy about race identity as portrayed by the inhabitants of a
bar in New York.

HANSBERRY, LORRAINE   *The Sign in Sidney Brustein's Window.* Longacre Theatre, October 15, 1964, 101 performances. Featured Gabriel Dell and Rita Moreno. A play about white Green
Village liberals who attempt to correct the disorder in their personal and public lives.

HUGHES, LANGSTON   *Black Nativity.* 41st Street Theatre, December 11, 1961, 57 performances. Featured Marion Williams and
The Stars of Faith. Subtitled "A Christmas Song Play," the work
is in two parts: the first, a retelling in gospel song and story of
the Nativity; and the second, a camp meeting revival in which
the gospel is spread.

HUGHES, LANGSTON   *Jerico-Jim Crow.* Sanctuary Theatre,
January 12, 1964, 31 performances. The history of segregation in
America from the time of slavery to the lunch-counter sit-ins told
in song and story.

HUGHES, LANGSTON   *Tambourines to Glory.* Little Theatre,
November 2, 1963, 23 performances. Adapted from the novel, the
play is a spoof on the life of a woman evangelist.

JONES, LEROI   *Dutchman.* Cherry Lane Theatre, March 23, 1964,
121 performances. Featured Robert Hooks and Jennifer Ward.
A one-act play about the murderous encounter of a black man
and a white woman in a subway. Made into a film with Al Freeman, Jr., and Shirley Knight.

JONES, LEROI   *The Slave* and *The Toilet.* St. Marks Playhouse,
December 16, 1964, 151 performances. Two polemic one-act plays
of violence and hate.

McIVER, RAY   *God Is a (Guess What?).* St. Marks Playhouse, December 17, 1968, 32 performances. Produced by Negro Ensemble
Company. Repeated at the World Theatre Season at the Aldwych
Theatre, London, May, 1969. A "minstrel morality" play with
routines from vaudeville and night clubs, the plot satirizes black-
white relations as it tells the story of Jim, who refuses to flee from
lynchers.

MILLER, RONALD   *Who's Got His Own.* American Place Theatre, October 12, 1966, 19 performances. Featured Barbara Ann Teer. A drama of the hostility sparked between family members living in a Detroit ghetto by the return of a wayward son.

II. ADDITIONAL READING

ABRAMSON, DORIS E.   *Negro Playwrights in the American Theatre, 1925-1959.* New York: Columbia University Press, 1969.

COUCH, WILLIAM   *New Black Playwrights.* Baton Rouge: Louisiana State University Press, 1968.

HILL, HERBERT   *Anger, and Beyond: The Negro Writer in the United States.* New York: Harper and Row, 1966.

HUGHES, LANGSTON and MELTZER, MILTON   *Black Magic: A Pictorial History of the Negro in American Entertainment.* Englewood Cliffs, N.J.: Prentice-Hall, 1968.

ISAACS, EDITH J. R.   *The Negro in the American Theatre.* New York: Theatre Arts Books, 1947.

MELTZER, MILTON   *Langston Hughes: A Biography.* New York: Thomas Cromwell, 1968.

MITCHELL, LOFTEN   *Black Drama: The Story of the American Negro in the Theatre.* New York: Hawthorne Books, 1967.

PATTERSON, LINDSAY   *Anthology of the American Negro in the Theatre,* Vol. III, *International Library of Negro Life and History.* New York: Publisher's Company, 1967.